THE
CLASSIC
COCKTAIL
SESSIONS

CLARKSON POTTER/
PUBLISHERS
NEW YORK

PHOTOGRAPHS BY
EMMA JANZEN

THE
CLASSIC
COCKTAIL
SESSIONS

A Bartender's New-Fashioned
Approach to the World's
Most Beloved Recipes

TOBY MALONEY

AND

EMMA JANZEN

We are craftsmen. We are not artists, nor mixologists, nor bar chefs. Just bartenders, doing something that, although quite simple, few bars can manage to do. We make cocktails as well as can be made, and that should not be such a big deal.

— SASHA PETRASKE, *MILK & HONEY*

The Prelude

The Prep

The Composition

SHOW

THE PRELUDE

An Invitation

ello! My name is Toby Maloney. I've been tending bar for over thirty years now. Recently, I've come to the confounding realization that I will never be as good at anything as I am at bartending.

Since 1992, I have done Malcolm Gladwell's ten thousand hours of practice more than six times over. I have tried to estimate how many cocktails I have made during this time. It's definitely more than 500k, but less than one million. Let's call it an Olympic swimming pool's worth. I've been behind the stick in New York, Chicago, Nashville, Philadelphia, Martha's Vineyard, Vancouver, Tokyo, and on Thai beaches, plying my trade in dives, clubs, restaurants, and cocktail lounges.

Of the hundreds and hundreds of thousands of cocktails I have mixed, I have invented (or had a hand in inventing) well over a thousand originals. Some, like Juliet & Romeo and Eeyore's Requiem, have been dubbed "modern classics" by contemporary cocktail scholars. That's flattering, but those inventions aren't what defines my craft. Instead, it is my proficiency with the classics that makes me the steadfast bartender I am today.

I love making Sidecars, Vieux Carrés, Crustas, and Cosmos. My Manhattan game is tight. I can stir an Old Fashioned to perfection with my eyes closed (along with five straw tastes), free-pour a Daiquiri, and add just the right amount of crème de violette for an Aviation rinse without thinking twice. I also tend to prefer drinking the classics: If given the choice to order the latest ten-ingredient feat of modern mixology or a Sazerac, nine times out of ten I'm going with the Sazerac. And I am not alone in this.

I know many jaded mixologists who will whip up a simple Martini for themselves after a long night of sphérification and pretentiousness. New bartenders gravitate back to a three-touch Gimlet when home alone. And enthusiasts, after trying out some snazzy cocktails from the latest buzz-worthy bar, will settle back with a Last Word when left to their own devices.

This is because the classics are the embodiment of "gimme the usual." Comforting. Contemplative. Versatile and steadfast. These cocktails are supernovas, the brightest stars in the galaxy of cocktails that bartenders have invented in the last two centuries. Most have been around for ages because they are damn delicious. Through poorly conceived prohibitions and global pandemics—and even the rise of flavored seltzers—they endure.

Classic cocktails are for everyone, everywhere. For any occasion. Like a Little Black Dress, drinks like the Mint Julep and Moscow Mule are ever fashionable. A Margarita can be dressed up so it looks chic at an opera or dressed down for a punk rock show. A mink or a motorcycle jacket is just a delicate coupe or red Solo cup. The classics are also never out of place: A New York Sour tastes equally delicious in your pajamas on the couch as on a 64th-floor skyscraper veranda in the twinkling glow of the Manhattan skyline.

Just as you should know how to make a grilled cheese that comes out perfectly gooey and crispy at the same time, you should be able to mix these drinks with aplomb, keeping pace while chatting with a friend or commiserating with your significant other about the details of their day. It is an important life skill, like ordering a properly cooked steak with the right bottle of chewy red wine or getting out of a parking ticket. Not because of the dizziness of the alcohol—if that were the case, you could serve someone room temperature Everclear and call it a day—but rather because the rites and rituals of the classics make life richer and more enjoyable for you, and for the people around you.

The classics are also of the utmost importance to the craft of bartending, because they are the building blocks of any good drink repertoire. When you take piano lessons, you learn Bach, Beethoven, and Mozart first, because those are the canonical classics that will make you a better piano player. With cocktails, once you know how to calibrate the right temperature, create good texture, tweak ratios for balance, and maximize good aromas in drinks like the Airmail, Hurricane, and Stinger, a world of mastery and improvisation opens up. I'm living proof of this. Without the Negroni, there would be no Eeyore. Without the Gimlet, no Juliet. This applies to many other drinks we consider "modern classics" today: You can't have a Benton's Old Fashioned without the Old Fashioned, or a Kingston Negroni without the Negroni.

My stance is that anybody, armed with a jigger of knowledge, a dash of technique, and a splash or two of common sense can make these cocktails well enough to wow your father-in-law or mollify your most evil nemesis. With practice and dedication, you, too, can get to the point where your Manhattan game is tight and you can stir an Old Fashioned to perfection with your eyes closed (along with five straw tastes), or free-pour a Daiquiri and add just the right amount of crème de violette for an Aviation rinse without thinking twice.

When you reach this precipice, slinging drinks becomes a pleasure instead of a chore. The bell curve of proficiency will become steeper, and more fun, and later you'll be able to show off your voice by inventing original cocktail recipes. At this point, you will be able to saunter into any bar in the world and feel confident in choosing a menu drink you'll enjoy, spotting riffs in the wild without hesitation. You will also acquire what people mysteriously call "good taste." That is, the palate of a practitioner.

The journey toward mastering these recipes will be even more delicious with someone like me standing at your shoulder, because I've already made all the mistakes a bartender can make with these formidable recipes. I know them inside and out and can share all the tips, insights, and course corrections I've learned myself over the decades. And that's why this book exists.

From the 20th Century to the White Russian, *The Classic Cocktail Sessions* is a deep dive into the inner workings of sixty-one of the world's most beloved classic cocktails. Each drink gets its own "session," where my coauthor, Emma Janzen, and I will explore what makes the cocktail unique and marvelous, accompanied by details of the nitty-gritty techniques and philosophies you'll need to make the most delicious versions possible. The point isn't simply to memorize specs and rehash histories but rather give insight into the way professional bartenders approach these foundational recipes, so the road toward elevating your skills from mediocre to marvelous becomes easier and more enjoyable.

Think of this as the younger sibling to our first book, *The Bartender's Manifesto* (which we lovingly refer to as *Manny*). It is not just a book of recipes, but rather a training manual for aspiring bartenders, where we'll teach you a hell of a lot about the technique and theory behind each cocktail. Unlike *Manny,* which was like hardcore bartending school, the goal with *Sessions* is to pursue this knowledge with the vibes of a casual Sunday jam sesh: It's midafternoon and the windows are open because it's summertiiiiiime and the living is easy. The jukebox is playing punk rock covers of Johnny Cash's greatest hits. There are no expectations of perfection; no judgment when you drop a shaker tin on the floor or spill green Chartreuse on the counter. We're here to have a little fun and learn a few cool things along the way. Ideally, you will achieve proficiency with these recipes quickly, with more than your fair share of enjoyment.

Our Approach

ozens of other recipe books also focus on classic cocktails, but this one is a little different. First, we're looking at these drinks through the lens of the twenty-first-century bartender, giving you slightly more modern takes on each one. The concept of "authenticity"—that is; the exact ratios and mannerisms in which these drinks were originally made—doesn't matter within this context. We want them to taste delicious to you NOW, with all the wild and wonderful and weird ingredients we have readily available. Think old drinks, new perspective.

To be clear: We're not treading into riffs territory with these specs. A riff is when you change the recipe so dramatically that its flavor and personality transform into something completely different. If you swapped the raspberry syrup for a blackberry syrup in the Clover Club, for example, it's a new drink. Or if you changed the crème de menthe to crème de banane in a Grasshopper, it's no longer a Grasshopper, right? In this book, the Tom Collins is still clearly a Tom Collins, the Bamboo, a Bamboo, and so on.

Our approach is kinda like when a musician covers a classic song by taking the melody up an octave, playing the chorus faster, or alchemizing the spirit of the tune with a different style or approach. See: The Ataris's punk spin on "Boys of Summer," or Sinead O'Connor's incomparable take on "Nothing Compares 2 U." Same songs, new energy.

Okay, yes, sometimes we add a bit of syrup or a dash of bitters to a spec, but only to amplify existing flavors instead of changing the fundamental nature of the drink. It's a fine line, we know, but bartenders all over the world personalize the classics in small and meaningful ways to communicate their style, so we're taking those tiny liberties as we see fit, critics be damned.

For the folks who invented these drinks who are still alive and thriving out in the world, bartending, writing, mentoring, and being consummate professionals: In many cases we are presenting our own versions of your recipes in these sessions, but NOT because your original isn't delicious already. We're doing this with the goal of showing the next generation of bartenders how they can take a classic spec and make it their own. So, when we modify a ratio, or change the garnish, or add a float of Peychaud's, it comes from a deep respect for your pioneering work; not us thinking that we're "improving" it.

We're also going to ignore the history and backstories of these drinks. These things mattered greatly at the beginning of the cocktail movement in the late '90s and early 2000s. We were just starting to change the paradigm back then, shifting from sour mix to fresh juice and picking up jiggers instead of free-pouring, so we needed to learn everything we could about "the good old days" of mixed drinks to set a foundation for creativity to follow. But in the "right here right now," you should be focusing on how the ingredients and the technique dovetail to make the best possible cocktail you can make at any given moment—not who invented the drink and what they were wearing that day and why they did it and how drunk they were at the time and in what bar.

I want to acknowledge something: When I say the "best possible" version of these drinks, I'm not suggesting there's a singular right or wrong way to make them. Deliciousness is subjective, so "best" is all about what tastes good to YOU. My Mojito tastes different—not better or worse, just different—than the one my friend Javier Villalobos Brenes puts on the bar menu at Pocket Food & Drinks in Escazú, Costa Rica, or the one Jessica Sanders mixes at DrinkWell in Austin, Texas, because we all have unique palates. That is what makes this craft so beautiful and compelling. And what makes it so fun to barhop around the globe, visiting different bartenders in different hemispheres along the way.

The idea is that by following along with how *we* reinterpret familiar classics, over time you'll naturally start adjusting specs for your palate—this is akin to "finding your voice" as a drinks maker. Once you're at the point where you're sketching preferred measurements in the margins, this book becomes personal to *you*. From there, the world is your oyster shooter.

To get you to that point a little faster, we give you a lot of information alongside each spec. First, we offer intel on how various brands of gin, rum, vermouth, and other liquid ingredients differ from one another, and why those decisions will make a huge impact on your cocktail. Then, in the mixing instructions, we detail how to create exceptional balance, texture, temperature, and aroma so the cocktail never tastes "too sweet," and it's always ice-cold and feels good on the palate. These instructions are loquacious, exacting, and full of purple prose, just as they were in *Manny*, because we believe that "shake or stir then strain" is not enough information to make the very best cocktail. Finally, we give suggestions for how to make these drinks extra personal, so you have a starting line for further developing your bartending identity. Read the whole session before you start mixing! It's (sorta) easier to put together an IKEA bookshelf after you have read all the instructions, and the same is (definitely) true of a cocktail.

Oh yeah, we also give you a guesstimate of the cocktail's alcohol content (in grams), to give you a sense for how boozy the drinks are compared to one another. We used Jeffrey Morgenthaler's handy ABV calculator to figure out the volume and ABV of each drink (after dilution), then plugged those numbers into Eric Roehm's alcoholic drinks calculator at NutritionHeart.com, which is how they do it at The Doctor's Office in Seattle. Unlike ABV alone, which just gives you an idea of the perceived booziness of a drink, the number of grams of alcohol tells you exactly how much alcohol is in each cocktail. For example, a French 75 has 11 percent ABV, while a Gimlet has 21 percent ABV, and yet both cocktails have about 21 grams of alcohol, so while one seems less boozy than the other, they both pack a medium-size punch. And while the Daisy de Santiago also has 11 percent ABV, it has even more alcohol in the glass than either cocktail: 26 grams! When you keep in mind that the US defines one alcohol-based drink as 14 grams of alcohol, you can make smart decisions about what to imbibe.

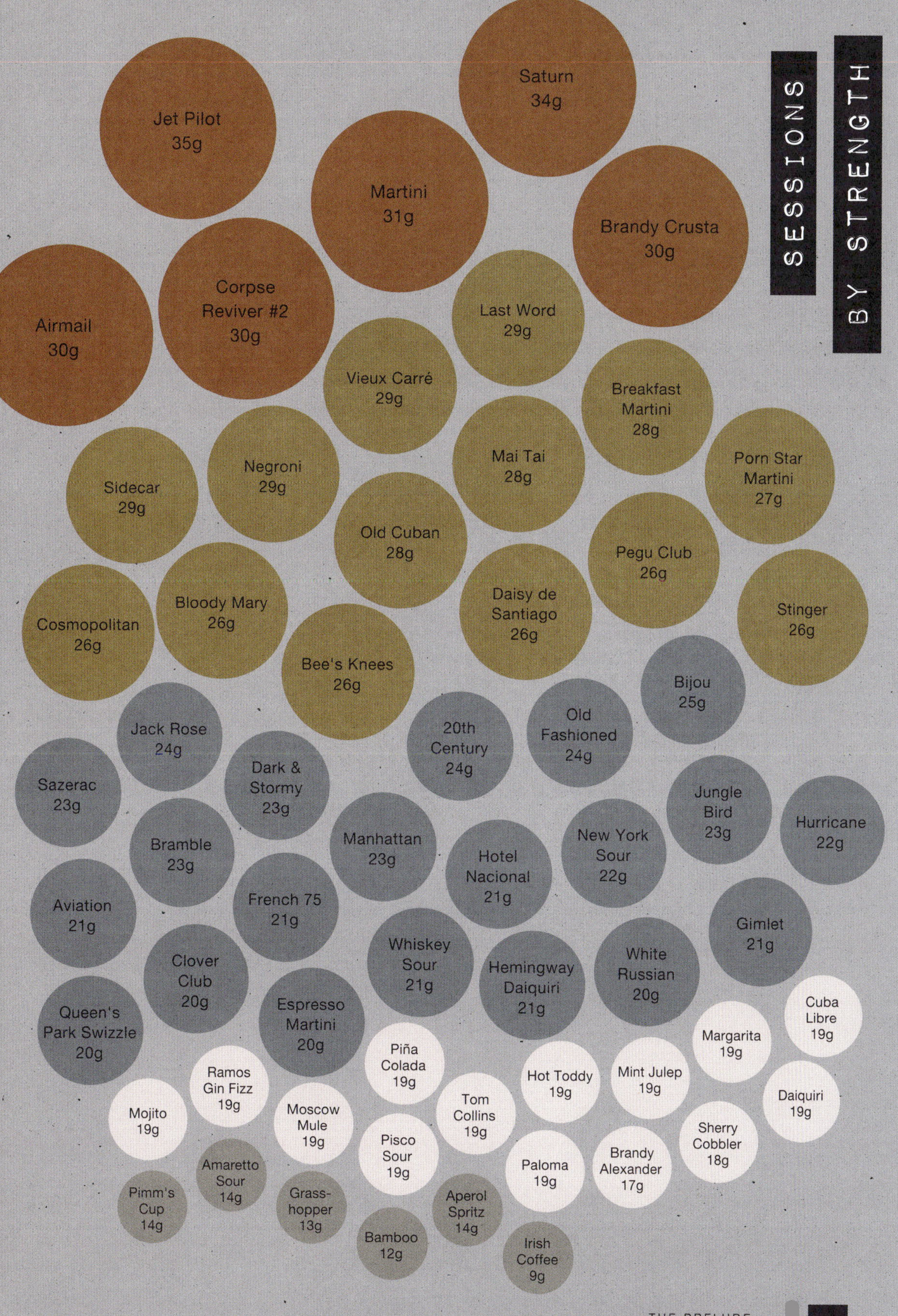
Jet Pilot
35g
Saturn
34g
Martini
31g
Brandy Crusta
30g
Airmail
30g
Corpse Reviver #2
30g
Last Word
29g
Vieux Carré
29g
Breakfast Martini
28g
Sidecar
29g
Negroni
29g
Mai Tai
28g
Porn Star Martini
27g
Old Cuban
28g
Pegu Club
26g
Cosmopolitan
26g
Bloody Mary
26g
Daisy de Santiago
26g
Stinger
26g
Bee's Knees
26g
Bijou
25g
Jack Rose
24g
20th Century
24g
Old Fashioned
24g
Sazerac
23g
Dark & Stormy
23g
Jungle Bird
23g
Hurricane
22g
Bramble
23g
Manhattan
23g
Hotel Nacional
21g
New York Sour
22g
Aviation
21g
French 75
21g
Gimlet
21g
Clover Club
20g
Whiskey Sour
21g
Hemingway Daiquiri
21g
White Russian
20g
Queen's Park Swizzle
20g
Espresso Martini
20g
Cuba Libre
19g
Ramos Gin Fizz
19g
Piña Colada
19g
Hot Toddy
19g
Mint Julep
19g
Margarita
19g
Mojito
19g
Moscow Mule
19g
Tom Collins
19g
Daiquiri
19g
Amaretto Sour
14g
Pisco Sour
19g
Paloma
19g
Brandy Alexander
17g
Sherry Cobbler
18g
Pimm's Cup
14g
Grasshopper
13g
Aperol Spritz
14g
Bamboo
12g
Irish Coffee
9g

HOW TO USE THIS BOOK

Some cocktail books are intentionally written for professional bartenders, while others target the home mixology crowd. We want to break down the barriers between the two and welcome all y'all to the table, because if schlepping *Manny* hither and yon has taught me anything, it's that home mixologists have just as much passion, enthusiasm, and skill as folks employed by a bar, and can achieve the same liquid genius when given the same education and tools. The only difference between at-home bartenders and professional bartenders is that the former are not making a few hundred drinks a night, so while their progress might be a bit slower, all will end up in the same place. That's why from here on out we are going to refer to anyone who is interested in learning to make drinks as bartenders—regardless of whether you stride the rubber mats in slip-resistant Danner boots or you do it in your kitchen in your house slippers.

For the casual dabbler, enthusiastic host, or jaded mixologist:

Pick up this book to find and mix your favorite drink. It will be useful if you have never made the cocktail before, or if you are in the weeds with guests screaming orders for Porn Star Martinis, Cuba Libres, and Last Words right at last call. Maybe you have made a Bramble half a dozen times and just need a cheeky reminder about how much crème de mûre to lace on top. We've organized the cocktails alphabetically to make this process easier to navigate and included a handy "mize" box at the top of each sesh, so you can see the basics of each build—serve, glassware, etc.—at a quick glance.

For serious aspiring pro bartenders and hardcore connoisseurs:

This book should be your Rand McNally atlas as you navigate your cocktail pilgrimage, the reference you turn to again and again as you work to perfect your craft. For you, each session could be three times as long as what we're able to offer in this book—there is just too much information to share. Our hope is that you can learn a new thing or two with each drink, then remember that thing and apply it to future cocktails. Let your knowledge build exponentially, apply it to other parts of your life, and watch your skill set expand and flourish.

Defining *the* Classics

We chose not to include every classic ever created in the pages that follow. Instead, we landed on sixty-one recipes we think both bartenders and civilians *need* to know. It's a lean and comprehensive group that feels definitive, and makes our lives, and the work of training aspiring bartenders, super easy.

Putting the list together was no small task. Over the course of more than a year, we expanded and contracted it more than a dozen times. We cross-referenced famous drink books and online publications. We trolled Facebook and Reddit groups and bar menus from Baltimore to Bangkok. We talked to friends and family members and esteemed colleagues in the bar world. Quickly, we realized that drinks scholars will argue until they are blue in the face over what exactly constitutes a "classic" cocktail, so we knew we'd need to create our own criteria for inclusion.

Some decisions were easy. The Bee's Knees and Pisco Sour are essential (pages 81 and 261). A Mind Eraser is not. Nobody needs to know the Bronx, or that if you add Ango it becomes an Income Tax. Other decisions were not so simple—do the Tuxedo #2 and the Hanky Panky deserve their own sessions, or is it better to nestle them into the Martini Friends & Family section (page 209) since they are made using the same techniques as the "mother" drink anyway? In those Friends & Family sections, we've included quick specs—not full sessions—for as many variations on the headliner cocktail as we could, so you have those available to reference when the mood for an Alaska (page 210) strikes.

Sometimes the two of us disagreed, so gauntlets were thrown, and concessions were made. For example, the White Russian is here because Emma made a strong case for how tricky the drink can be to get right texturally, plus the options for customization are ample (page 309). Yet we have killed the Corn & Oil, because I think it's a drink with a crappy name and deplorable balance, and it's as ugly as the industrial sludge pool of a petroleum factory. The Caipirinha and Ti' Punch don't require a session because they are just Daiquiris made with different techniques, and the Monkey Gland is not included, because fuck orange juice. Plus, that name is entirely out of order.

We've thrown a few curveballs into the mix for good measure. For example, the Porn Star Martini, the Breakfast Martini, and Old Cuban were all invented at the very dawn of the 2000s, which might not seem old enough to qualify as a "classic" in the same way an 1800s-era Old Fashioned does, but these drinks were ahead of their time, added something to the conversation at large, and have proved their staying power. We feel confident they will be shaken and stirred for decades to come. (Find those sessions on pages 265, 105, and 237, respectively.)

Plenty of armchair mixologists will argue that we've made some terrible decisions in the process. Or that there are more cocktails that deserve space in this book. I'm sure you have opinions as you start digging in, too. To each their own! Send a letter to the editor and maybe she'll let us write a B-sides version of this tome down the road.

OUR CRITERIA

1 **The drink must be of a certain age.** We've set the creation period from 1862 to 2002, which spans from Jerry Thomas's first iteration of *The Bartender's Guide*—the first proper cocktail book ever published—to Dale DeGroff's pivotal text *The Craft of the Cocktail,* which was *the* reference book for the modern cocktail revolution. This is not to say great drinks haven't been invented since 2002—it just felt like a solid place to set a cap, since what followed was an entire era of new ideas.

2 **The drink must have proven staying power.** Whether the recipe was invented in 1862 or 2002, these drinks have clearly stood the test of time. They aren't just recipes you find in obscure vintage recipe books. Instead, their names still grace the pages of countless menus around the world today. They have inspired endless numbers of riffs and/or have large family trees that can be traced back to the original recipe.

3 **The drink must be instantly recognizable and distinctive.** These are the cocktails you have on the tip of your tongue without thinking about it, ready to call out without fear when it's three deep at the bar. No one will argue that a Martini or Daiquiri is a classic cocktail. A Tailspin or a Blackthorn? If you can't quickly remember what's in the drink or how it is supposed to taste, it's probably not covered here.

4 **The drink must be delicious.** Yes, this point is subjective, as some people are Mai Tai drinkers, some Pegu Club drinkers, and others have the eclectic tastes of an autodidact. As industry professionals we aimed to think as objectively as possible, positioning decisions within the context of many decades of experience. It's not that we love all of these drinks equally or even have some of them in our regular rotation, but we can agree that every cocktail in this text has something that's worth enjoying or at least appreciating.

THE
PREP

Curating a Hi-Fi Booze Collection

here are two types of booze collectors. One has a tightly curated assortment of bottles because they like only Daiquiris and Negronis and drink the occasional small-batch spirit straight. The other has every bottle known to humanity, brashly spelunking dusty old liquor stores and bringing back obscure treasures from trips abroad. Neither approach is wrong, but if you're starting from scratch, it's wiser to build a small collection of liquors and liqueurs that you know you love and have many applications.

Professional bars *need* a lot of bottles because a lot of different people come into bars wanting different things. At home, you probably don't need three types of vodka, plus brandy, eau-de-vie, white dog, aged and unaged tequila and mezcal and bacanora and sotol, Irish whiskey, Scotch whisky, bourbon whiskey, Japanese whisky, multiple rums from far-flung locales, all the amari, forty-two liqueurs, and ten kinds of bitters.

Start with your favorite one or two classics and buy what you need to make those first. If you dig a Daiquiri, start with rum. Once you've nailed that, add yellow Chartreuse for the Daisy de Santiago. If you like Negronis, start with gin, Campari, and sweet vermouth. Then buy whiskey to make a Boulevardier or Manhattan, or rum to make Jungle Birds. When you acquire ingredients cocktail by cocktail, eventually you'll have a nice tight assortment that serves your actual needs, not your aspirational ones.

Of note: We often call out recommended brands in the sessions—that is not because these brands paid us to mention them, but because we know they are made with integrity and work reliably well in cocktails. You don't *have* to use the same brands we do—in fact, experimenting is half the fun and will teach you a lot about your palate in the long run—but knowing what bottles worked well for us might help give you a starting point for your own mixing adventures. And for transparency: While we paid out-of-pocket for a ridiculous amount of product for recipe testing each classic, several brands sent us samples (at our request) to help us lower the costs. Big kudos to Fords, Planteray, Ferrand, Giffard, and Tempus Fugit for the assist.

Here's a quick cheat sheet for how many times each spirit or liqueur or syrup or pantry item or bitters or wine is used to make all sixty-one classics in this book, so you can make informed decisions about what to buy. A bottle of gin, for example, will give you the ability to make far more drinks than if you were to buy a bottle of pisco or absinthe. Maybe you don't need sloe gin in your cabinet, but dry curaçao will be suuuper handy. You get the idea. Flip back to the index to discover what drinks you can make with each ingredient.

SPIRITS

Gin	19
Rum	15
Whiskey	9
Cognac/Brandy	8
Vodka	5
Agave	2
Absinthe	2
Pisco	1

LIQUEURS

Dry curaçao	7
Maraschino liqueur	4
Crème de cacao	4
Passion fruit liqueur	3
Campari	2
Green Chartreuse	2
Crème de menthe	2
Falernum	2
Herbsaint	1
Bénédictine	1
Fernet-Branca	1
Yellow Chartreuse	1
Coffee liqueur	1
Aperol	1
Crème de violette	1
Crème de mûre	1
Amaretto	1
Apricot liqueur	1

WINES

Sparkling wine	5
Sweet vermouth	4
Blanc vermouth	3
Cocchi Americano	3
Sherry	2
Dry vermouth	1
Red wine	1

BITTERS

Orange bitters	15
Angostura bitters	14
Peychaud's bitters	7
Angostura cacao bitters	1
Grapefruit bitters	1
Bittercube #2 Jamaican bitters	1

SYRUP

Simple syrup	22
Demerara syrup	13
Orgeat	2
Honey syrup	2
Grenadine	1
Raspberry syrup	1
Cold brew syrup	1
Cinnamon syrup	1
Vanilla syrup	1

PANTRY

Fresh lime juice	22
Fresh lemon juice	20
Soda water	6
Egg white	6
Heavy cream	5
Grapefruit juice	3
Pineapple juice	3
Ginger beer	2
Cranberry juice	1
Coca-Cola	1
Orange marmalade	1
Coffee	1
Grapefruit soda	1
Coconut cream	1
Orange flower water	1

Turning Up
the Volume
on Syrups

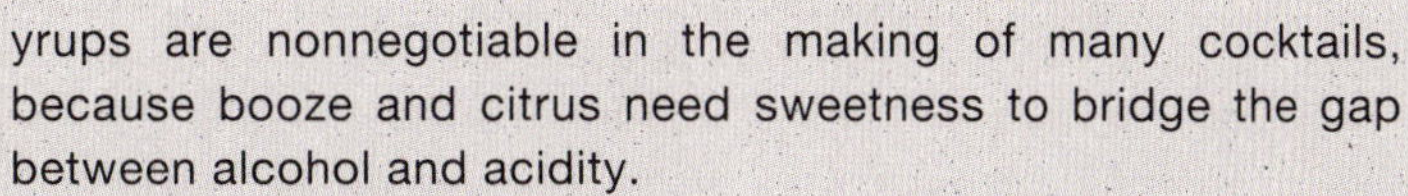

yrups are nonnegotiable in the making of many cocktails, because booze and citrus need sweetness to bridge the gap between alcohol and acidity.

I make most of my syrups in a blender with room-temperature water instead of heating them on the stove. Why? First, and I have no scientific proof of this, but heated syrup feels slick and sweet, which is not the texture you want in most cocktails. Also, there is the very real possibility that you will lose water to evaporation, throwing off the sweetness ratio and ruining the balance of the cocktail. Finally, if your syrup is hot, you must chill it, which takes 10 minutes in a bath of water, ice, and salt. Longer if you put it in the fridge. This is a waste of precious time that you could be drinking.

If you own a house, take out a second mortgage and buy a Vitamix. Its brawn is second to none. If not, buy any middle-of-the-road priced blender, but don't cheap out with a bottom-shelf model, because it will be frustrating to use. And if work is toil, you won't want to do it. Get one with a lid that disengages and pops out, so you can add things into the mix while frappéing.

In the following pages you'll find recipes for all the syrups you need for this book. Commercial versions of these syrups can also be found in stores and online. This is great because those typically have good consistency from batch to batch, which is hard to create yourself at home when only making syrups occasionally. I recommend everything coming out of Small Hand Foods and Liber & Co., but I'm not going to hold it against you if you stray from those brands.

SIMPLE SYRUP

This is the syrup you will make the most of: an everyday workhorse that adds texture and sweetness, without adding flavor. Measure 1 cup sugar and 1 cup room-temp water independently of one another (i.e., in separate measuring cups) to keep the right ratios intact. Pour the water into a deli container (or a large mason jar), then add the sugar to the water. Put the lid on tightly and shake vigorously to combine. Test the texture. It should feel plump and silky smooth. If not, shake it again, test, and repeat until the liquid is sans graininess.
Yield: ~1½ cups

DEMERARA SYRUP

The heftier, sweeter alternative to simple syrup, "Dem" is a great option for supporting aged spirits in drinks. In a blender, pour in ½ cup room-temp water first. Then add 1 cup of Demerara sugar. Blend on low until incorporated. Funnel into a bottle, cap, and let cool.
Yield: ~1 cup

HONEY SYRUP

Honey's inherent texture is outrageously thick, so we dilute it with room-temperature water to reach a consistency that will flow easily from a speed pourer. We use the ratio of 1 part water to 4 parts honey. To make 1 cup total, add ¼ cup water to a mason jar or other container with a lid, then add ¾ cup honey and shake until no clumps are left.

Yield: ~¾ cup

Use this to make the Airmail (page 61), Bee's Knees (page 81), and maybe the Hemingway Daiquiri (page 153) or the Whiskey Sour (page 305).

GRENADINE

Our grenadine is half fresh and half cooked for extra dimension, as we made it at The Violet Hour. Measure 1 cup POM pomegranate juice into a saucepan on the stove. Measure another 1 cup and set aside. Peel 1 orange into as many strips of peel as possible and add the peels to the saucepan. Heat over medium heat until the liquid has reduced by about half, so you end up with about ½ cup, 13 to 14 minutes, depending on your stove. Pull out the orange peels. Add the reserved 1 cup pomegranate juice to the reduced portion. Measure the outcome. You should have a little less than 1½ cups. Add 5 dashes each of Angostura and Peychaud's bitters, then 1½ cups of sugar. Stir until the sugar has completely dissolved. (Or shake in the mason jar or deli container you'll use to store the syrup.)

Yield: ~2 cups

Use this to make the Jack Rose (page 173), and maybe an Old Fashioned (page 241).

CINNAMON SYRUP

This is a total showstopper in tropical drinks, and others made with aged spirits like Cognac and whiskey; you can also use this recipe with other spices if you're feeling frisky. Follow the instructions on page 29 to make a batch of Simple Syrup using 1 cup sugar and 1 cup water; set that aside. Crackle up 23 grams of cinnamon bark (about 2½ thick sticks). You don't need a precise and even method, just break up the sticks into chunks large enough to get caught in a sieve. Toast the cinnamon in a skillet over low to medium heat, hot enough to release the oils in the cinnamon but not enough to scorch the bark. When you start to smell wisps of toasted cinnamon (not smoke! That's too hot!), pull it off the heat and dump the bark into the syrup. Set aside to infuse for 15 to 20 minutes, checking on the flavor every few minutes. When the liquid starts to change color and the flavors taste saturated, you're on the right path. As soon as you think the flavor is bold enough, strain and discard the cinnamon bark. If you pull it too soon and the cinnamon syrup is feeling kinda wimpy, you can toast more cinnamon and steep again.

Yield: ~1½ cups

Use this to make the Jet Pilot (page 177) and maybe an Old Fashioned (page 241).

VANILLA SYRUP

Vanilla is a great subtle addition to drinks made with aged spirits, like añejo tequila or rum. It's also a banger alongside passion fruit. First, make a batch of Demerara syrup using 2 cups Demerara sugar and 1 cup water, but this time use the stovetop method. In a saucepan, combine the two ingredients and slowly bring the mix up to a boil. Reduce the heat to medium-high and stir until the sugar is dissolved. Remove from the heat. Add a 2-inch piece of vanilla bean to the syrup and set aside to infuse for 15 to 20 minutes, checking on the flavor every few minutes. When the liquid starts to change color and the flavors taste saturated, you're on the right path. As soon as you think the flavor is bold enough, strain out all the bits. Let cool before using.

Yield: ~2 cups

Use this to make the Porn Star Martini (page 265) or maybe a Hot Toddy (page 161).

ORGEAT

The most classic tiki sweetener of all time. You have two options for how to make it:

The long route: Spread 33 grams of almonds over a sheet pan and roast at 400°F for 25 minutes, shaking the pan every 5 minutes or so to ensure the nuts don't burn. Crush the roasted almonds by either tossing them in a shaker and muddling or bashing them with a sauté pan on a cutting board. Pour 1 cup water into a medium bowl, add 2 cups sugar and the almonds, and let the mixture sit overnight. Force-strain the liquid through a Superbag or a fine-mesh sieve. Measure the amount and add 13 drops of orange flower water per 1 cup.

The easy route: Combine equal parts unsweetened almond milk with Demerara sugar by adding the dry ingredient, aka the sugar, to the wet ingredient, aka the almond milk, so that the two integrate well. Run it through a blender until the sugar dissolves and then add 1 ounce of orange curaçao and a barspoon of orange flower water.

Yield: ~2 cups

Use this to make the Saturn (page 277) and the Mai Tai (page 189).

RASPBERRY SYRUP

This fresh berry syrup can also be made with strawberries or blackberries or, hell, even marionberries if you please. Into your mason jar or 1-quart deli container, measure 1 cup sugar and add 12 to 15 fresh berries (we always use fresh, but at home you can use frozen if they are 100 percent thawed and not hot from a quick microwave). Muddle lightly, then add 5 dashes of Peychaud's bitters to the mix. Let sit for about 15 minutes, enough time for the bitters to really soak into the berry/sugar combination. Then add 1 cup water, cover, and shake until the sugar has dissolved. Force-strain through a fine-mesh sieve, pressing on the berries with a spoon or muddler to extract as much liquid as possible. Some of the pulp will make it through, and that's a good thing, because it creates a nice round and voluptuous texture for the syrup.

Yield: ~1½ cups

Use this to make the Clover Club (page 109) and maybe the Bramble (page 93) or Sherry Cobbler (page 285).

FASSIONOLA

This is the original syrup used to make Hurricanes, before passion fruit became the norm. I like using it in drinks that sing with fresh fruits, or as an interesting alternative to grenadine. In a pot, combine 1 cup passion fruit pulp or puree and 1½ cups water and heat to 190°F over medium-high heat. Add 2 tablespoons guava jelly and 2 cups sugar and stir until they have fully integrated into the mix. Remove from the heat. Add ¼ cup dried hibiscus leaves. Let rest (at room temp) overnight. Remove the hibiscus before bottling.

Yield: ~4 cups

Use this to make the Hurricane (page 165) and maybe the Saturn (page 277).

ALWAYS LABEL SYRUPS WITH THE DATE YOU MADE THEM, BECAUSE YOU WILL FORGET. STORE IN THE REFRIGERATOR, WHERE THEY WILL STAY VIABLE FOR ABOUT TWO WEEKS.

The Deep Cut Guide to Glassware

here are no hard-and-fast rules when it comes to gathering glassware. Most decisions come down to personal choice. I will happily drink a double Tom Collins out of my sturdy Guinness pint glass or pour a French 75 into this weird highball I found at a thrift store—the cheat, or base, on that bad boy is as thick as a '70s disco diva's platforms—for example. But I would rather drink out of a jagged, rusty, partially opened soup can that's been passed around the filthy paws of a smack of rabid raccoons than sip an Old Fashioned from a green, square rocks glass.

My biggest piece of practical advice is to prioritize substance over style, because the shape, size, and material of your glass will influence the temperature, aroma, and balance of the drink in question. For example, super-thin cocktail glasses look fancy, but they shake off cold temps fast and can disintegrate in your hands when washing or polishing. Thicker glasses are more durable and will stay colder for longer. At home, you can usually get away with having just a few standard Double Old Fashioneds and coupes, because that covers a wide range of drink styles. At the bar, find a glassware manufacturer that delivers on time, has a wide variety of options, and rarely discontinues a line, so you have fewer things to worry your pretty head about every night behind the stick.

Think about how the cocktail will be served—we've listed the styles out for you here—then choose a vessel that best supports its temperature, aroma, and texture.

COCKTAILS SERVED UP

Examples: Last Word, Martini, Bamboo
Glass: Coupe or Nick & Nora (sometimes a sidecar)

Always serve "up" cocktails in glasses with stems, like coupes and Nick & Noras. First, because the shape stops the cocktail from flash-flooding both sides of your mouth, as can happen with the garish V-shaped Martini glasses if you aren't paying attention. The stems also prevent your grubby little mitts from warming up the glass. Bonus points for a narrow opening, because the more surface area, the faster the liquid warms up. The exception to this is drinks made with egg whites—see egg white cocktails (page 35) for more intel.

Sidecars: For times when your cocktail has more liquid than the glass holds, you need a tiny carafe or sidecar to hold the leftover liquid on the side. When stored on ice or in your freezer while you sip, it keeps that little extra bit of cocktail nice and frosty, until you are ready to top off the glass with more. Audrey Saunders—who opened the pioneering cocktail bar Pegu Club in NYC, which has since sadly closed—sells hand-blown glass versions via Cocktail Kingdom online. For my bar programs, I buy them through Libbey—to find these, you can google "Libbey 735 glass wine decanter, 6½ ounces" and you'll find the right size and shape.

COCKTAILS SERVED DOWN, OR ON THE ROCKS

Examples: Sazerac, Old Fashioned, Vieux Carré
Glass: Double Old Fashioned

Much like Russian literature, which should be read out of a gargantuan hardback, cocktails like the sturdy Sazerac or serious Old Fashioned should be housed in a heavy glass to match the vibe and keep temps cold for a long time. Choose Double Old Fashioned glasses that have a clunky cheat—the solid part at the bottom, named as such because it makes the drink look fuller, i.e., "cheating" the guest out of more booze—so your fingers don't warm up the glass.

I like tall DOF glasses, because the collar—the area between the surface of the drink and the lip of the glass—is prime real estate to add an aromatic component. Take the Sazerac, for example: The absinthe you use to rinse the glass before pouring in the cocktail will disappear into the drink if there is no collar to stick to. With a large collar, you get a powerful punch of aroma. (The Collar Theory also applies to drinks served up in a coupe that call for rinses, like an Aviation, page 73.) Note that tall DOF glasses will need extra-long citrus peels to sit above the rim.

COCKTAILS SERVED ON CRUSHED ICE

Examples: Mint Julep, Queen's Park Swizzle
Glass: Metal Julep cup, Collins, or footed Pilsner

Metal Julep cups conduct a frightening chill, which is why they're perfect for crushed ice drinks that you want to sip slowly. You can also use a Collins or a footed Pilsner, but it's not as cool-looking, and the glass material won't hold the same icy chill for as long.

CARBONATED COCKTAILS

Examples: Aperol Spritz, Cuba Libre, French 75, Moscow Mule
Glass: Highball or Collins

Highball glasses are tall and narrow, best suited for two-ingredient drinks like Scotch and Soda or Gin and Tonic. Collins glasses hold more liquid (at least 4 ounces of "cocktail" plus sparkling water), so they are perfect for cocktails like the Tom Collins (hence the name). Both styles come in many sizes, so think about what ice you're using—if you have regular home freezer ice machine ice, the glass will need to be bigger than if you have long, thin single shards of ice cut for service. For recipes that include Champagne instead of sparkling water or soda, you're typically adding less carbonated liquid to the glass, so the glassware should be smaller (unless crushed ice is involved, in which case a highball works well).

HOT COCKTAILS

Examples: Hot Toddy, Irish Coffee
Glass: Irish Coffee glass or ceramic mug

You can serve hot drinks in your favorite coffee cup, because ceramics retain heat well. If you want more visual appeal, go clear with an Irish Coffee glass. Like the ones they use at The Buena Vista café in San Francisco, this is a stemmed 6-ounce glass that looks like a Nick & Nora had a major growth spurt. Always get a mug with a handle, so you don't burn your fingers when holding on to the hot, hot glass.

EGG WHITE COCKTAILS

Examples: Clover Club, New York Sour, Pisco Sour
Glass: Shallow, wide coupe

Egg white cocktails dressed up to the nines with an aromatic garnish will always smell better than naked ones. This is typically achieved via festooning the surface with bitters or atomizing something delicious over the surface. Shallow, wide coupes are great, because the expansive surface area creates plenty of room for aromatic garnishes to float undeterred toward one's inquisitive proboscis. These glasses don't keep the cocktail very cold for very long, though—there is always give and take in these equations—so the drink should be consumed quickly.

TROPICAL DRINKS

Examples: Jet Pilot, Zombie, Long Island Iced Tea
Glass: Tiki mug, footed Pilsner, or Hurricane glass

When your cocktail is a muddy orange or brown color, throw it in a quirky tiki mug! I love the textures of these, some smooth as a river stone, others rougher than a cat's tongue. I love the whimsy, too, as some resemble parrots and sharks and peacocks, while others look like pirates and grim reapers, and famous cocktail personalities like Paul McGee. Oh my! Also, there is really no glass better at sealing in the cold and combating unwanted condensation than a tiki mug. If you don't want to invest in a newly minted one—they can be somewhat pricey if you're not lucky enough to score an old cheap one at an antiques mall—or if the drink has an electrifying color that shouldn't be hidden, you can use a footed Pilsner or Hurricane glass for these cocktails.

COMP

THE COM-POSITION

The Step-by-Step of Mixing Cocktails

he study and practice of making drinks is like stepping in a river—it's never the same twice, and that makes it a fascinating, intellectual pursuit. To get to the point where you're acting on instinct and shaping your materials into something beautiful without much effort, as most craftspeople do—think about the best ceramicist or pianist or woodworker you know—you must know the craft inside and out. The way you get to this point is to establish good habits and practice them every time you step up to the plate.

In the sessions, we're going to teach you how to make each drink in painstaking step-by-step detail, but there are some universal tenets and techniques you can apply to your practice, so we're going to walk you through those first. These are the "hows" and "whys" of every step of drink-making. All of these add up to create a balanced drink. Consider every step as important as using a manual to defuse a bomb or build a soapbox car—you want to do everything in the proper order, and for the love of god don't leave anything out.

SET YOUR MISE EN PLACE

If you've ever worked in a professional kitchen, or watched an episode of *Top Chef*, you already understand the importance of mise en place when cooking. Mize, as I call it, also applies to the trade of cocktails. The word roughly translates to "organizing the stuff you need to get shit done," and refers to the prepping and gathering of ingredients and tools so you can mix cocktails stress-free and FAST. There is nothing more frustrating when you reach for a bottle and discover it's only got half an irksome amount of liquid in it, or when you discover your salt is all clumped up and unusable, or when there's nary a bar towel in sight and you just spilled heavy cream all over the counter. All of these things impede the flow of making drinks, which is absolutely crazy making. Everything should be within arm's reach to maximize speed and cleanliness.

Good mize starts before you even *think* about mixing a drink. First, choose a logical place to mix. If I'm not working on a wooden bar top, I set up my mize on a bar towel or a Silpat (silicone baking mat), paired with a cutting board that's easy to wash. I hate bar mats with every fiber of my being. They aren't as sturdy as I want them to be and they collect spillage. Fuck those things. It's also important to ergonomically organize your station between the sink and the ice, because you will need to grab ice once or twice while making drinks, and you need a place to dump it after mixing, too.

Second, don't have shit you don't need in your station! You'll spend all your time knocking it over or pushing it aside, wasting valuable energy. Sure, that dusty bottle of rare 23-year-old Scotch is impressive, but unless you are

We live in a miraculous time where we can buy citrus year-round at the grocery store or local market. But it fluctuates in quality, depending on how far away it comes, what the rainfall was in the days and weeks before harvest, and if it was packed well, and rotated right. If you are hand-picking out fruits at the supermarket, make sure they are large and soft. Juicy, but not squishy! Room-temperature fruit will give more juice, so if your fruits are cold, let them float around in a bowl of room-temp—not hot—water for a few minutes to come up to a better degree before juicing. Finally, taste your juice before you mix a drink! Fresh citrus should taste bright and bouncy, with a hint of sweetness—if it tastes flat, dull, or borderline acrid, use another lemon or lime for the cocktail.

banging out Rob Roys (page 199) with it, put it in a cabinet alongside the other expensive and esoteric bottles and backups. Same with gimmicky barware or equipment. The vintage ice crusher stays on the shelf until you are making Mai Tais (page 189).

I'm going to give you a checklist to set up the mize for every session in this book. One more word of wisdom first: For the most seasoned barkeeps, good mize is a state of mind. It is visualizing what you will be doing and knowing all the steps so well that you can see what's missing from your station, or the process, in a heartbeat or single glance. You could extend this metaphor to developing consistency in your mixing practice. Always read the full recipe from start to finish before embarking on it—you could call this cocktail due diligence—to make sure you have everything you need to make that drink and have a general understanding of everything you will encounter in the act of making the cocktail. Then when mixing, think two steps ahead, always, and especially when you're serving drinks to other people. Your practice will benefit from it in the long run.

TASTE YOUR INGREDIENTS

At some point when training bartenders I tell them they need to taste every bottle behind the bar, and when they are done, to start at the beginning and do it again. I see fear and wonder in most of their eyes at this moment, because knowing even a little bit about all those bottles is both Herculean and Sisyphean. You can no more know every wave in an ocean than you can know every distillate, fortified wine, liqueur, amaro, and sparkling wine on terra firma. But it's important to taste everything, because knowing your ingredients inside and out makes them easier to work with in the long run.

To have a practitioner's palate, you need to build an arsenal of taste knowledge in your brain. Taste voraciously and with great fervor. Take notes! Look for the things that you don't expect as you do this, like the sugary part of lime juice and the flowery parts of Scotch. What the fuck is so soft in that amaro, which is otherwise just a lion's roar of bitterness? This is the big-picture palate work, so squirrel all this intel away for future use.

When you are ready to mix—after all your mize is arranged at your station and before you do anything else—sneak a quick taste of the ingredients you are about to mix with, again. Even if you *think* you are familiar with how they taste, memory is a fickle thing, so a refresher never hurts. During these tastes, you're looking for sweetness, acidity, and proof, and how those things come together in balance or imbalance, so you can adjust a cocktail when you find it's too dry or too sweet on the second straw taste (page 48). Flavor is the last thing you need to consider in this moment, because if you're using high-quality products, the makers of these liquids have already created great flavor foundations for you. You just need to know how to work with them.

Also look for freshness during this quick taste. This is especially

☐ **Refrigerate your wines and bubbles.** Sodas and sparkling wines will not hold a fizzy structure unless they're really fucking cold, and fortified and aromatized wines like vermouths and sherries will oxidize faster at room temp. Chill these ingredients in the freezer or refrigerator—or the back patio like Chicagoans do in the dead of winter—to get them as frosty as possible before mixing.

☐ **Check your eggs.** To ensure your eggs are fresh enough to mix with, fill a clear bowl or large cup or 1-quart deli container with cold water (big enough for the egg to not touch the sides). Gently place the egg in the water. If it sinks and lies on its side, it's super fresh. If it sits on the top or bottom end, it's fine. If it floats . . . time to pick another cocktail to make.

☐ **Chill your glassware.** This happens in one of two ways: For drinks served in a coupe or Nick & Nora, chill in a freezer for at least 5 to 10 minutes. Five will give you a nice light frost, while ten will hold a solid chill for much longer. For Double Old Fashioned glasses and Collins glasses, which are harder to keep in a freezer and more apt to slip from your fingers, fill the vessel with ice and water and let it sit for a similar amount of time at your station. Cold glass, full hearts, can't lose!

☐ **Temper your ice.** If your ice is too cold— i.e., straight from a home freezer—it will not melt fast enough in the shaker or mixing glass, meaning you end up with an underdiluted cocktail. Or it will shatter when you start to shake it, which creates overdilution. Both scenarios result in off-kilter balance. At home, temper for at least five minutes. When it's ready, the ice will look slick or a little sweaty, like it's gotten home from a tough day and is kicking back in a recliner, relaxed.

☐ **Grab your bar towels.** Like six of them, for when you need to clean up spills. Clean and folded. If it's summer, keep them in the fridge. This is an old line cook's trick. When the kitchen is hot, a cool towel is pure joy, like pulling on dry socks after playing in the rain.

☐ **Arrange your ingredients.** I line ingredients up from cheapest to most expensive, so I can grab each one in order of how they go into the tin or mixing glass. Floats and "bottom" liquids are the exceptions—line them up in the order you add them to the glass. (The mixing instructions will tell you when this happens, if you are unsure.) Have fresh citrus and fresh herbs on hand for garnish prep, too. Make sure the herbs are pleasing to look at. No brown edges! Those are an affront to all things beautiful. Remember: We drink with our eyes, too.

☐ **Ready your tools.** Everything should rest within hand's reach. Knives with the sharp edges pointed away from your money makers. Jigger? Present, clean, and ready as always. Do you have your Hawthorne, Julep, and fine strainer at hand? Good. This mize also includes tasting straws and a place to put them after they are used (aka a trash bin), because you will taste each cocktail twice before all is said and done.

☐ **Pull up your trash can.** Keep it close to your station, so you can throw things away without hesitation. Put it back under the sink after all drinks and cleanup are finished.

☐ **Have your "seasonings" at the ready.** I always grab simple and Demerara syrups, plus the holy trinity of bitters—Angostura, Peychaud's, and orange—for my station because sometimes I need to adjust a recipe to taste. Adding syrup to a cocktail is like adding butter to a dish even when it's not in the recipe (called monter au beurre in the cooking world), it adds a bit of "fat" that plumps up the texture nicely. Adding a dash of bitters is like sprinkling flaky sea salt on a steak before serving—one dash brings a tiny spider bite of flavor and complexity to the cocktail.

pertinent advice for dairy products, because bad cream will ruin a drink faster than a mixologist in a tiki bar will tell you their Zombie spec. Sell-by dates are generally reliable guidelines, but you can often use dairy beyond the date stamped on the packaging, especially in the case of really high-quality, locally sourced stuff (if you have the privilege of access to these things). Trust your instincts.

MEASURE PRECISELY AND CONSISTENTLY

A cocktail with precise balance is a thing of beauty. In cooking, chefs balance Salt, Fat, Acid, and Heat (according to the brilliant Samin Nosrat), but in cocktails it's more like: Booze, Bitter, Sweet, Sour, and Water. Not nearly as catchy, I know, but when you spin these plates in the right alignment, the cocktail becomes seamless and elegant. If you do it really well, it can be awe-inspiring.

Always measure using a jigger, because precision is key to creating balance. Specifically, I use the Leopold jigger with hash marks for ¼ ounce, ½ ounce, ¾ ounce, and 1 ounce when full on the small side, and 1½ ounces and 2 ounces when full on the big side, which tend to work universally for the ratios I'm pouring. This jigger is almost indestructible, and I also like how it feels in my hands: The weight is satisfying, and when you accidentally tap it against the bar top or metal tins or a belt buckle, it sings.

To jigger precisely, hold the jigger between your index and "fuck you" fingers so you can easily pour liquid from the jigger into your tin. I touch my ring finger to the edge of the tin I'm pouring into, because I spill less that way. Hold the jigger completely level when you pour the liquid inside, because more than one positive meniscus will add up to ¼ ounce of liquid if you aren't careful, and then your drink will be topsy-turvy instead of balanced. Only Tony Hawk is allowed above the rim!

There are exceptions to this rule: Sometimes in a recipe we'll add a + or − next to a measurement (see the Mai Tai, page 189, for example) to indicate that you should measure the liquid slightly above or below the hash-mark of the jigger. These "bold" and "shy" measures are all in service of adding a bit more (or less) of an ingredient, but not a full ¹⁄₁₆ ounce. There aren't too many of those in this book because it's a more advanced technique, but it's something worth considering for a beat or two as you get started.

CUSTOMIZE YOUR SHAKE OR STIR

Shaking or stirring a drink does two things: It chills and adds water, which fuses together the booze, sugar, and (sometimes) acid into one cohesive melody. Some people call this process "dilution," but that sounds like we're watering things down instead of bringing them together in sparkling harmony. I prefer to call it buffering, like when you buff a glass or mirror until it shines— it's what transforms disparate ingredients into a cocktail.

Shaking adds lively effervescence, making the cocktail look riled up and opaque. Stirring creates silky smoothness and a calm and clear(ish) appearance, because less air is injected into the mix. The difference between the two styles also begs for two different drinking experiences: a Daiquiri freshly shaken should be quaffed with dispatch, but a Manhattan, stirred to viscous cold, should be sipped with reverence.

Shake drinks that include juice, egg, or dairy, because these components need an aggressive bashing to fully integrate. Stir those made with distillates, vermouths, amari, and other fortified and aromatized wines, because spirits and their ilk tend to hook up without much encouragement. (The Espresso Martini and Stinger are notable exceptions to these guidelines—find out why on pages 137 and 293, respectively.)

THE TOOLS AND MECHANICS OF SHAKING

I like using Toby Tins—yes, they are eponymous, see *Manny* for the full story—where a small metal shaker fits inside a larger one, because they seal well, are easy to clean, and keep ingredients nice and cold. They come in different sizes, so make sure the two sides fit together, and the combo feels proportionate in your hands. Japanese companies like Koriko make great ones with a weighted bottom that don't tip over easily.

Always use a consistent amount of ice to shake. Always! This creates a foundation for you to make intuitive decisions about when a cocktail is ready to strain into the glass. When you are just starting out, use 5 cubes. It's a very Goldilocks number—not too few, not too many. There are exceptions to this, of course. I use 3 cubes for an egg white drink like the Clover Club (page 109), or if the proof is really low like a straight-ahead Pimm's Cup (page 253), because it doesn't need as much dilution to come into balance.

Physically, when I'm shaking, I engage the biggest, strongest, and most muscles possible. You don't want all the work to land on your elbows and forearms, because this will get you tennis elbow to the point you can't button a shirt. I sink down a little, knees bent, engage my core and think about using my shoulders and back while I move. I try to switch between my dominant and nondominant hand as well, so I am not using only one side of my body all night. Always make sure that you have both hands on both sides of the shaker. Hook a pinkie and a thumb on each bottom so the tins don't unseal and shower you, and the folks nearest to you, with liquids.

Pacing-wise, with 80-proof spirits in the drink, songs that are 120 beats per minute, like "Seven Nation Army" by The White Stripes, or "Come as You Are" by Nirvana, are a great pace to aim for with your movement. With high-proof spirits in play, try 180 BPM songs like "Modern Love" by Bowie. And sometimes, like with the Stinger (page 293), you need to shake to the frenzied beat of KMFDM "A Drug Against War."

After you've shaken, I encourage you to "wring and tap" before you strain, to make sure every drop of cocktail makes it into the glass. (Yes, Wring & Tap sounds like the new speakeasy behind the laundromat.) Pour the cocktail from the small tin into the large one, twirling (wringing) the tin as you do this. Then tap the lip of the small tin against the big tin to propel the remaining drops out.

When I worked on the opening staff of Pegu Club in 2005, owner Audrey Saunders taught us one of the litmus tests she used to decide which of our hairbrained recipes would make the menu. First, she would take a sip of the cocktail to make sure it's delicious right away. Then she'd let the drink sit and "die" a little bit before taking another sip to make sure it still tasted good, in the event the drinker wanted to sit with it while they chat with friends. She'd do this a third, and fourth, and sometimes fifth time, when nobody in their right mind would conceivably consume the drink anymore because all the ice has melted or the temperature has warmed beyond what is appropriate in a civil society, to see if the drink still held its structure and general deliciousness. This is what I now call the "narrative arc" of the drink: how its flavor, texture, and temperature change in the glass over time. Each cocktail has a unique arc as the water eats the sugar and the booze, and time forces the aroma into the ether. The best bartenders anticipate the way this will happen and adjust their mixing technique accordingly, so that each sip tastes great. (Narrative arc also applies to the journey every sip takes you through, too—the nose, attack, and finish, which we'll talk a bit more about in the sessions.)

SERVED WITH ICE

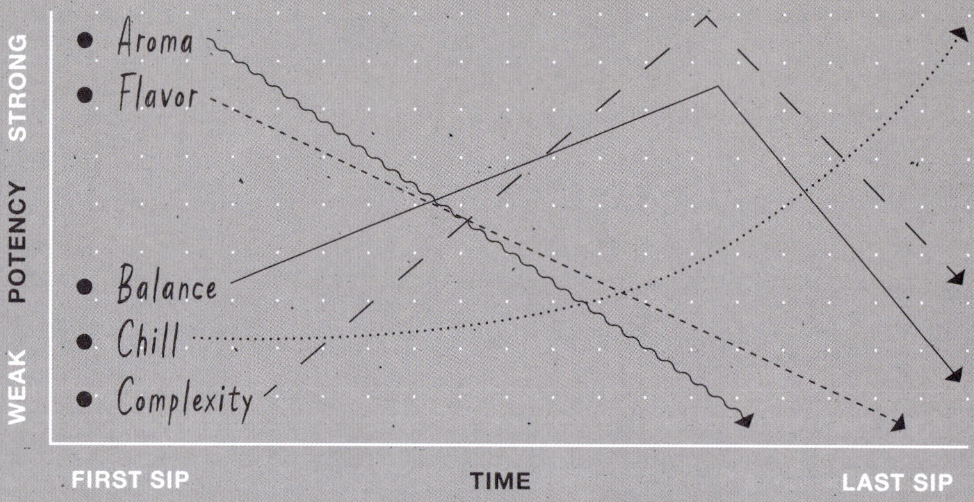

SERVED WITHOUT ICE

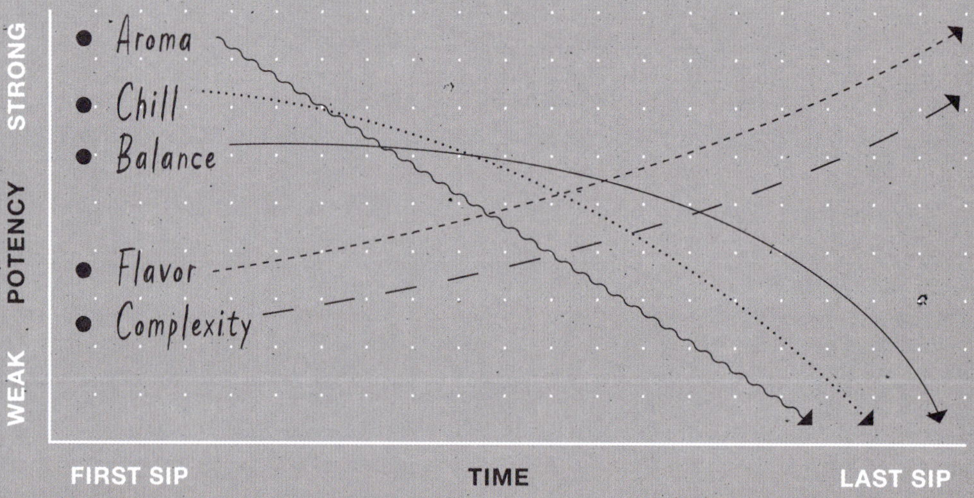

The greatest myth about shaking and stirring is that you can use the same length and intensity of shake or stir for every cocktail. This is flat-out false. Cocktails are not static things—the temperature, balance, texture, and flavor all change from first to last sip, depending on a whole host of factors. I call this progression "narrative arc," stealing from the literary term that explains how a book or movie plot progresses from beginning to end. The key to making a cocktail taste great from start to finish is to anticipate its arc and adjust your shake or stir accordingly.

SHAKE STYLES

Mime Shake 🍶🍶🍶🍶 + Coupe Shake 🍶🍶🍶🍶🍶

When shaking egg white drinks, we shake in two phases: first without ice (Mime Shake) to whip air into the egg whites, which helps them mesh seamlessly with the other liquid ingredients. Other bartenders call this a "dry shake," but that makes zero sense because we're working with wet ingredients. After you've mime shook for a minute or so, set the tin down and take a beat—like, a full minute at least—to let the citric acid of the citrus juice denature the proteins of the egg whites, making them fluffier. The second shake, done with ice, is to get the cocktail cold and add water content. We use the Coupe Shake for the second shake, whether the drink is served in an iceless coupe or in a Double Old Fashioned glass over a large ice cube or multiple cubes; we do this because even though there is ice in the DOF, it takes a bit of extra time to get those egg whites nice and cold. See the Amaretto Sour (page 65), Clover Club (page 109), and New York Sour (page 233) for a few examples of when to Mime Shake + Coupe Shake.

Coupe Shake 🍶🍶🍶🍶🍶

Drinks served up in a coupe, like a Gimlet (page 145), will not gain further dilution as they sit in the glass because there is no ice in play, so shake for a good long time to get a lot of water content into the mix and achieve balance. You also shake for a long time to get the cocktail suuuper cold, since it will only warm up in the glass over time. That first sip should send shivers up your spine. Listen for the ice in the tin to sound like it's turning into slush, then shake for a few beats longer. This sonic moment sounds like when you tell your friend Malört is a great substitute for red bitters in a Negroni and you're confronted with a sharply arched brow and a: "SHHHHHH, don't say that out loud."

Rocks Shake ▮▮▮▮

On the opposite end of the spectrum, drinks served over ice cubes (like the Margarita, page 201) gain a good amount of ice melt over time as they swim in the glass, so they need a medium-length shake to chill the ingredients and give them a slight dilution. Stop shaking when the tin feels cold to the touch.

Collins Shake ▮▮▮

With a highball or Collins cocktail, most of the water content exists in the form of sparkling water, so you don't need to shake the "body" of the drink for very long. This shake just pulls the heat out of the room-temperature ingredients, so that when the cocktail hits the ice and carbonated liquid inside the glass, it doesn't warm up right away. Shake for 4 or 5 beats, then quit and strain.

Whip Shake ▮▮

Intended for drinks served over crushed ice, this is the shortest shake, because there is so much chill and dilution that will happen in the glass! Typically, you only need an ounce or two of crushed ice in the tin—shake until the ice becomes quiet, and then you are done. No need to strain if the drink will have a straw. "Rock and roll" it directly into the glass!

THE TOOLS AND MECHANICS OF STIRRING

To stir, you're going to need a mixing glass and a barspoon. If you want to be old-school, I recommend a 22-ounce Imperial pint glass that is tempered, which means it can go from hot to cold, or cold to hot, quickly, and without shattering. The glass should have a little T, for "tempered," on the bottom to indicate this. Make sure it holds more than 16 ounces, otherwise it will be too small to properly mix two cocktails at a time—an occasion that often arises at home and at the bar. Buy a few, they aren't pricey. Or go for the insulated metal mixing "glasses" now available, which will last forever, and get cold super-fast.

For the spoon, I was brought up with the "Red Tipped" barspoon, which is clunkier and harder to use than the sleek, fast Japanese spoons that are all the rage now, but I would recommend getting a cheap barspoon first and once you get comfortable with that, you can use something more professional. You want the spoon to feel natural in your hands as you stir, or else you'll be wrangling the spoon instead of having the spoon wrangle the drink. Not ideal. The shaft should be smooth like a barber's pole in three dimensions, as it will spin easier in between your fingers.

Before you add anything to the mixing glass, make sure the vessel feels room temperature to the touch. If you stir in a frozen mixing glass, it will take forever to get the right water content, and if the glass is right out of the dishwasher, it'll melt the ice too fast. Both scenarios will make the balance of the cocktail off-kilter. When stirring, hold onto the very base of the vessel (the cheat) with your nondominant hand, so that your body temperature doesn't warm up the glass. It's also more secure this way.

As with shaking, you want to establish consistency regarding how much ice you use to stir. I typically fill up the glass three-quarters of the way and keep adding fresh ice along the way to shock the drink with an electric chill. I will often add a few cubes to the top just before the cocktail is ready and

then strain over those—the extra cubes help the Julep strainer hold its position, and give a tiny blast of H_2O and chill to the cocktail as it exits the vessel.

Motionwise, a stir should be suave and controlled. If you're using a Red Tipped barspoon, which has a large bowl, aim for a stir that lands around 120 beats per minute, like "How Will I Know" by Whitney Houston. If you've got a smaller Japanese-style barspoon, aim for more like 180 BMP, like "Blitzkrieg Bop" by The Ramones.

Know that stirring is the hardest technique to master. You are going to be BAD at it when you start. Sure, you have stirred a coffee, or a stew simmering over a hot stove, or maybe even the feelings of someone's heart (this is trickier), but stirring a cocktail requires a totally different motion. Hold the spoon between your fingers like you would hold a pen, then pull the bottom of the spoon with your top finger and then pull the bottom of the spoon away from you with the lower finger. Steady your hand and wrist so it moves as little as possible.

To polish your stirring skills and develop intuition for the practice, straw taste the cocktail as you stir. First, as soon as the drink is put together in the mixing glass, so you know what the cocktail tastes like without chill and water content. Then straw taste every 20 to 30 rotations to see how the "heat" of the booze mellows, and the other ingredients get chattier. Eventually, figuring out when a cocktail is "done" and ready to strain into the glass becomes as natural and intuitive as driving to work without a GPS or showing up at the airport with just enough time to fill up your water bottle before boarding.

STIR STYLES

Coupe Stir //////
Drinks like the Martini and Manhattan need a long, luxurious stir to gain enough water content to taste delicious from first sip to last. Stir until the drink looks to have doubled in volume. It should taste as smooth and dry and cold as your ex's heart, because as it warms in the glass, its complexity and flavor will blossom. If it's not cold enough on sip one, the final sip will taste overly sweet and flabby.

Chunk Stir ////
When a cocktail is served over one large glacial cube or sphere of ice, the drink will continue to chill and soften in the glass as the ice melts into its cold embrace. That first sip should be big and bold to accommodate for this arc. Stir about two-thirds as long as a Coupe Stir. The drink is ready when the liquid feels cold in your mouth but not "lightly chilled" as it did during the first one or two straw tastes. Think the difference between wine at cellar temperature and Champagne in an ice bucket. You want this drink ice bucket cold!

Rocks Stir //
With cocktails served over a handful of ice cubes, the goal of the stir is to combine the ingredients and get the drink cold enough so that it doesn't immediately melt the ice in the glass. Think wine cellar temp. You don't need to stir until the ice cubes look diminished and wimpy. Stop when you take a straw taste and the booze has stopped making you wince. It should still taste spirit-forward, but mollified.

STRAW TASTE (AT LEAST) TWICE

After putting the ingredients into the shaker tin or mixing glass, taste to make sure you have everything in the vessel before you shake or stir. You might laugh here as a home mixologist, because how could you possibly forget an ingredient if you're not working under duress in the chaos of a bar? Well, maybe the dog is teasing the cat, maybe the UPS person is leaning on the doorbell, maybe you forgot your syrup in the kitchen and you're making drinks in your basement bar. I don't know. Just do it.

The first taste also gives you a chance to get a sense for what the cocktail tastes like before dilution. This is like looking at the big picture. Like seeing George Seurat's *A Sunday Afternoon on the Island of La Granade Jatte* from five feet away. You get the idea and the shapes at this stage, and you'll use that intel to make informed decisions about the ratios and balance later.

The second taste comes after you've shaken or stirred (or sometimes along the way). This is when you think the drink might be ready, but you need to double-check to make sure. Look for how the texture feels, how the balance is, whether it's cold enough or not. Ask yourself: Does one ingredient stick out like a sore thumb? Too boozy? Too watery? Too sweet? Too acidic? Too bleh? Or is it nice and evenly balanced, with all the ingredients in sync with one another? (Not 'N Sync.) This is when you adjust the cocktail.

Grab a clean straw, stick one end into the liquid, close the other end with your thumb to trap the liquid inside the straw, then taste the contents. Throw that straw out so you don't accidentally introduce bacteria to the next taste.

ADJUST FOR BALANCE

After you've diagnosed the state of your shaken or stirred drink, only tweak one thing at a time. Most of the time I'm adding one dash of bitters or a barspoon of syrup or juice—more bitters to bring extra structure or complexity, more syrup if it's too spiky and acidic, or more juice if it's too sweet—but I'll give you more specific guidance in the mixing instructions of each session, so try not to sweat this too much right now.

STRAIN (ALMOST) EVERY DRINK, EVERY TIME

Strainers are the first line of defense in keeping ice and other flotsam out of the glass, which is why we strain (almost) every cocktail. The exception to the rule is crushed ice cocktails, which you whip shake with a few ounces of crushed ice until the ice melts in the shaker, leaving only liquid ingredients to pour. In this instance, we typically just roll, or pour, all of the contents of the shaker tin directly into the glass.

A well-equipped bar has three types of strainers at the ready: the Hawthorne, Julep, and fine strainer. Each one serves its own purpose.

HAWTHORNE STRAINER

Used to strain shaken cocktails. I like ones with a tight coil to keep the ice inside the tin and a wide gate that allows a free flow of liquid. Avoid the cheap and flimsy ones if you can, but if you are stuck with a budget version, pair it with a fine strainer to catch what the Hawthorne misses.

When ready to strain, place the Hawthorne on top of the shaker so it sits flush inside the lip. Hold the handle between your index and fuck-you fingers to avoid bending your wrist like a T-rex with rickets. This grip also positions your finger on the gate—the opening near the rim of the shaker—so you can "open" or "close it" to control the pour. A poorly gated cocktail floods out like Niagara Falls, whereas a well-poured one will resemble pouring ribbons, with the viscous liquid spinning out like a giggle of children around a maypole. If your cocktails aren't coming off the center of the Hawthorne, you're more likely to make a huge mess.

JULEP STRAINER

For stirred drinks, use a Julep strainer, which is shaped like a large spoon with little holes in the cup. This strainer sits inside the vessel, convex side up or down, depending on how much ice is in the glass. Big and heavy is the way to go, and it should fit snugly inside the mixing glass, so ice doesn't sneak around the sides or bully the strainer out of the way.

FINE STRAINER

Used to double-strain. There are three scenarios in which I do this. First, if the drink has muddled stuff in it, because nobody needs mint shreds or raspberry seeds in their teeth. Second, drinks made with egg white, cream, or pineapple juice taste better with tight bubbles and a silky texture, like a perfectly poured Guinness. Straining has this effect on a cocktail. Finally, when the drink has no straw, forcing lips to touch the rim of the glass, I double-strain to stop floating ice chips from bumping against teeth.

Your fine strainer should be big—larger than the stream of liquid that flows out of your Hawthorne—and conical. A severe angle is important because the flatter the bottom, the slower the liquid will strain through. You want that liquid to flow into the glass quickly, so it doesn't warm up along the way.

To double-strain: Put a Hawthorne strainer on the tin as you normally would, and hold a fine strainer below it, sending the liquid cascading through both strainers from tin into the glass.

GARNISH FOR AESTHETICS
AND AROMA

We devour things with our eyes first—it's why chefs go to great lengths to make food look like art. The same applies to cocktails. Pretty cocktails just taste better, and a cocktail made with good aesthetics serves as a bat signal that the bartender cares about your enjoyment. (Just beware the "aesthetics

When cutting citrus or fruit or herbs for garnish, keep your knives as sharp as a razor! Many finger cuts happen when the knife slips off what you're cutting because it's dull. When not in use, keep knives in a safe and secure spot, like nestled on a towel at the top of your cutting board, handle pointing toward your dominant hand, AT ALL TIMES, so you don't stab yourself when reaching for it. When cutting, keep your thumb tucked up away from the path of the knife so you don't slice yourself. And finally: A falling knife has no handle. Step back fast and far, and let it hit the ground.

for aesthetics' sake" establishment, doing it for the likes on social media; that's a crude and lazy marketing tactic that needs to go down the drain ASAP.)

Most important, a drink should have an inviting aroma, like a scented candle in a cozy foyer in a beautiful house. Our sense of taste is 70 to 90 percent dependent on our sense of smell, so that first aromatic impression matters. The cocktail must smell good and make sense with what's inside the glass.

Smell is also most closely linked to memory and emotions, so fiddling with aroma can create deeper meaning in a drink or make the drinking of said drink stick in the mind for years to come. The first whiff should spark the imagination and stir up curiosity, or prompt feelings of wonder and nostalgia. These are all stupendous things that make a cocktail an *experience* instead of a thirst-quenching glass of booze.

I'm not saying that *every* cocktail needs a garnish. If the cocktail has an intriguing aroma already, like the Last Word (page 185) or the Jungle Bird (page 181), you don't want to mess with that. If it wears a cloud of neutral-smelling egg whites, as is the case with the Clover Club (page 109) or Whiskey Sour (page 305), a little citrus oil will go a long way. (As an aside, a pet peeve of mine, like Siegfried & Roy's pets, is that I fucking hate dehydrated citrus as garnish. It adds no aroma to the cocktail, and it just ain't that pretty.)

In other cases, like the Manhattan (page 193), a garnish can add a new layer of intrigue if you choose an aroma that juxtaposes the flavors in the body of the cocktail. For example, when I was coming up in bartending, the cherry—like the kind on top of a kiddie sundae—was the de rigueur choice, but I have always thought citrus oil is more exciting. Like tossing fresh parsley or basil on top of a lasagna, a bit of lemon or orange oil will add a layer of surprise and intrigue to a glass of whiskey and vermouth.

Tools-wise, when prepping garnish, you'll need a large cutting board to work on; a 4-inch paring knife for cutting herbs and trimming peels for fancy drinks; an offset serrated knife for cutting fruits from limes to pineapples and watermelons; a channel knife for pulling pigtails; and a Y-peeler (or vegetable peeler or cheese slicer) for pulling citrus peels.

Each session will detail exactly where and how and when to place garnishes, but as a general rule of thumb: with all garnishes, be intentional about where you place them in the cocktail. Garnishes should not make the drink hard to drink, or bob about like a Band-Aid in a pot of soup, brushing up against your teeth and lips.

CITRUS GARNISHES

DISK

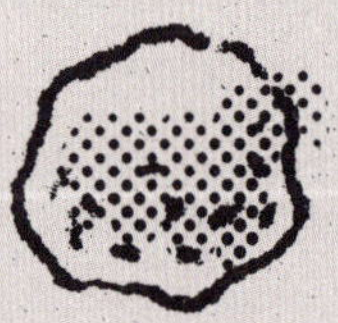

This small circle/coin of citrus peel should be cut to the size of a silver dollar, using a paring knife or offset serrated knife. I use them when I need a jolt of oil over the top of the cocktail as aromatic garnish, but I don't want the citrus rind to serve an aesthetic purpose. You could use a "peel" for this, too (see below), but I find disks more efficient because they are smaller and easier to pinch to express the oils (always pinch the disk with skin side facing the cocktail, so the oils land on the surface of the drink). A peel is like five times the size of a disk, so there is also less waste. These are always discarded after use.

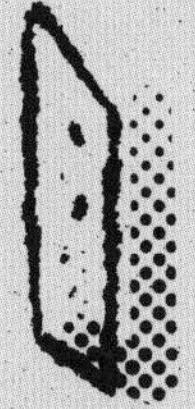

PEEL

Peels are usually 5 to 6 inches long and about 1 inch wide, cut into the shape of an awkward-looking rectangle, or rhombus, if you trim the edges into sharp angles. Use a vegetable or Y-peeler to do this—the OXO is a favorite because it has a solid rubber grip, and the blades don't snap off easily. (Jeffery Morgenthaler recommends a Boska cheese slicer for beginners, which I agree with if you are nervous about using the sharp as hell Y-peeler.) Peels are used instead of disks when a drink calls for a garnish that gets inserted into the drink. This makes cocktails look pretty and also serves a secondary function: Ice traps this garnish against the side of the glass, allowing the oils on the skin to affect the drink throughout its time on earth. A little squeeze will reactivate the brightness.

I like to peel my citrus from pole to pole on a 45-degree angle. You get less peels out of the fruit, but they also come out longer and stand up better in Double Old Fashioned glasses. Keep the ring finger and pinky of your noncutting hand tucked well under the fingers that are holding the fruit for safety. Pull gently and evenly toward yourself to make the peel. Put the tip of your nonpeeling hand on the peel as soon as it pulls up from the fruit. When you are about halfway through, move the fruit in the hand you're holding it in away from the peeler so you can safely and cleanly finish the peel.

PIGTAIL

A pigtail is a long (6 to 7 inches), thin curlicue, like the little winding pigtails you see in old cartoons. They are pleasing to look at, and when you cut one over the top of a cocktail, the oils from the peel cascade over the surface of the drink, adding an aromatic component. Unlike the disk or peel, this garnish is cut using a channel knife, so the width of the peel is narrow. Pigtails grace the rim of any drink that doesn't have ice in it, like a 20th Century (page 57) or Bamboo (page 77). The curve of the twist will hang on the side of the glass, keeping the garnish away from the intake manifold that is your mouth. You can also use these pretty twists on crushed ice drinks and rocks drinks.

To garnish: Once the cocktail is strained into the glass, position the lemon about 6 to 7 inches above its surface. You do this so the amount of oil that lands on the drink resembles a subtle touch, not a Silkwood shower. Hold the fruit with the poles horizontal and the channel knife toward you on the far side, so you can't see the business end, start pulling the channel knife toward you while rotating the bottom part of the arrangement away from you. This will scatter a heavy sheen of oil across the surface of the drink. Turn the lemon 90 degrees so you can see the groove you have created and keep turning the lemon, so you have circles as tight as possible. Put down the lemon and twist the peel in a tight coil. For coupe drinks (like the French 75 on page 141 for example), lower the coil onto the lip of the glass with three-quarters of it in the drink, one-quarter hanging outside. For crushed ice drinks, nestle the coil into the mound of ice.

THE SESSIONS

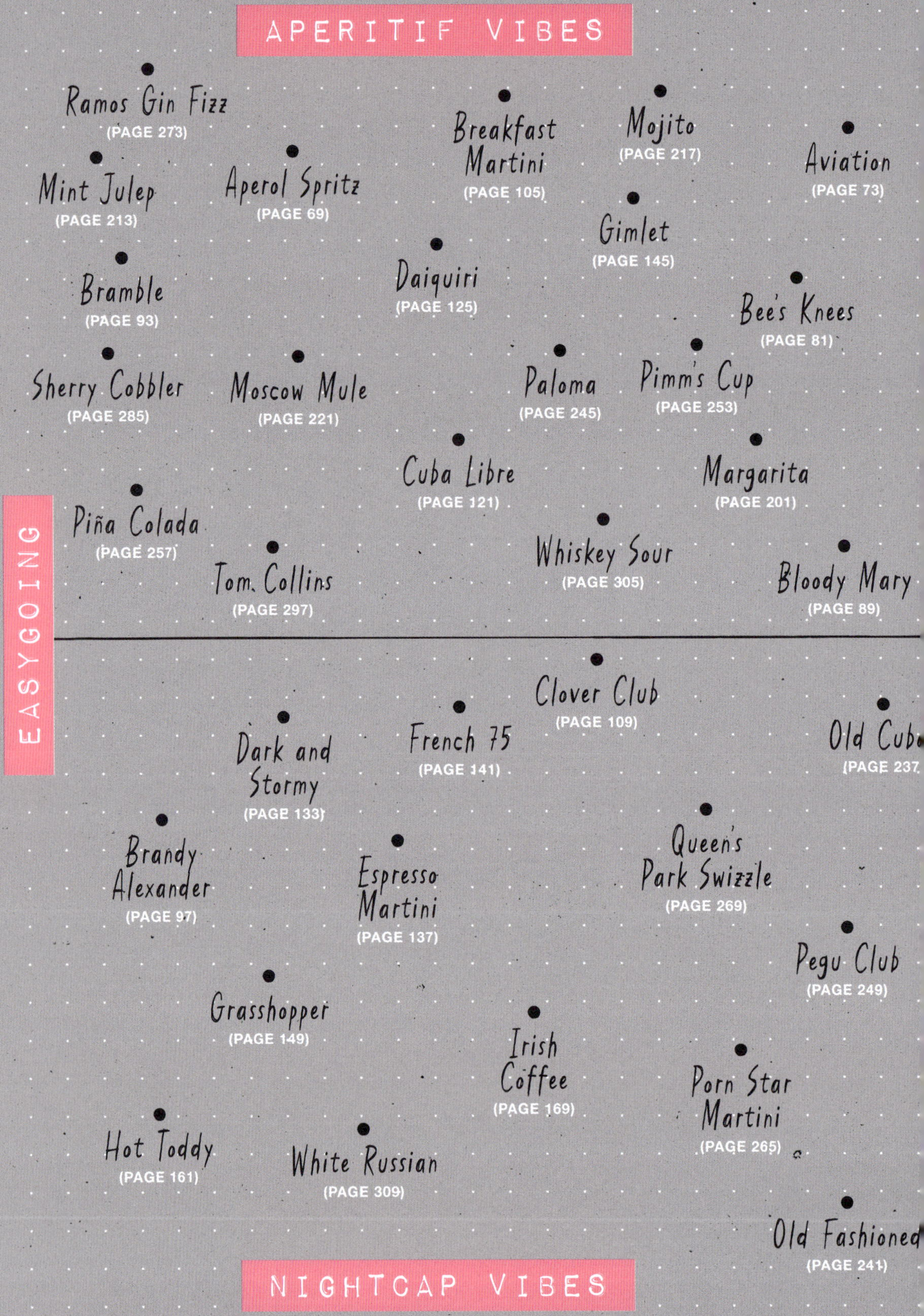

APERITIF VIBES
NIGHTCAP VIBES
EASYGOING
Ramos Gin Fizz (PAGE 273)
Breakfast Martini (PAGE 105)
Mojito (PAGE 217)
Aviation (PAGE 73)
Mint Julep (PAGE 213)
Aperol Spritz (PAGE 69)
Gimlet (PAGE 145)
Bramble (PAGE 93)
Daiquiri (PAGE 125)
Bee's Knees (PAGE 81)
Sherry Cobbler (PAGE 285)
Moscow Mule (PAGE 221)
Paloma (PAGE 245)
Pimm's Cup (PAGE 253)
Cuba Libre (PAGE 121)
Margarita (PAGE 201)
Piña Colada (PAGE 257)
Whiskey Sour (PAGE 305)
Tom Collins (PAGE 297)
Bloody Mary (PAGE 89)
Clover Club (PAGE 109)
French 75 (PAGE 141)
Dark and Stormy (PAGE 133)
Old Cub (PAGE 237
Brandy Alexander (PAGE 97)
Espresso Martini (PAGE 137)
Queen's Park Swizzle (PAGE 269)
Pegu Club (PAGE 249)
Grasshopper (PAGE 149)
Irish Coffee (PAGE 169)
Porn Star Martini (PAGE 265)
Hot Toddy (PAGE 161)
White Russian (PAGE 309)
Old Fashione (PAGE 241)

20th Century
(PAGE 57)

Corpse
Reviver #2
(PAGE 113)

Jack Rose
(PAGE 173)

Airmail
(PAGE 61)

Bamboo
(PAGE 77)

Last Word
(PAGE 185)

Pisco Sour
(PAGE 261)

Cosmopolitan
(PAGE 117)

Daisy de Santiago
(PAGE 129)

Hurricane
(PAGE 165)

Hemingway Daiquiri
(PAGE 153)

Hotel
Nacional
(PAGE 157)

Martini
(PAGE 205)

CONTEMPLATIVE

Amaretto Sour
(PAGE 65)

Sidecar
(PAGE 289)

Jet Pilot
(PAGE 177)

Jungle Bird
(PAGE 181)

Negroni
(PAGE 225)

Brandy Crusta
(PAGE 101)

Saturn
(PAGE 277)

Sazerac
(PAGE 281)

New York Sour
(PAGE 233)

Manhattan
(PAGE 193)

Vieux Carré
(PAGE 301)

Mai Tai
(PAGE 189)

Stinger
(PAGE 293)

Bijou
(PAGE 85)

NIGHTCAP VIBES

20TH CENTURY

*A beguiling battle between
juniper and cacao*

I would lie down in traffic for this drink. Like the Corpse Reviver #2 (page 113), it has all the components one might need if the night before intrudes on your morning like an onerous houseguest. It is light on the palate, but with intriguing undercurrents of bitterness and dark sweetness—a melding of sequins and tweed. It's also a real head-scratcher the first time you have it, because of the surprising inclusion of crème de cacao alongside the gin and lemon—the way those ingredients tussle and work in counterpoint is wondrous. Juniper is so spiky and emerald, but cacao is the opposite: round and luxurious. On paper, it looks like it shouldn't work, but it's a dynamite combo. I can't think of many other cocktails that evoke both comfort and curiosity with such casual aplomb. A great fit for folks who prefer the ephemeral and eclectic over the obvious.

MIZE

Serve:
Shaken, up

Tools:
Jigger, shaker,
Hawthorne
strainer,
channel knife

Glass:
Coupe, chilled

Garnish:
Lemon pigtail

RIYL:
Corpse Reviver #2
(page 113),
Grasshopper
(page 149),
Brandy Crusta
(page 101)

SPEC

Gin	2.0 oz
Cocchi Americano	1.0 oz
Crème de cacao	.25 oz
Fresh lemon juice	.75 oz
Simple syrup (page 29)	.25 oz

OUR APPROACH

To send this drink to art school, we take a few liberties with the ingredients and ratios. First, I like my 20th Century with a suspicion of chocolate, because I enjoy the sneakiness of it. It's almost like an inside joke, or a riff in the background of a favorite song that has striking beauty and humility. (There is some subtle guitar work on the edges of Bonnie Raitt's "Angel from Montgomery" that makes me giddy, for example.) So, we dial back the amount of liqueur to make the cocktail sparkle. Cocchi Americano also comes into play instead of Lillet Blanc, because it does double-duty by adding bitterness *and* complexity to the mix. None of these flexes change the drink's character exponentially, they just finesse the periphery in a way that I find extraordinarily pleasing.

CHOOSE YOUR INGREDIENTS

First, think about how barbed you want the gin to taste. Should it poke out from the glass (like a Beefeater or Tanqueray), or do you want it to swim softly alongside its companions (like a more subtle Plymouth or Sipsmith)? I like an even-keeled London dry like Fords because of the way it cozies up next to the Cocchi Americano. For the liqueur, skip the bottom-shelf crap and aim for a cacao that's made with craftsmanship and care. Most historic recipes use white crème de cacao; if you want to go this route, Giffard makes a demure version with a pretty citrus note and subtle milk chocolate character, making for a bright, bouncy version of the cocktail. If you want to delve into more mysterious territory, try Tempus Fugit's dark crème de cacao. Made with Mexican vanilla in addition to Venezuelan cacao, its flavor reminds me of rich folks' version of s'mores. It brings a full-bodied, cashmere texture to the drink.

- **MEASURE.** Now, we mix. Start by adding the simple syrup and lemon juice to your shaker tin and follow with the crème de cacao, Cocchi Americano, and gin. In that order, because if you fuck up the measurements early on, you have only wasted the cheaper ingredients in play and not the expensive liqueur and spirit. Remember to measure each ingredient so they are level in the jigger—not above or below that razor's edge—for balance.

- **STRAW TASTE.** To make sure everything is in the tin, and to get a sense for what the drink tastes like before ice comes into play. You'll want this data in your head in a few minutes.

- **SHAKE.** Add 5 ice cubes and Coupe Shake (page 45). This sour requires a pretty standard Coupe Shake to get right if you're using a normal 40-proof gin. If you choose a higher-proof gin, shake it longer to bring more water content into the mix—this helps smooth out the rough edges of the spirit and brings it together with the other ingredients seamlessly. Once you hear the ice in the tin turning to slush—like when you are at the beach and a wave retreats—that's when you stop.

- **TASTE, ADJUST, AND STRAIN.** Open your tins and straw taste again to make sure you've shaken for the right amount of time. How do you know? All the sharp corners of each ingredient will calm down once the cold water has melted off the ice and into the mix. The texture should feel energetic, and not too thick or too thin. If it's still spiky or rough or feels askew, shake a bit longer, or add a barspoon more of simple syrup. When it tastes pleasing, strain into the glass.

- **GARNISH.** For drinks that call for a pigtail, we cut the citrus *after* mixing the drink. This is because when you are cutting your tight spiral from the lemon for the pigtail garnish, the peel shoots citrus oil off the front of the channel knife while also making the svelte shape. This is a good thing, because it creates a lovely aroma. See the Pigtail instructions on page 51 for the step-by-step on how to do this.

There are no aromatic bitters included in the original 20th Century, but I like the way a few dashes of Peychaud's helps sync up the gin and cacao. Why Peychaud's? There is an old baker's trick where adding a splash of vanilla makes things more chocolatey and vice versa, and Peychaud's bitters have a bountiful vanilla note. I also like how the fennel notes of the bitters bolster the botanicals in the gin and Cocchi Americano. You could add orange bitters to the party instead, if you dig that chocolate-orange vibe—start with one dash and ramp up to taste.

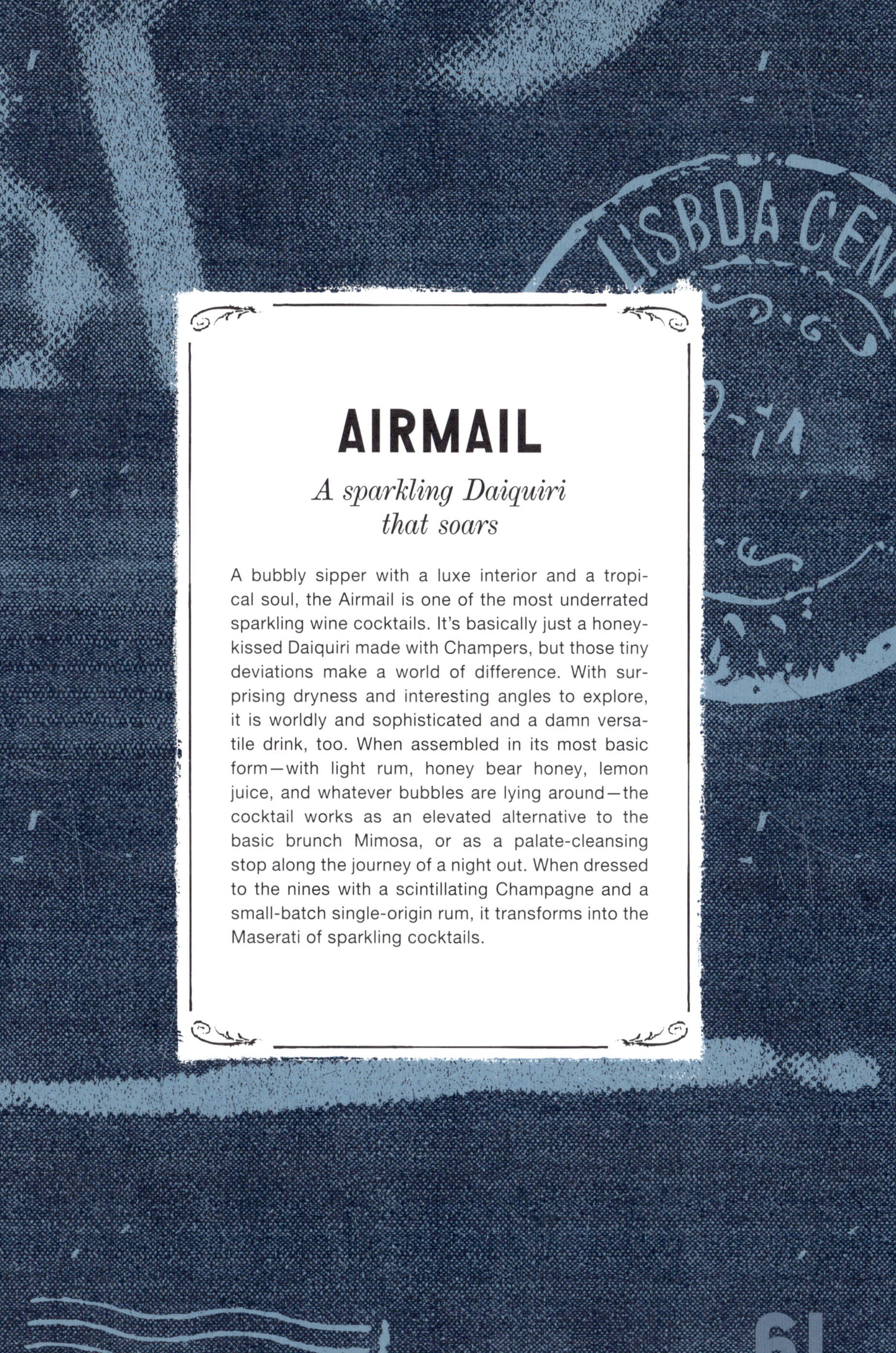

AIRMAIL

*A sparkling Daiquiri
that soars*

A bubbly sipper with a luxe interior and a tropical soul, the Airmail is one of the most underrated sparkling wine cocktails. It's basically just a honey-kissed Daiquiri made with Champers, but those tiny deviations make a world of difference. With surprising dryness and interesting angles to explore, it is worldly and sophisticated and a damn versatile drink, too. When assembled in its most basic form—with light rum, honey bear honey, lemon juice, and whatever bubbles are lying around—the cocktail works as an elevated alternative to the basic brunch Mimosa, or as a palate-cleansing stop along the journey of a night out. When dressed to the nines with a scintillating Champagne and a small-batch single-origin rum, it transforms into the Maserati of sparkling cocktails.

Serve:
Shaken, up

Tools:
Jigger, shaker,
Hawthorne
strainer,
channel knife

Glass:
Wine glass, chilled

Garnish:
Lemon or orange
pigtail

RIYL:
French 75
(with Cognac)
(page 141),
Daisy de Santiago
(page 129),
Pegu Club
(page 249)

SPEC

Rum	2.0 oz
Fresh lime juice	.75 oz
Honey syrup (page 30)	.75 oz
Sparkling wine, to bottom	4-ish oz

OUR APPROACH

The traditional recipe doesn't really need tweaks to taste as delicious as the day it was invented, so the spec we're giving you does not stray too far from square one. Its integrity lies with the ingredients you choose, and the technique you harness to assemble the drink. That said, I believe that a Champagne flute is an abomination to all things holy. This drink should be served in a big honking wine glass over ice cubes, so it stays spry and cold over the course of a long, leisurely sipping session.

CHOOSE YOUR INGREDIENTS

You could make this drink with different combos of honey and rum for ages and still discover something new to love every time. I recommend Planteray 3-Star throughout these sessions as an excellent baseline white rum—it's got a nice round balance and subtle sweetness but also good structure and vibrancy. Once you get to know how *your* base rum sets a tone for this cocktail, start swapping in more interesting options to see how it changes depending on the rum, ron, or rhum you pick. A funky dark Jamaican rum gives this drink a deep commanding sweetness, whereas something more light-bodied, like an aged blend from Barbados, will keep it more laid-back, for example. Regarding the sparkling wine, don't use anything you wouldn't drink on its own on a weeknight. If it's a special occasion, splurge and use a brut Champagne. And for the honey, clover honey (kinda boring) is way different than wildflower honey (kinda floral); and buckwheat honey (kinda bold) has deep pancake-like flavors that taste delish. (See the Bee's Knees, page 81, for more honey thoughts.) I personally like a funky Jamaican rum with leatherwood honey from Tasmania.

HOW TO MIX

● **MEASURE.** Grab your shaker tin to make the "body" of the drink—the honey Daiquiri, if you will. Measure the honey syrup precisely into your jigger and then dump that into your tin, followed by the lime juice and rum. In that order. (Read more about why we use honey syrup and not straight-up honey on page 30.)

- **STRAW TASTE.** To make sure everything is in the tin. Notice how warm and unsweet this drink tastes at this stage—once the honey gets whipped into the mix during the shake, it'll taste more like a real cocktail. Set the tin aside.

- **BOTTOM THE WINE.** Most recipes will tell you to add the bubbles last, "to top," but by "bottoming" them in the glass instead—that is, measuring them into the vessel before you add the rest of the cocktail—you're ensuring all the ingredients will integrate seamlessly when you pour the contents of the shaker tin into the glass. For this drink, dump out the ice and water you've used to chill the wine glass (because you did that as part of your Mize, right? Page 39). Insert your ice of choice, then add 4 ounces of sparkling wine. Set that aside and focus your attention back on the contents of the shaker tin.

- **SHAKE.** I always give drinks with wildly different viscosities a quick Mime Shake (page 45) first to be sure everything is copacetic before I add the ice and the whole thing seizes up with coldness. I do that with the Airmail because of the honey syrup, which is thicker than normal simple or Demerara syrup. After the Mime Shake, add 5 ice cubes to the shaker and give it a Collins Shake (page 46), going just long enough so the ingredients have chilled slightly, but not so long that your hands start to stick to the hoarfrost on the tin. Set this aside for a sec.

- **TASTE, ADJUST, AND STRAIN.** For the second straw taste, consider how balance is sometimes about understanding the negative space in a cocktail. The things that have yet to come. In this case, you are trying to anticipate how the contents of the shaker tin will taste once they collide with the sparkling wine. Sparkling wine is a damn dry ingredient. Even ones that lean to the sweet side when sipped solo dry out cocktails more than anything I know. You want the body of the cocktail to taste achingly sweet at this stage (that is why we only shake for a brief period). If it does, strain the contents of the tin into the glass. If it's not (because maybe you shook too long; no worries), add a barspoon or so more syrup to the mix and give it a swirl before you strain—if you want more honey flavor in the drink, use honey syrup for this. If you just want to fix the texture and balance alone, use simple syrup, which brings sweetness to the mix without adding flavor.

- **GARNISH.** The aromatic component of your garnish will change your perception of how the cocktail tastes, so that's a cool sleight of hand you can pull out when you want to change things up. Both lemon and orange will brighten the aromas of the cocktail, but lemon will pull out the beautiful citrus notes of the lime juice, while an orange peel will make the drink seem warmer and more velveteen—a great option for après-ski sipping. When ready to cut, use your channel knife to pull a thin strip off your citrus fruit—do this above the surface of the cocktail, so the drink catches some of the waves of oil that fly from the fruit—and nestle the pigtail on the side of the glass. Be sure to get some on the straw below where one would sip out of it, for extra oomph.

If you like a sweeter Airmail, swap out the lime juice for lemon juice. The two fruits are surprisingly swappable in cocktails—especially rum drinks, which seem to be amenable to every type of citrus—but lemon has less acidity, and in this case, it harmonizes well with the sparkling wine.

AMARETTO SOUR

Nutty luxury with a splash of nostalgia

I get a cavity and a headache thinking about how poorly bartenders made this drink in the '90s, when they drizzled syrupy stone fruit liqueur from a clunky rectangular bottle followed by sour mix off the gun. Thankfully, it's one of the few dessert-ish classics that has evolved beyond the gauntlet of shitty TGIF drinks and into the modern era, where we've found ways to transform the once certified hot mess into a delicious, well-balanced cocktail that will slay even the most die-hard "not too sweet" motherfucker. I love the look of wonder that appears when a skeptic takes their first sip of one made with good skill and technique.

Serve:
Shaken, up

Tools:
Jigger, shaker,
Hawthorne
strainer,
fine strainer,
paring knife

Glass:
Coupe, chilled

Garnish:
Lemon or
orange disk

RIYL:
Brandy Crusta
(page 101),
Mai Tai (page 189),
Whiskey Sour
(page 305)

SPEC

Lazzaroni amaretto	1.5 oz
Rye whiskey	.50 oz
Fresh lemon juice	.75 oz
Demerara syrup (page 29)	.25 oz
Egg white	1

OUR APPROACH

The standard spec is a sticky disaster, so I split-base the amaretto liqueur with a little bit of whiskey—a move pioneered by Portland bartender Jeffrey Morgenthaler and beloved by many of us modern barkeeps. I use this technique all the time, because the split-base is a simple way to slightly change the character of a classic without shifting the drink's personality so much that it becomes a riff. The key to doing this well is choosing bandmates that play well together. In some drinks (like the Margarita, page 201), that means tequila and mezcal; in others (like the Mai Tai, page 189), it might be two styles of rum. In this case, the flavors of the whiskey—vanilla, oak, earthy grain—complement the nutty marzipan notes of the amaretto. Split-basing is especially useful in this drink because amaretto is low-proof, so the cocktail can taste a bit wimpy without a little boost of proof from the whiskey, which barrels in with a wild *yee-haw* energy.

CHOOSE YOUR INGREDIENTS

I've specified Lazzaroni amaretto because it bears great balance and complexity, which makes sense when you think about how the family have been making the product in Italy since the 1800s. They've done all the hard work in giving us great flavor to mix with; we just need to not fuck it up with poor technique. It's also relatively easy to find in most states; you're welcome! The whiskey plays backup singer in this drink, not soloist as it does in the Whiskey Sour (page 305), so choose your brand accordingly. You don't need to break the bank for something too fancy or expensive, which might get lost in the mix. A solid workhorse rye like Rittenhouse will hold up its end of the bargain effortlessly. Finally, choose whether you want to use a lemon or orange disk to garnish this drink—lemon will make the drink seem drier, which is helpful if you find the build too sweet for your palate. It also makes the lemon juice in the cocktail pop! Orange will make it seem sweeter, and I also like the way its warmth snuggles up with the nutty notes of the liqueur. There is no wrong choice here, just different choices depending on what you desire in this moment.

HOW TO MIX

• **PREP THE GARNISH.** Cut a disk of citrus from the fruit. Choose lemon oils if you want to brighten the aromas and emphasize the lemon juice in the cocktail; orange oils will make the drink seem warmer and

sweeter. You get to decide which route to take. Set aside. Remember good eggtiquette (see page 234). Egg white cocktails are all about that gossamer texture, but they require a few extra considerations. First, you want to make sure you're not getting any yolk into the mix, so crack the egg over your shaker, then plop the yolk into the big side and the white into the small tin. Put the yolk in a container in the fridge to use later for something yummy. Save the whites in the small tin. If there is a little bit of shell in your whites, don't waste your time or clean hands trying to fish it out of the tin, because you are going to double-strain it out at the end to keep the texture of the drink nice and dense.

● **MEASURE.** Into the large tin, measure and add the Demerara syrup and lemon juice. Then stack the amaretto and the rye in your jigger, in that order, and pour that into the tin. The method I call "stacking" is adding two ingredients to the jigger at the same time so that the total amount of that ingredient doesn't exceed its measure, a cool little "checks and balances" moment. I use this for spirits when we split-base, but most commonly for liqueurs and syrups, because if you accidentally measure out too much sugar your balance will fall off a cliff quickly.

● **STRAW TASTE.** To make sure everything is in the tin.

● **SHAKE.** First we are going to use what I call a Mime Shake (page 45), where you shake the drink without ice to get the whites integrated with the liquids. After the Mime Shake, you're going to shake with ice: The bulk of this drink is low-proof liqueur and not a full 2 ounces of 80-proof whiskey, as is the case in the Whiskey Sour (page 305), so you need to use fewer ice cubes (3 instead of 5) to get the right balance of booze and dilution. Less water entering the picture means you will need to shake harder and longer to get the right chill and aeration. Got it? Go forth and add 3 cubes and Coupe Shake (page 45) until the tins feel cold to the touch and the ice starts to shatter.

● **TASTE, ADJUST, AND STRAIN.** Crack the tin, wring and tap (page 45), and then tap the tin against the surface of your counter five times to get the liquid cohesive. You don't do this with every drink, but definitely the ones with egg whites, because that stuff is CLINGY. The tapping will get all the contents in the tin to settle down nicely. Straw taste. Is it sweet and too boozy? Shake a bit more to get more water content into the mix, which softens those qualities. Is it sweet and somehow acidic? Add a bit of Demerara syrup and give it a quick stir or swirl. Once you've got it where you want it, double-strain into the glass over a handful of newly minted ice cubes.

● **GARNISH.** We talk more about the theory of garnishing egg white cocktails in the sessions for the Clover Club (page 109) and the Pisco Sour (page 261), so go read those if you want to learn more about the hows and whys of that practice. For now, trust the process as you express the oils of the citrus disk over the top of the drink and discard before drinking.

For an even more gussied-up version of the Amaretto Sour, you can add bitters for complexity. I like to think of bitters like mirepoix (the French cooking base for many dishes, made with carrots, celery, onion, parsley, and thyme), because they lay down a foundation of flavor that is then expanded upon by all the other components of the cocktail. I like Angostura and Peychaud's together for this job (well, okay, for most cocktails), because for some reason they always seem to sing together. Always use bitters sparingly at first and add more later if you think they are needed. Literally, go dash by dash to see how quickly they amplify flavor.

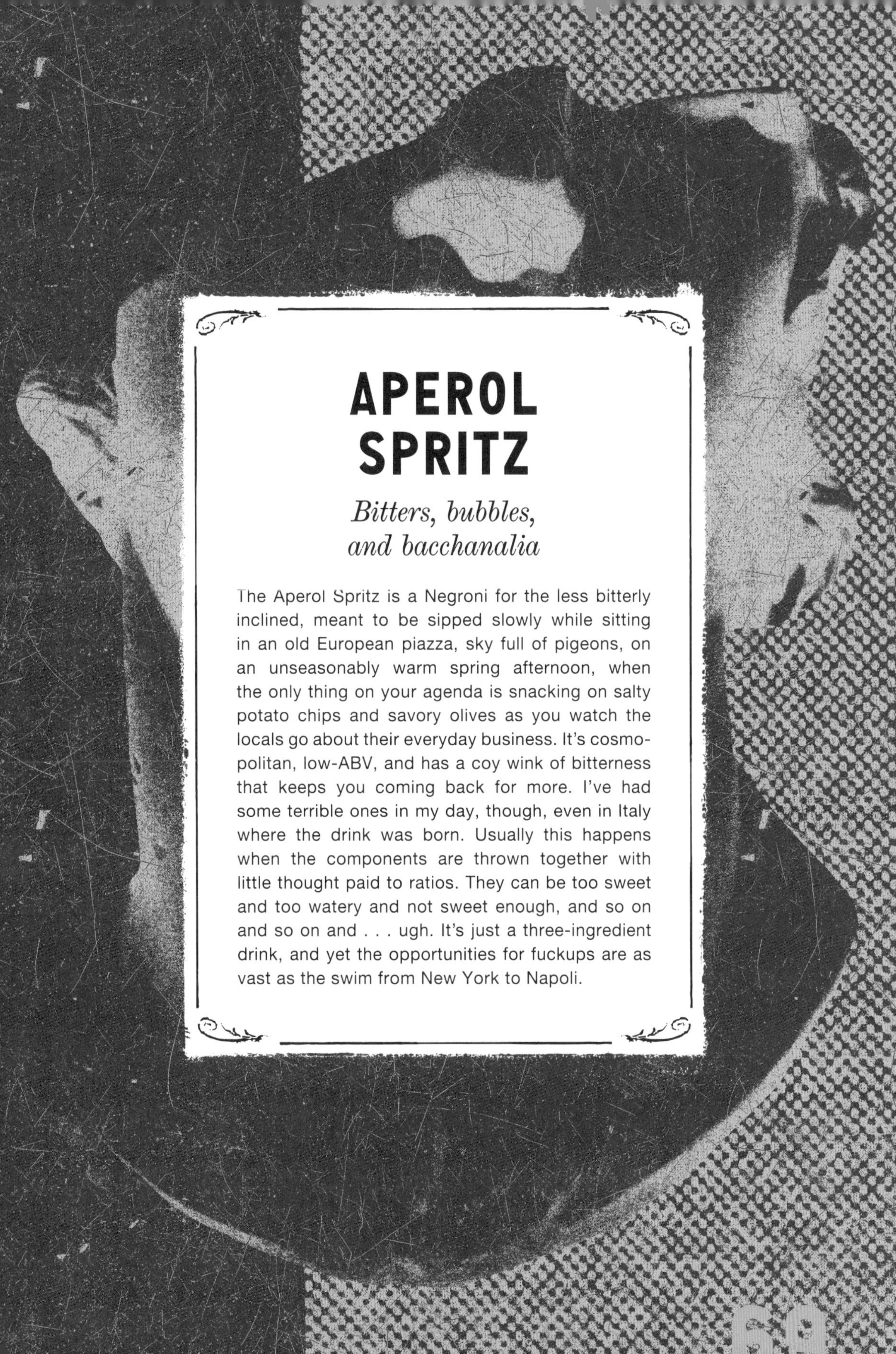

APEROL SPRITZ

*Bitters, bubbles,
and bacchanalia*

The Aperol Spritz is a Negroni for the less bitterly inclined, meant to be sipped slowly while sitting in an old European piazza, sky full of pigeons, on an unseasonably warm spring afternoon, when the only thing on your agenda is snacking on salty potato chips and savory olives as you watch the locals go about their everyday business. It's cosmopolitan, low-ABV, and has a coy wink of bitterness that keeps you coming back for more. I've had some terrible ones in my day, though, even in Italy where the drink was born. Usually this happens when the components are thrown together with little thought paid to ratios. They can be too sweet and too watery and not sweet enough, and so on and so on and . . . ugh. It's just a three-ingredient drink, and yet the opportunities for fuckups are as vast as the swim from New York to Napoli.

Serve:
Built in the glass,
on the rocks

Tools:
Jigger, barspoon,
offset serrated
knife, paring knife

Glass:
Wine glass or
spritz glass, chilled

Garnish:
Half orange wheel

RIYL:
Jack Rose
(page 173),
Pimm's Cup
(page 253),
Ramos Gin Fizz
(page 273)

SPEC

Aperol	2.0 oz
Prosecco	3.0 oz
Sparkling water	2.0 oz
Fresh lemon juice	.25 oz
Orange disk, expressed and discarded	

OUR APPROACH

To make a classic Aperol Spritz with dry wit and the propensity to wander around cobblestone streets with glowing curiosity, I add a suspicion of lemon juice to balance out the sweetness of the original. We also add a bit more sparkling water than the traditional 3-2-1 ratio, to further give the axe to the syrupy-ness of the liqueur. You can play with different ratios to find the balance you like the most. The key to making this drink its best self lies in maintaining a bright, effervescent carbonation, because a flat spritz is an affront to all things holy. First, make sure your Prosecco and sparkling water are colder than the Rink at Rockefeller Center in mid-January, because cold carbonated beverages hold a tight fizzy bubble longer than lukewarm ones do. Really! It's science. Then, to keep those cold frisky bubbles intact, pay close attention to best practices listed out in the mixing instructions.

CHOOSE YOUR INGREDIENTS

The classic Aperol Spritz hinges on the use of Aperol and Prosecco. Use good-quality Prosecco and not the cheapest bottle you can find. Believe me, there is a big quality gap between $10 and $20. The good stuff will have a tight structure and softly sweet honey note. The sparkling water you use in a spritz is also super important—did you know different sparkling waters have different carbonation levels? They also have different mineral contents, which will impact the flavor in addition to the texture of the drink. It's easy to go with San Pellegrino or Lurisia for the Aperol Spritz, both great waters from Italy, but don't sleep on Singha sparkling water (from the Thai beer maker) or the good old Topo Chico, which is the chingón of mineral waters with bubbles that last for days (okay, maybe not days, but at least an hour or two in the fridge). An outside-the-box choice could be Vichy Catalan, which has a distinct saltiness. (It also tastes great with espresso because the salt wrangles the bitterness.)

- **PREP THE GARNISH.** Grab an orange and cut off a disk. This will be used only for aromatics. Set aside. Then, with your offset serrated knife, cut one pole of the orange off the fruit. Then cut one wheel of orange. Cut the wheel in half. This will be used to make the drink look pretty. (You can also snack on it after the cocktail has vanished, if you please.) Set aside.

- **MEASURE.** We're building this one in the glass. First, add ice cubes. Then I like to put the orange wheel in before the liquids, because I don't want to disturb all the bubbles later. Slide the wheel along the inside of the glass, into the middle of the ice, at a slight angle. Then add the lemon juice. Be frugal! You shouldn't be able to taste lemon in the drink; it's just acting as a drying agent. Then measure out the sparkling water; use the fancy technique of dribbling the liquid down the barspoon into the glass, so the bubbles stay intact (see the Ramos Gin Fizz, page 273, for more on this). Do the same with the Prosecco. Measure your Aperol and add it to the glass—with this pour, I make an infinity (∞) movement, so the liqueur incorporates into the other ingredients well.

- **STRAW TASTE AND ADJUST.** An Aperol Spritz is meant to be lingered over, so it should taste a little bold and boozy on the first few sips—it will mellow over time as the ice melts. If you need another 1 ounce of sparkling water or a skoosh of lemon to temper the sweetness or add a pop of brightness, add that now. If you think it needs a bit more staying power without more sweetness at this point, splash a bit of Prosecco into it to add just a "chef's kiss" of alcohol. This'll make the narrative arc of the drink long and winding, with the last sips tasting as gleeful as a romp in the Trevi fountain.

- **EYEBALL THE WASH LINE.** A good spritz is one that's filled almost up to the top of the glass. If you need more ice to make the glass look full, now is the time to add a cube or two. Remember: The more ice you add, the waterier the drink will become as it melts—this can be a good thing or bad thing, depending on how you look at it. If you don't want to sip on a watery drink in a few minutes, sip faster. If you like the way the extra dilution makes the drink taste light and unassuming, do like The Cranberries and have no shame as you let it linger!

- **GARNISH.** Give the orange disk a squeeze over the top of the glass so some of its oils spray over the top, then discard it. I always marvel in the way this orange-oil aroma pulls out the orange notes in the Aperol. A beautiful echo of orange flavor. Toss in a straw, then hurry up and relax.

There's absolutely nothing wrong with Aperol, but these days there are shelves dripping with new-wave red liqueurs so you can choose one or two or three to mix for your own personal blend. With a deeper red hue, a more defined structure, and brushstrokes of complexity, Select is one of Emma's favorites. It also has a lush, rich texture that Aperol lacks, making the drink simultaneously more robust and elegant. Drinking one in its origin city of Venice is downright transportive. Cappelletti is another great option—with a wine base instead of neutral spirits, it has an uncommon unctuousness that sits lavishly on the palate. If you are wary of trying out something new, try introducing 1 ounce of another red bitter to 1 ounce of Aperol to dip your toes in before fully committing.

AVIATION

*An Alpine hike, phone
set to airplane mode*

The Aviation is like the eccentric grandmother who has a mysterious past, maybe working in the French Resistance in WWII, and now quirkily wears violet perfume and rattles her gold bangles at passersby from her stoop. Ha! Okay, but seriously, when Haus Alpenz imported a respectable version of crème de violette from Rothman & Winter in the early 2000s, we mustachioed bartenders went crazy with it. It was Aviations for all our friends, all the time. I think there was a moment where my fingernails were turning purple, I was drinking so much of the stuff. These days, the Aviation isn't as popular as it used to be, as our collective palates have shifted more toward big bold bitter flavors, but it's still worth knowing because it's one of the most classic classics out there. When made with a few modern flourishes, it tastes downright magnetic.

Serve:
Shaken, up

Tools:
Jigger, shaker, Hawthorne strainer, fine strainer, paring knife (optional)

Glass:
Nick & Nora, chilled

Garnish:
Grapefruit disk

RIYL:
Cosmopolitan (page 117), Hotel Nacional (page 157), Last Word (page 185)

SPEC

London dry gin	2.0 oz
Fresh lemon juice	.75 oz
Luxardo maraschino liqueur	.25 oz
Simple syrup (page 29)	.50 oz
Peychaud's bitters	3 dashes
Crème de violette, to rinse or atomize into the glass	

OUR APPROACH

Crème de violette is a bully—an ingredient with an intensity of flavor so loud it pushes others out of the way—so this drink can taste like a flower bomb if too much enters the equation. I personally don't love drinks that taste like grandma's linen drawer. I want a *nuanced* cocktail, not a mouthful of steel mothballs; so in this version I use an atomizer (or I rinse the glass) to get just a fleeting smooch of the liqueur into the mix. The ingredient still exists within the theater of the drink, just not in the way you might expect. I also reduce the amount of maraschino liqueur. Doing these two things minimizes the amount of sweetness in the drink, though—because liqueurs contain both sugar and booze—so to keep everything in balance I add simple syrup. I throw a few dashes of Peychaud's bitters in there too, because I love the way the vanilla and fennel traits complement the cherry notes of the maraschino.

CHOOSE YOUR INGREDIENTS

Don't grab the neon purple bottle of crème de violette from the bottom shelf. I know, it's cheaper, but then your drink will come out tasting cheap, too. I recommend Rothman & Winter, which is made from violets grown in the Alps by a liqueur-making family that tends to use less sugar than others. It's also higher proof, which concentrates the flavor and aromas nicely. Tempus Fugit also has a new-school (pink!) one made in Switzerland using French violets from the Côte d'Azur that is fabulous—while it changes the color, its floral qualities sync up swimmingly with the maraschino and gin. In my experience, a soft New American gin will help the wildflower notes shine, while a workhorse London dry like Fords or Hayman's will stand up and be counted more notably. You could also swap out the Italian Luxardo maraschino for the less funky Croatian version of the liqueur called Maraska, if a more floral cherry flavor is your jam.

HOW TO MIX

● **PREP THE GARNISH.** A grapefruit oil garnish adds a cool contrasting citrus note to all the botanicals in the drink, so it's a clever way to upgrade the experience of the cocktail with a quick twist of the wrist.

You don't *have* to go this route though, because the violet liqueur has a powerful aroma of its own—it's your choice which aromatic route to pursue. If you do decide to use a grapefruit peel garnish, cut a disk right now, before you mix the drink. Set aside for later.

● **MEASURE.** Usually, we build drinks from the cheapest to the most expensive ingredient, but in some cases, we change the mixing order to make sure too much booze or sweetness doesn't sneak its way into the tin. That's the case in this drink, where we'd normally add the bitters first, then syrup, then lemon juice, maraschino liqueur, and gin. It's so important to keep the sweetness in this drink in check though, so instead we're going to start with the bitters, then stack the simple syrup and maraschino in the jigger so that neither measure accidentally ends up being too heavy. If your jigger doesn't have the right marks to make this happen, that's fine—just measure both independently, then follow those with the lemon and the gin.

● **STRAW TASTE.** To make sure everything is in the tin, give it a straw taste. You do this also to get a sense for how floral the drink tastes at this moment (due to the maraschino), before it gets iced. The drink will taste like an awkward half-baked version of an Aviation at this stage, but it'll come together in the end. Trust!

● **AROMATIZE OR RINSE.** Spray a few mists of crème de violette into the chilled glass using an atomizer. If you don't have an atomizer, do a rinse instead: Pour a very small amount of the violette in the glass and roll the liqueur around as close to the lip as possible. When the entire surface is coated, ditch the excess liquid into the sink. Put the glass down, let the last droplets of liqueur gather at the bottom, then toss those, too. For a fun exercise, try making the drink both ways, to see how the rinse differs slightly from the atomizer. (Rinsing is also suggested to tame absinthe in the Corpse Reviver #2 on page 113.) Set the glass aside.

● **SHAKE.** Add 5 ice cubes to the shaker tin. Pause to note the proof of your gin. If it's more than 80-proof, you'll need to shake a bit longer than you normally would. There's no hard and fast amount of time I can give you for this because everyone's shake is a bit different. Figuring out the timing takes time and practice. For now, give it a Coupe Shake (page 45). As you do, listen carefully to the way the ice breaks down: It starts off rattly and sharp and then tapers off to slight slushy *shhhhhhh*, like a bike wheel going fast in the rain. This is when you stop and taste the contents of the tin again.

● **TASTE, ADJUST, AND STRAIN.** It should taste evenly balanced at this point. Tight and cold. If the texture is too thin, you can add a bit more simple syrup to boost the thickness. If it's too sweet, shake longer—the more water content that enters the cocktail, the better its balance will be. Once it tastes good, double-strain into the glass.

● **GARNISH.** If using, express the oils of a grapefruit disk over the top of the drink and discard the disk. If you feel the need for something else to make the visuals pop, a maraschino cherry skewered is a cool move.

Crème de violette is the crux of this drink, so that's the ingredient to fiddle with when customizing the recipe to your taste. If you love the flavor, you could do a heavy rinse instead of a light one, by adding more liquid to the glass and leaving a puddle of purple in the bottom so the flavor and aromas get integrated at a louder volume. Or you could go the opposite route and aromatize just a tiny spritz over the top of the drink instead of coating the glass first, so the aroma turns into more of a memory of violet versus a clear picture of the thing itself. It's only a few drops between those two things, so measure and spray with intention.

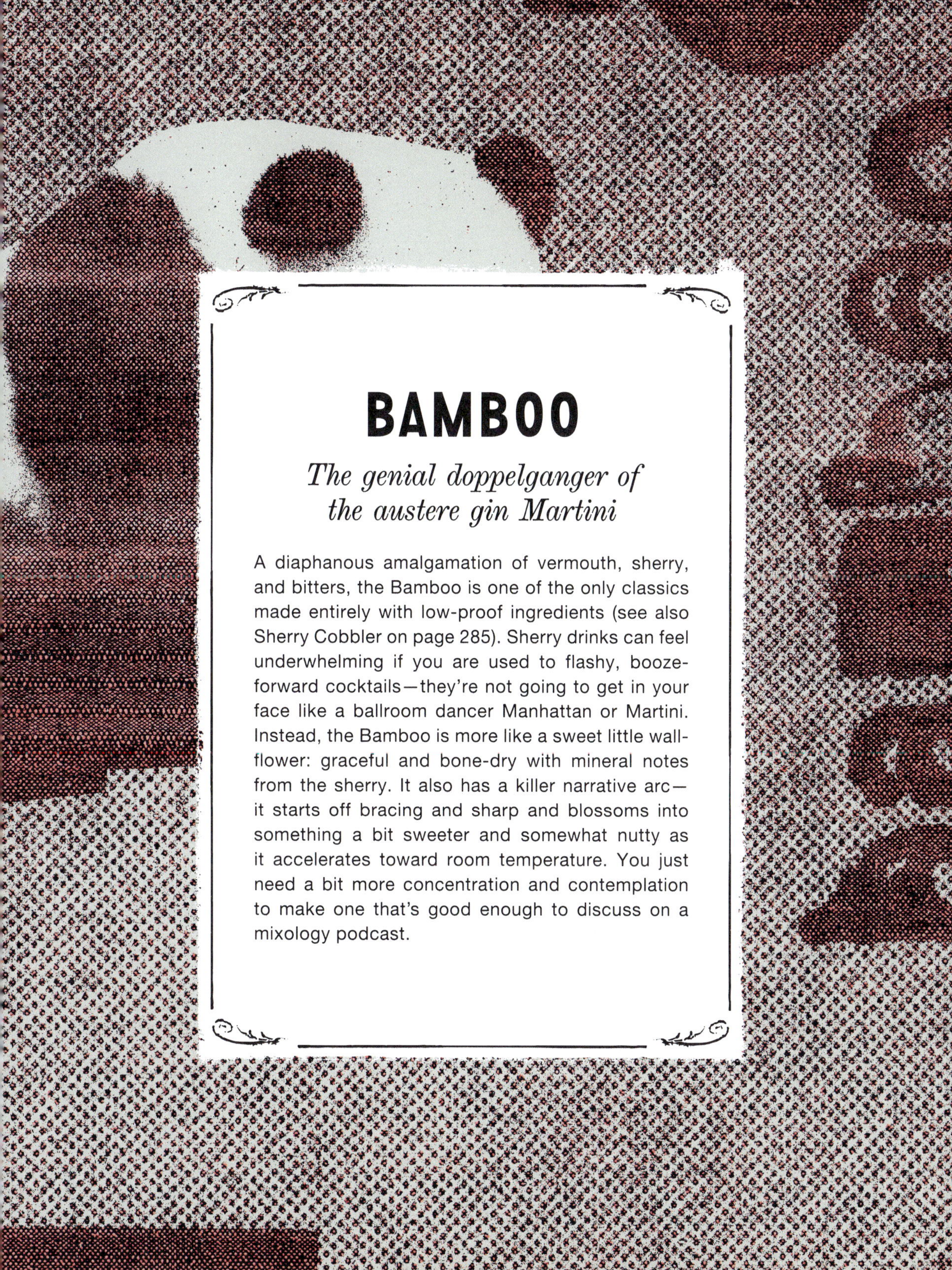

BAMBOO

The genial doppelganger of the austere gin Martini

A diaphanous amalgamation of vermouth, sherry, and bitters, the Bamboo is one of the only classics made entirely with low-proof ingredients (see also Sherry Cobbler on page 285). Sherry drinks can feel underwhelming if you are used to flashy, booze-forward cocktails—they're not going to get in your face like a ballroom dancer Manhattan or Martini. Instead, the Bamboo is more like a sweet little wall-flower: graceful and bone-dry with mineral notes from the sherry. It also has a killer narrative arc—it starts off bracing and sharp and blossoms into something a bit sweeter and somewhat nutty as it accelerates toward room temperature. You just need a bit more concentration and contemplation to make one that's good enough to discuss on a mixology podcast.

Serve:
Stirred, up

Tools:
Jigger, mixing glass, barspoon, Julep strainer, channel knife

Glass:
Nick & Nora, chilled

Garnish:
Orange pigtail

RIYL:
Martini (page 205), Sherry Cobbler (page 285), Hemingway Daiquiri (page 153)

Fino sherry	....	2.0 oz
Dry vermouth	....	.50 oz
Blanc vermouth	....	.50 oz
Orange bitters	....	2 dashes
Angostura bitters	....	1 dash

OUR APPROACH

The original Bamboo was made in equal parts, which I understand, because its components are more alike than different, so when they meld together it creates a beautiful flavor constellation. That said, I like sherry more than vermouth, so I up the sherry a notch and reduce the vermouth a skosh. I also split-base the dry vermouth with blanc vermouth, which buffers the texture and complexity while adding a touch of sweetness. (See our approach to the Amaretto Sour on page 65 for more on the split-basing theory.) These modernizations make for a real classy Bamboo—one with clean edges, slightly fruity notes from the blanc vermouth, and a Sharks-and-Jets-style balance. I find it a touch sweeter—necessary for such a bracingly dry drink—and far more interesting than the original.

CHOOSE YOUR INGREDIENTS

We're not talking about cooking sherry here, so you can tuck away those frightful memories of sneaking sips from your grandparent's liquor cabinet. Instead, the variety of high-quality fortified wines we have at our fingertips now is vast and varied and compelling—modern cocktail bartenders have been trying to make sherry cool for a couple of decades because of this, and they're not wrong—so it's easy to make an elegant version of this drink without much effort. Just do not be frugal with your picks! The extra cash you put into buying a better bottle of fino sherry will make a profound difference, so reach for bottles from Lustau, Valdespino, Tio Pepe, or González Byass for delicious results. Make sure you get fino sherry for this drink, though, because if you grab a cream sherry or an oloroso or a PX or manzanilla or amontillado, you're creating an entirely new cocktail. Style matters. Details matter! The same goes for your vermouths, which play supporting characters in the drink—skip the crappy stuff and grab a bottle of Dolin, Noilly Prat, Carpano, or perhaps something cool from Spain to match the origins of the sherry, like Lustau blanco vermouth, made with a base of fino sherry and muscatel wine.

- **MEASURE.** In the mixing glass, add ice until it is three-quarters of the way full. Then dash in both of the bitters, aiming to slide them down the sides of the ice instead of haphazardly on top, because you need to taste them integrated with the other ingredients on the second straw taste when you decide if you want to add more bitters or sugar or not. Then add both vermouths and the sherry. Be precise in your measurements, because there aren't that many ingredients in this cocktail, so every measure matters. Give it a brief stir to incorporate.

- **STRAW TASTE.** To make sure everything is in the glass. Notice how dry and disjointed the drink feels at this stage. Mark this information in your brain, so you can track how it changes upon subsequent straw tastes.

- **STIR.** Because this is served up, we're going to give it a shorter than usual Coupe Stir (page 47). Techniquewise, cocktails made with only vermouth and/or aromatized wines need a little more concentration and contemplation because they are easy to overstir. This drink specifically needs a fraction of the amount of stirring time as a Martini. It's not going to get as cold, but it doesn't need to because your ingredients are more understated anyway. They will become beautifully expressive and interesting as they warm.

- **TASTE, ADJUST, AND STRAIN.** Straw taste every 20 rotations or so as you stir, to witness how the drink transforms into something suave as it chills and absorbs water from the ice. This will also help make sure you don't overstir. After a taste or two, use some brainpower to decide whether the drink might need an extra dash of Ango. How do you know? If the drink tastes a bit watery, a small dose of bitters should help snap it back into place. Once it's nice and coooool (and still balanced), strain it into a Nick & Nora glass.

- **GARNISH.** Pull an orange pigtail using a channel knife. Do this about 6 inches above the surface of the drink, gently so you're not blasting the face of the cocktail with too much oil. If you are a Martini drinker and live for the driest cocktails out there, you could garnish with a lemon pigtail instead, which will make the drink read as less sweet. Either way, place the pigtail on the rim of the glass as garnish before you take that first sip.

You could split-base the fino with a dram of another dry sherry like manzanilla or amontillado, which share a similar minerality. You could also drop the Angostura entirely and lean into the Martini vibes. Eat some Manchego while you do this! I would just caution against swapping in sweet sherries like oloroso or PX, or changing the dry vermouth to sweet vermouth, because then the drink becomes more like an Adonis (fino sherry, sweet vermouth, and orange bitters) and not a Bamboo.

BEE'S KNEES

A buzzing glass of merriment and nonmonogamy

When you're in the mood for an easygoing sour with a little more intrigue than a Gimlet (page 145) or Daiquiri (page 125), the Bee's Knees is a beguiling option. This drink, round and tasting of meadows and flowers, is the opposite of a Martini (page 205), which is all cold pine needles and arctic tundra. The Bee's Knees is also fun because while most classic cocktails are about elevating the spirit (a man-made component) to center stage, this cocktail puts more of a spotlight on the honey. The product of those busy little bees is really a miracle substance: it never goes bad, it expresses a sense of terroir, and it is the best tasting medicine of all time. When you make a cocktail with the fruits of their labor it's akin to turning a nursery rhyme into an epic trilogy.

Serve:
Shaken,
on the rocks

Tools:
Jigger, shaker,
Hawthorne
strainer, fine
strainer, Y-peeler,
paring knife

Glass:
Double Old
Fashioned, chilled

Garnish:
Lemon peel

RIYL:
Clover Club
(page 109),
French 75
(page 141),
Hotel Nacional
(page 157)

SPEC

Hayman's Royal Dock gin	1.5 oz
Barr Hill gin	.50 oz
Fresh lemon juice	.75 oz
Honey syrup (page 30)	.75 oz
Orange bitters	2 dashes

OUR APPROACH

Most Bee's Knees cocktails are served up in a coupe with no ice. I like this when I'm thirsty and ready to down a round quickly, but—I know this might sound blasphemous to some—I also love a Bee's Knees on the rocks. Especially in the summer when it's hot and I want to hang out with the cocktail for a bit. To make this taste great over ice, I use Navy Strength gin because its extra proof will hold up to the dilution, plus a second gin for added layers of intrigue. I also add a few dashes of orange bitters, because their sturdy botanical profile hooks into the gin and drives up the complexity of both, with gusto. You want the cocktail to taste big and bold on the first sip but still hold its integrity as the ice in the glass melts—bitters help create this narrative arc.

CHOOSE YOUR INGREDIENTS

This is a great drink for cocktail newbies and folks who don't know they like gin yet. I call for Hayman's and Barr Hill in my version—the latter of which is distilled with honey, channeling the floral sensations of Vermont in the summer—but you can split that measurement with whatever gins you fancy. If you want to win over skeptics, try Dorothy Parker—the hibiscus in the botanical profile highlights the wildflower notes of the honey. Gins with citrus and fennel notes like Citadelle Jardin d'Été will also shine, because they tend to be softer and more gentle than big juniper-driven ones like Tanqueray or Copper & Kings The Moons of Juniper, which is usually what folks refer to when recalling a "ginsident" in their past. Weirder gins also work: Think low Christmas tree notes, big other flavors, be it cucumber and rose (Hendrick's) or bog myrtle and meadowsweet (The Botanist). The honey you choose will dictate how this drink drinks, just as much, if not more, than the style of gin. Think about the sweetener in terms of seasonality: wildflower for summer, buckwheat for fall, Tasmanian leatherwood for winter, and any kind in the spring, because it's a weird in-between season that can skew cold and rainy as fast as it does warm and sunny. Decide if you want the cocktail to be a patio pounder or a sipper best suited for an overstuffed armchair next to the fireplace, then let the thermometer be your guide. (And for a bit more intel on different kinds of honey, see the Airmail session on page 62).

- **PREP THE GARNISH.** Cut a nice swath of lemon peel from the citrus and set aside. For the love of all things holy, make sure there's no ugly freckles or flaws or blisters or discolored bumps on the peel. Seriously, nothing that makes the drinker think about stigmata instead of leisurely sipping. Trim those edges with a paring knife!

- **MEASURE.** Always dash the bitters into the tin before the other ingredients. I make this a habit because it's easy to forget that dash or two when you're distracted or in the weeds. Do it every time and it'll become rote. Now, jigger out the stickiest ingredients (honey syrup) before the other liquids, because the ones you measure afterward will help loosen up any tiny residual gunk. Hold the jigger upside down above the tin for an uncomfortably long time so there isn't a puddle of honey taking up space when you measure out your citrus juice. Now into the tin goes the lemon juice and both gins. If any of the syrup seems stuck to the bottom, stick your barspoon in there and give it a swirl to loosen up.

- **STRAW TASTE.** To make sure everything is in the tin.

- **SHAKE.** Take a gander at the bottle and see what the proof of your gin is—if it's high-proof (that is, more than 40% ABV), you will shake for a longer amount of time than if it's an 80-proof. Anticipate this in your mind, then add 5 ice cubes and Rocks Shake (page 46). If you are just beginning this wild and weird bartending journey, do this as an experiment: Make one of these drinks with 80-proof gin and one with Navy Strength gin, at the same time. Shake them both for the same amount of time, and taste both to see how the proof withstands the ice melt. In theory, you'll see that the one made with Navy Strength feels a bit boozy at this point, so you'll need to shake it a bit longer so that it eases into balance in the same way as the 80-proof version.

- **TASTE, ADJUST, AND STRAIN.** Straw taste. Are the edges sharp and rough, with a sandpaper-like quality drying out the tongue? Add a little more honey syrup; if the drink already tastes too much like honey, bring in simple syrup here for sweetness and texture instead. Add just a small amount to start, because you can always add more later. Another scenario: If your honey is skewed sweet so the drink is really sugary right now, add a bit more lemon juice. If the drink tastes too thin and wimpy because you overshook it, add ¼ ounce of the spirit. Once it's Goldilocks good, double-strain into your chilled DOF glass over ice cubes. Does it need one more cube to look appealing? Make little adjustments now, before you garnish.

- **GARNISH.** Squeeze your prepped peel over the top of the drink and marvel in how this motion expels oils all over the top of the glass. Might wanna do this from relatively high up, so the drink doesn't totally bathe in oils—you just want a little kiss of that quality for best aroma. Insert the peel. Go forth and get buzzzzzzzzed.

For your version of the Bee's Knees, you could fuck around with subbing in different kinds of bitters. I know that a dash of Peychaud's will go well with the lighter honeys like clover and wildflower. If you have a honey that reads deeper, like buckwheat, why not go chocolate bitters? (If you like it, then go whip up the 20th Century cocktail on page 57 and see how they compare.) For both scenarios, try hitting the top with a citrus peel that isn't lemon. Orange or grapefruit will do nicely.

BIJOU

*A Gregorian chant
echoing in the rafters*

The Bijou is a marvel. The liquid embodiment of a spellbinding chanteuse or beguiling traveler in a Dashiell Hammett novel. It just feels old and worldly in a way many other classics don't. I think this is because it's a higher-proof cocktail featuring only ingredients that have a rich sweetness and dizzying array of botanicals, so when stirred together the sum of its parts becomes quite decadent. And because of all this complexity (and booze and sugar), the opportunities for fucking one up are as numerous as termites in the desert, or krill in the ocean—if not handled with grace, it can escalate into an unpleasant situation quickly. I don't say these things to scare you off! With patience and a lot of straw tastes, it can be one of the most impressive cocktails in your arsenal. It's just one of those drinks suited best for the nerdiest of cocktail nerds (said as a card-carrying nerdy cocktail nerd).

Serve:
Stirred, up

Tools:
Jigger, mixing glass, barspoon, Julep strainer, paring knife

Glass:
Nick & Nora or coupe, chilled

Garnish:
Skewered cherry, lemon disk

RIYL:
Brandy Alexander (page 97), Manhattan (page 193), Saturn (page 277)

SPEC

Fords gin	1.0 oz
Hayman's Royal Dock gin	.50 oz
Green Chartreuse	.50 oz
Cocchi di Torino sweet vermouth	1.0 oz
Orange bitters	3 dashes

OUR APPROACH

The Bijou has such a hefty syrupy sweetness. Even if you stir the fuck out of it, it's still bombastic. To take its lavish texture and elevate it into something ethereal, we approach its character and assembly as if it were a dry Martini. This begins by upping the ratio of base spirit to set a foundation for the other ingredients to layer upon, splitting the measure between two gins with higher-than-usual proofs. Then we reduce the Chartreuse portion slightly, to slim down the amount of sweetness the liqueur adds to the mix. It's still an imposing drink, but these little adjustments create spectacular spiderwebs of complexity.

CHOOSE YOUR INGREDIENTS

For the purposes of this book, we tested many different variations of gin and sweet vermouth, and a beautiful harmony unfolded when pairing Hayman's and Fords with Cocchi di Torino sweet vermouth—the way the velvety cherry notes of the vermouth soften the gin, and wink at the Chartreuse, is magical. Generally speaking, an even-keeled London dry will set an almost neutral tone for the bombastic Chartreuse and vermouth to layer upon, so try your everyday go-to gin here, or let the Monk Magic (Chartreuse is made by the Carthusians) take the lead with something subtle like The Botanist or Sipsmith. The sweet vermouth is where the biggest opportunity for customization comes into play—because each option on the market has a slightly different botanical profile and level of sweetness, swapping in Dolin for Carpano or Cocchi for Cinzano will change the demeanor of the drink in a nanosecond. Mess around and see what sticks. Finally, green Chartreuse is really the crux of this drink, so do your best to not fuck with this sacred elixir.

HOW TO MIX

● **PREP THE GARNISH.** Carve out the lemon disk and set aside for future use. Don't skip this step! I'll talk about this more at the end, but here's a teaser: For me a lemon oil garnish always makes a sweet cocktail read as less sweet, so it really helps establish good balance in this recipe.

- **MEASURE.** Ice your mixing glass first, three-quarters of the way full with cubes. Then add the bitters and the sweet vermouth, followed by the green Chartreuse. This order of measuring—cheapest to most expensive ingredients—is especially important in this drink, because Chartreuse is hard to come by these days, and pricey to boot. If you fuck up the bitters or vermouth, you've still got a chance to dump the mix before you waste any precious Monk Juice. Flip the jigger and coax the gin out of the bottle. Carefully. Precisely. Precision is even more important in this drink because its balance is so precarious. Drizzle that in. Give this mix one or two rotations with a barspoon, to get the ingredients mixed together for the first straw taste.

- **STRAW TASTE.** To make sure everything is in the glass. Bookmark how sweet the cocktail tastes right now; it'll be a good learning experience to watch and see how that sweetness reduces as you stir.

- **STIR.** Coupe Stir (page 47) this with the patience of a saint. Straw taste, religiously. Look for how the complexity of the cocktail shuffles forth as the temperature drops. Look at how the Monk Magic is doing three things: adding complexity, sugar, and booze. I need your brain in the future here, also thinking about how this is going to warm in the coupe. You need to get it to the point that the hundred or so botanicals in the cocktail aren't overwhelming when its garnish has worn off and your inquisitorial schnozz is sunk in the glass, and a whirlwind of aromatics attack. Stir longer than you would a normal Martini—until your wrists start to hurt and your fingers feel on the verge of a cramp. The volume of the drink should have almost doubled by the time you finish.

- **TASTE, ADJUST, AND STRAIN.** Ideally, if you're new to this cocktail, you've been tasting occasionally to track how the drink dries out as you stir. It's magical, watching how the simple addition of cold water transforms a glass of ingredients into a cocktail—a thing that is greater than the sum of its parts. So how do you know when it's ready to serve? In this case, the drink no longer has thick viscous ribbons of sweetness, but instead the resemblance of a tight, cold, sorta Martini. I doubt you could overstir this one, but on this final straw taste check and see how you enjoy its balance of flavors: If you need to sneak in a bit more Chartreuse for a rounder texture and more honey notes, do it. There? Strain into your glass.

- **GARNISH.** The garnish is crucial on this drink. What's in the glass is a stew of sweet and dark flavors, a "something wicked this way comes" kind of vibe, so you need a bit of sunshine on top to balance out the broodiness. I call this "juxtaposition." The aroma you get from the lemon oils sets up an expectation of brightness, and once you take the first sip, that brightness shines for a quick second before fluttering away into the darkness. A cool moment of surprise and delight. Lemon disk oil also sets up an expectation that the cocktail will taste somewhat dry, which helps mute the cocktail's sweetness. Discard the disk after expressing its oils over the top. Skewer (or sink) your cherry as a final touch of garnish.

With a drink this technically challenging to make, I'd suggest keeping personalization as simple as possible. You could play with split-basing the sweet vermouth with different brands, as long as the measurement adds up to 1 ounce. Cocchi also makes a vermouth-amaro hybrid called Dopo de Teatro, which brings a twitch of bitterness to the build. You could also improvise with the garnish, because different types of citrus will change the aromatic entryway into the drink. Do this as an experiment: Make one cocktail but split it into three different coupes, then express a grapefruit peel over one glass, an orange over the second, and a lemon peel over the third to see what aromatic combo you like best. I'm always amazed how well grapefruit works on things you don't expect it to, so keep a special eye on that combo. And sure, if you want to get super hipster and use yuzu, Meyer, mandarin, or calamansi, go for it!

BLOODY MARY

*Savory Sunday-morning
hair of the hound*

The Bloody Mary—which looks like cocktail sauce but tastes like a boozy gazpacho—is a common-sense drink, guzzled out of necessity more than anything else. It gets some nutrition into your nauseous stomach when you are about to shrivel up like a snail on the Bolivian salt flats the morning after you ignored Dorothy Parker's excellent advice about Martinis—"two at the very most"—the night before. You need sustenance and a cocktail. Why not both at the same time?

Serve:
Shaken,
on the rocks

Tools:
Jigger, shaker

Glass:
Pint glass, chilled

Garnish:
Whatever your
heart desires
(consider celery
sticks, pickled
peppers, lemon
peel); plus one
7-ounce pony of
beer, such as Little
Kings or Miller
High Life

RIYL:
Aperol Spritz
(page 69),
Espresso Martini
(page 137),
Pimm's Cup
(page 253)

SPEC

Gin or vodka or aquavit or tequila	2.0 oz
Mother's Ruin Bloody Mary Mix (recipe follows)	5.0 oz
Citrus juice	.25 oz

OUR APPROACH

The beauty of the Bloody is that everyone has their own preferred version—some fussy and overwrought, others terrifically basic and straightforward. This spec, pared down a bit for ease of assembly, is an amalgamation of all of the recipes I've bumped into over the course of my career. It's a devil-may-care, kitchen-sink approach: one with a bunch of unusual ingredients that tickle your palate. What I like most about it is the tornado of flavors, textures, and sensations. Seriously, a sip of this will whip you right to OZ (the one where the wizard lives, not the abbreviation for ounces). It is sweet from tomatoes, salty from Worcestershire, spicy from Sriracha and horseradish, tangy from tamarind and citrus juice, and umami from mushroom bouillon and Worcestershire. I like to make a batch the day before I need it—like a good marinara, the flavor will be better after it sits for 24+ hours, and it will be colder, too.

CHOOSE YOUR INGREDIENTS

You might already know that vodka usually stars in the Bloody Mary. If a different spirit steps in, the cocktail assumes a different persona: Red Snapper for gin; Bloody Maria for tequila; Bloody Viking for aquavit, and the Bloody Caesar features vodka and clam broth. Any of these versions pairs well with the Bloody Mary mix sketched out here, so the base spirit is up to your whim and whimsy. Sometimes I choose based on what I'm eating: if you are having huevos rancheros for breakfast, use tequila, Cholula, and lime. Red Snappers pair swimmingly with all types of brunch food, and I'll be damned if a Bloody Viking isn't a sublime match for a meat and cheese board with pickled herring and rustic bread. For the citrus component, I find that lemon juice works with every spirit *except* for tequila and mezcal, in which case I'd recommend lime.

HOW TO MIX

• PREP THE GARNISH. Choose and prep what you want to use now, so you aren't wasting precious minutes assembling the army of garnishes after the drink is ready to sip. Don't forget the pony! I love how a little sip of beer here and there cleanses the palate and readies the soul for more boozy tomato soup.

● **MEASURE.** Grab your Bloody Mary mix from the fridge. Then, in a shaker tin, combine the citrus juice with the mix and your spirit of choice.

● **STRAW TASTE.** You're looking for balance of salt to spice to savory to sweet to acid to booze in this first straw taste. Seriously, apply the same lens to this drink as you would to any other cocktail in this book. Does the acidity level match the intensity of the sweetness of the tomato, the richness/umami character, and the spice levels? Adjust now to taste. If the mix has sat overnight, it will often need a pinch of salt or a bit of ground pepper before shaking.

● **SHAKE.** The best bloodies are shaken. You want all the components to be integrated, and because you have some wildly different textures, things need to get comfy with one another. Fill your glass with ice about three-quarters of the way full, then roll that ice to the shaker. Rocks Shake (page 46) the shit out of this.

● **TASTE AND ADJUST, THEN ROLL.** During shaking, the texture of this drink should have lightened up a bit as the flavors tightened together. You can add ¼ ounce of fresh lemon or lime juice à la minute to brighten it up, if it's tasting kinda muddy. A dash of Angostura could help add complexity, if it's a bit one-dimensional. Give it a quick shake one more time just to make sure everything is integrated, then roll the whole contents back into the glass. There should be a finger or so of wash line available at the top of the glass so you can fit your cornucopia of garnish without overflowing. If there isn't, use a spoon to take out a few ice cubes to make room.

● **GARNISH.** Go wild! Nothing is off limits.

The Bloody Mary is one of the most customizable drinks ever invented, but there should at least be some sort of liquid tomato product, some spices, and something tangy included. Beyond that, the world is your Rocky Mountain oyster. Acid can come from lemon/lime juice or vinegar or red wine. Why not all three? Anchovies, fish sauce, and Worcestershire are your friends. Bring the fucking noise! You want heat? Toss in a few different hot sauces, from a few different countries. Add peppers and horseradish, wasabi, too. Fuck yeah! Spices, you ask? Black pepper, celery salt, dill, oregano, bay leaf are all fair game. I would just shy away from basil as the drink just might end up tasting more like a lasagna than breakfast.

BLOODY MARY MIX

Science has proved that time makes flavors more complex, creating new molecules that make the food more pleasing, like how a multifarious barroom of characters from all walks of life is more interesting than a homogeneous soirée. So: Make the Bloody Mary mix at least 24 hours ahead of time. Store in the fridge until ready to use. Use within two days, otherwise the flavors will become too intense. PS: I have always used Sacramento tomato juice for this mix because I like the balance between the acidity and the sweetness. It is a great blank canvas to slather other flavors on. It's also readily available everywhere. If you want to cut it with some V8 to add a bit of background vegginess, gopher it. **Makes 12 ounces**

1 (7.2-ounce) can Sacramento tomato juice
2 tablespoons plus 2 teaspoons red wine
1 tablespoon pickle juice
1 tablespoon pineapple juice
1 tablespoon Worcestershire sauce
1½ teaspoons fresh lime juice
¼ ounce fresh lemon juice
1 teaspoon Sriracha
3 dashes Cholula hot sauce
1 tablespoon horseradish
½ teaspoon mushroom bouillon base, such as Better Than Bouillon
2 teaspoons freshly ground black pepper
1 teaspoon kosher salt
½ teaspoon Old Bay seasoning
½ teaspoon sugar

Pour the tomato juice into a large bowl. Add the rest of the components, whisking together as you go. Transfer to a large bottle, labeled with the date, and refrigerate for at least 2 hours before using. Use within 2 days.

BRAMBLE

*Crushable adult lemonade,
painted pink*

Whimsical and smashing, the Bramble was born in the debauchery of SoHo, but I prefer to think of the drink as the definition of refinement and prudence. A simple sour, but one with decidedly more panache than a Gimlet (page 145). The drizzled purpleness of the mûre (that is, blackberry liqueur) is as pretty as a Dover Sunrise. It is a cocktail that does more with less, packing an outsized punch of flavor, considering its modest assembly. I love batching them for a spring picnic. Or drinking them in a dark bar in the middle of summer. If it's hot and muggy, or you are dancing your ass off in a club and want something that delivers Antarctic cold with tranquil quaffability, the Bramble is an excellent choice.

MIZE

Serve:
Shaken,
on crushed ice

Tools:
Jigger, shaker,
paring knife

Glass:
Collins or Double
Old Fashioned,
chilled

Garnish:
Fresh blackberry,
mint bouquet,
lemon disk

RIYL:
Jack Rose
(page 173),
Pimm's Cup
(page 253),
Paloma (page 245)

SPEC

Fords gin	2.0 oz
Fresh lemon juice	.75 oz
Simple syrup (page 29)	.25 oz
Giffard crème de mûre, to lace	.50 oz

OUR APPROACH

This is one of those "no notes" kinda cocktails and I don't see a reason to fuck with a good thing, so my spec is a standard, straightforward Bramble. It's wicked dry, like the acerbic wit of Sarah Silverman. If you are wondering how it's wicked dry when there's simple syrup *and* liqueur in play, it's because the crème de mûre is surprisingly dry (and adds proof). The simple is added to buff up the texture of the drink, which is lacking thanks to said dryness, without adding flavor on its own. That little measure of simple helps the whole cocktail stand up to the blast of dilution from the crushed ice better. Speaking of crushed ice, it's one of my favorite things about this drinking experience, because it adds texture you just can't get out of a regular sour, and a sound that instantly makes me thirsty. Finally, a spry shower of lemon peel oil over the top of the cocktail serves as icing on the cake: It echoes the lemon juice in the drink and makes the first sniff screamingly bright and fresh.

CHOOSE YOUR INGREDIENTS

The Bramble is classically made with a blackberry liqueur called crème de mûre, but I have taken liberties with strawberry syrups and sloe berry syrups and currant liqueurs and raspberry ones. I have made them deep and dark and fit for a chilly fall day. I have also made them light and flirty, like a summer dress looking for a breeze to blow it up. For this version, I find that Giffard's mûre has a lovely antique personality reminiscent of blackberries plucked from the fields of an English farm. But like the kind of farm with an old farmhouse with ivy crawling up the walls and a sun-soaked library filled with dusty old books. You can match this with a big gin like Beefeater, which'll make its presence known in the glass, or you can go the opposite route with a more subtle gin like The Botanist or Fords, if you want the syrup to serve as more than mere pocket square.

HOW TO MIX

● **PREP THE GARNISH.** Select a beautiful blackberry, because it needs to look pretty on top of the crushed ice. Grab a lush bouquet of mint. No holes or rips or tears in any of the leaves. Cut a disk from a fresh lemon. Set aside for later.

- **MEASURE.** Make the "body" of the cocktail in the shaker first by measuring and adding the simple syrup, then the lemon juice and the gin. You will add the liqueur later, so for now just make sure it's nearby and ready to pour.

- **STRAW TASTE.** To make sure everything is in the tin. After you've done this, prepare your Double Old Fashioned glass by filling it with crushed ice about four-fifths of the way. If it is totally full, the drink will end up all over your station and not in the glass. Not ideal.

- **SHAKE.** Okay, back to your shaker tin—add 2 ounces of crushed ice. The goal is quick and deliberate chilling, not adding a full buffer of ice water as you would with a Coupe Shake (page 45), because this cocktail tastes best when it's strong-ish on the first few sips, then mellows into the crushed ice over time. Whip Shake (page 46) until you can't hear any ice rattling around in the tin anymore.

- **TASTE AND ADJUST, THEN ROLL.** Taste for balance; remember that you will be adding another sweet component with the crème de mûre later, so it should stay on the dry and tart end of the spectrum. The temp should feel lightly chilled—not ice cold—so the cocktail doesn't melt too much crushed ice when it hits the glass. Roll the drink gently into your prepped glass.

- **LACE.** Some people call this a float, but "lace" makes more sense to me when it comes to liqueurs drizzled over crushed ice cocktails because the liquid creates a delicate pattern as it weaves down into the drink. The goal is to get a fine stratum of the laced ingredient on top of the crushed ice without dripping any down the sides of the glass. To do this, make sure the crushed ice sits below the lip of the glass; you can add more after you lace. Slowly pour the syrup out of a jigger in one spot, as close to the lip of the glass as you can without spilling it, and turn the glass 360 degrees until there is a line of liqueur all the way around the edge that'll sink slowly down, like an inebriated octopus looking for the next whiskey bar.

- **GARNISH.** Put a straw in the drink. Insert the mint bouquet and nestle a blackberry in its embrace. Then grab your lemon disk and pinch it, skin side facing the cocktail, to spray its oils over the top of the crushed ice, mint, and blackberry. Take a sniff and marvel at the way all three garnish components come together to tell a really cool aromatic story. Always serve with a napkin and let the drinker know it's gonna get slippery as ice sheaths the outside of the glass.

In my ultrapersonalized spec, I muddle fresh blackberries instead of using blackberry liqueur (or I use jam if the fruit is out of season) to put all that good fruit flavor directly into the mix, then add a bit more simple syrup than usual to keep the sweetness in balance. The gin, lemon, and berries come together in a way that communicates the full spectrum of the cocktail's flavor in every sip. Same cocktail, different experience. (See the Clover Club, page 109, as another good candidate for this treatment.) I also love tossing in some Angostura, because it complements the fresh blackberries so well. Like Laurel and Hardy!

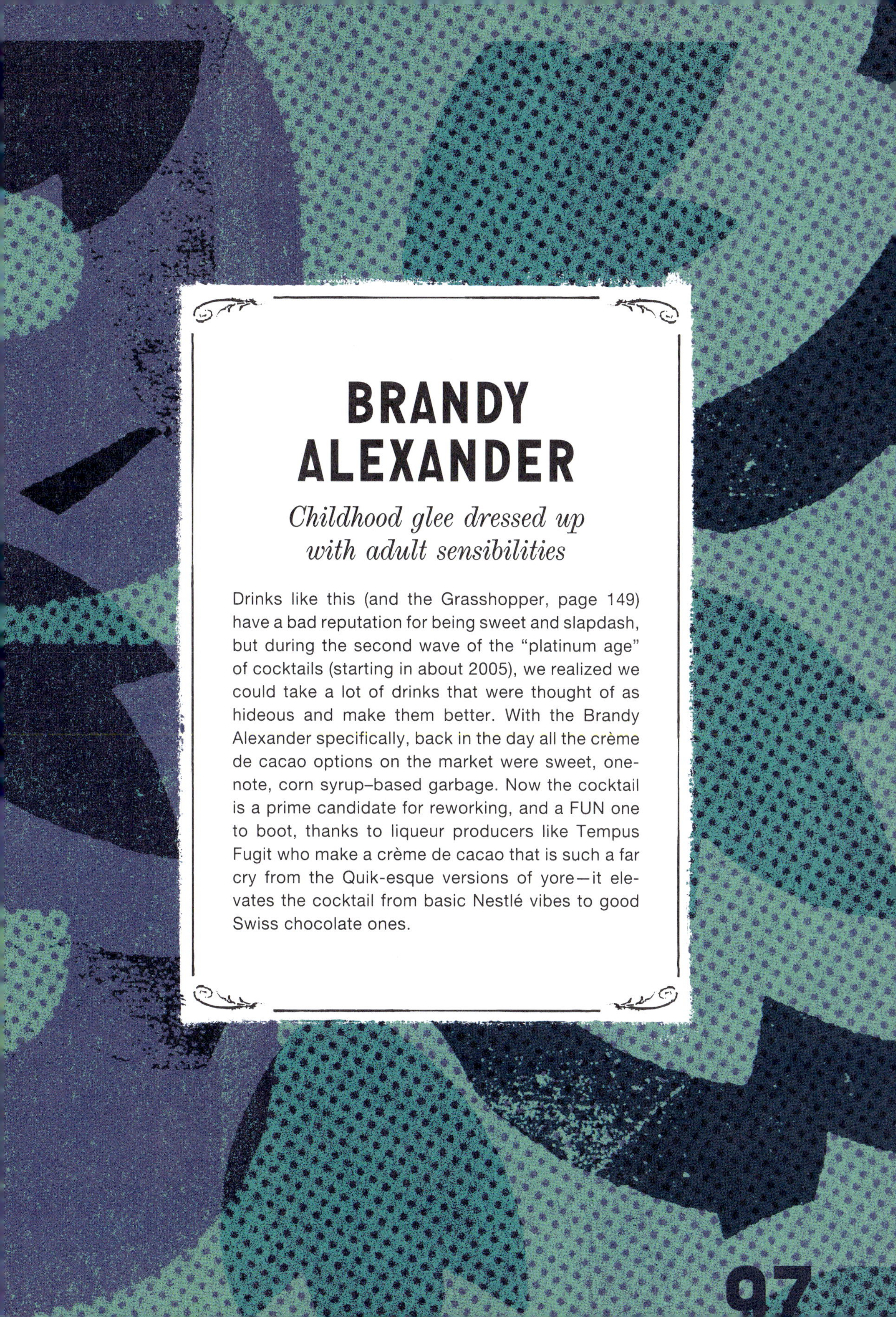

BRANDY ALEXANDER

*Childhood glee dressed up
with adult sensibilities*

Drinks like this (and the Grasshopper, page 149) have a bad reputation for being sweet and slapdash, but during the second wave of the "platinum age" of cocktails (starting in about 2005), we realized we could take a lot of drinks that were thought of as hideous and make them better. With the Brandy Alexander specifically, back in the day all the crème de cacao options on the market were sweet, one-note, corn syrup–based garbage. Now the cocktail is a prime candidate for reworking, and a FUN one to boot, thanks to liqueur producers like Tempus Fugit who make a crème de cacao that is such a far cry from the Quik-esque versions of yore—it elevates the cocktail from basic Nestlé vibes to good Swiss chocolate ones.

Serve:
Shaken, up

Tools:
Jigger, shaker, Hawthorne strainer, fine strainer, Microplane, paring knife

Glass:
Coupe, chilled

Garnish:
Grated nutmeg, orange disk

RIYL:
Grasshopper (page 149), Stinger (page 293), Ramos Gin Fizz (page 273)

SPEC

Ferrand 1840 Cognac	1.0 oz
Tempus Fugit crème de cacao	1.0 oz
Heavy cream	1.0 oz
Angostura cocoa bitters	2 dashes

OUR APPROACH

The Brandy Alexander is a dessert drink, not a nightcap (yes, there is a difference), but our goal is to yank it out of the world of the milkshake and into the realm of respectable indulgence, like a world-class tiramisu or tres leches. We do this by focusing first on the integrity of the ingredients in the glass—just by upgrading the quality of the liqueur and elevating the brandy to a world-class Cognac, the level of sophistication increases exponentially. Then we lean into the "bitterness" of chocolate liqueur by adding . . . bitters! Bitters can be like ambient sound in a cocktail, where they just add a soft buzzing background hum. In this drink specifically, I like chocolate bitters for how they echo the chocolatiness of the crème de cacao. Finally, a kiss of warm, aromatic orange oils as garnish serves as an unexpected entryway into the cocktail—there's no orange in the drink, so when you get that surprising whiff before you take the first sip, it's a super cool little moment of surprise and delight. I love using invisible garnishes like this to spark awe or curiosity in an unsuspecting drinker.

CHOOSE YOUR INGREDIENTS

I think a lot of people see the Alexander as a frou-frou drink because it has heavy cream in the mix, but it has potential to be the belle of the ball if you're using good ingredients. Start with the spirit: I love a good Cognac and how it can swing in all classy and deep in a Vieux Carré (page 301) or Sidecar (page 289) and then get all playful in a Stinger (page 293) or Alexander. It is so underrated. I like Ferrand 1840 Cognac, Brandy Sainte Louise, and the Butchertown from Copper & Kings, a brandy maker smack dab in the middle of the Bourbon Trail in Louisville, Kentucky, for this cocktail. All of them can stand up to the heavy texture of the cream and the richness of the cacao. Chocolate bitters come in a range of flavors as well: Angostura has a milk chocolate vibe that tastes great in this cocktail, but if you like dark bittersweet chocolate better, try the bitters from The Bitter Truth. Bittermens Xocolatl Mole bitters or Bittercube Chipotle Cacao bitters would also be a wicked cool flex if you want to add a whisper of dried chile pepper notes to spark a "what's that flavor?!" moment. For the liqueur, revisit the 20th Century cocktail (page 57) for notes on how Giffard and Tempus Fugit—our preferred options—compare. Finally, check your heavy cream NOW, before you start mixing anything. If your heavy cream smells fresh, you're good. If it doesn't, run to the store real quick. You could use half-and-half in a pinch, but the texture won't be as luxurious, because it has a lower fat content—it's up to you to go the extra mile, here.

- **PREP THE GARNISH.** Cut a small disk from the peel of an orange. Set aside. Grab your nutmeg and Microplane. If you've got a really banging single-origin nutmeg, that'll match the intensity of the Cognac and high-quality liqueur. Preground nutmeg out of the jar will taste less vibrant—sometimes even stale or dusty depending on how old it is—so that will bring down the quality of the cocktail as a whole, but you could use a pinch, in a pinch, if you must, just to get the job done.

- **MEASURE.** Start by dashing the bitters into the tin. Then the heavy cream. When you're pouring dairy into the tin, let the jigger hover upside down over the shaker for a couple seconds longer than you would with booze or juice, to make sure every drop lands inside. Every drop matters! Now add the crème de cacao and the Cognac. You can stack them in the 2-ounce side of the jigger, if you like, for better precision. I usually only stack ingredients of the same ilk (like booze and booze, or syrup and liqueur), to ensure the full measure of two ingredients doesn't exceed what's called for, but you can do this with any ingredients if you're practicing jiggering with precision.

- **STRAW TASTE.** To make sure everything is in the tin. It's going to kinda taste like melted ice cream in this moment. That's okay! It'll change after you shake.

- **SHAKE.** This is a CREAMY drink, which you'd think you need to shake to death to get the cream incorporated with other ingredients, but when you do that, the cream actually gets whipped to the point of too much froth. So don't overthink, don't overshake. Instead, add 5 cubes and use a Coupe Shake (page 45), and a relatively quick one at that: like a horse galloping one long lap around a racetrack. It might take a few tries to get a feel for this, so the first few you make, shake for a bit, crack the tin and straw taste, concentrating on how the drink feels on your tongue, so you develop a sense memory. It should feel weighty without being too ponderous. Eventually you'll be able to use your intuition to figure out when it's frothy but not too whipped.

- **TASTE, ADJUST, AND STRAIN.** Straw taste: If it is not chocolatey enough, add a shy ¼ ounce more of cacao. If it doesn't seem decadent enough, add a shy ¼ ounce of Demerara syrup—this will buff up the texture without changing the flavor of the drink. Such a cool trick to have in your arsenal. Remember to shake briefly again, or swirl the tin around, to incorporate whatever you might have added. Did you shake too much, causing the bitters to fade away into the background? You can add an extra dash now. Or two, maybe, but start with one first and taste, then add more if needed. You can always add, but you can't subtract! Double-strain into the coupe.

- **GARNISH.** Grate fresh nutmeg on top. Express a bit of orange oil over the spices. Discard the orange peel disk.

BRANDY CRUSTA

*A flamboyant dandy peacocking
on the promenade*

The Crusta, as its name sort of suggests, is a bone-dry drink, sharp as a straight razor straight from the strop. It's not necessarily straight-up delicious, but it's fascinating. Like having a chat with Jerry Thomas at his bar just south of Madison Square Park in the late 1800s. Or so I imagine. Anyway, it is also a confusing drink. I mean, on paper it's just a Sidecar (page 289) with the addition of maraschino liqueur. But that one little change makes a cocktail that's both more interesting and more polarizing than the popular Sidecar, which I often call the most versatile drink I know. A small but mighty flex.

Serve:
Shaken, up

Tools:
Jigger, shaker,
Hawthorne
strainer,
fine strainer,
paring knife

Glass:
Coupe + sidecar,
chilled

Garnish:
Lemon or orange
disk, orange peel,
sugar rim

RIYL:
Aviation
(page 73),
Sidecar
(page 289),
New York Sour
(page 233)

SPEC

Ferrand 1840 Cognac	....	2.0 oz
Fresh lemon juice	....	.75 oz
Ferrand dry curaçao	....	.50 oz
Luxardo maraschino liqueur	....	.50 oz
Simple syrup (page 29)	....	.25 oz
Orange bitters	....	2 dashes

OUR APPROACH

This can be a bit of a fussy drink, thanks to the seriously extra garnish and the dramatic sugar rim. Some people love these things, putting care and craft into their assembly, others can't be bothered. I get it! Sometimes I want a less persnickety version, too. Luckily, this drink can totally be a lovely little tipple that's easy to bang together and great for a quick happy hour. First, I'm giving you a nice middle-of-the-road spec. Not too sweet, not too dry. I'm ditching the overwrought orange peel garnish in favor of a quick spritz of oils, and you can ditch the sugar rim entirely, if you fancy. Onward, we go!

CHOOSE YOUR INGREDIENTS

The Crusta has a singular place in my heart because it's how I learned to love maraschino cherry liqueur (albeit in small amounts). You could describe its flavor as "adult cherry." Like a deep, funky, stewed cherry and not the "fresh red cherry" of Minute Maid cherry limeade. For this drink, I recommend Luxardo maraschino, a liqueur made with all parts of the cherry—the pits, the stems, the leaves, the whole shebang—because it captures a full-aperture vision of Italian cherry flavor. For the other ingredients: The combo of Ferrand 1840 Cognac and Ferrand dry curaçao creates a swirling vortex of complementary flavors. The stone fruit and vanilla of the Cognac and the orange and clove notes of the curaçao together are simply glorious.

HOW TO MIX

• PREP THE GARNISH. You have two options here. If you want to lean into the "simple" side of this drink, just carve out a regular lemon or orange disk that you can express and discard later. If you prefer a full Horse's Neck garnish, do your best to pull one single peel from the entire citrus; this super-long peel makes for a pretty visual, but getting good at pulling them can take some practice.

- **SUGAR ON THE RIM.** I didn't always appreciate the sugar rim. For the last twenty-five years, I'd lick and chew the sugar before drinking the drink and I HATED it, like I hate sand in a PB&J for lunch at the beach. But recently while drinking a killer Crusta at Jewel of the South in New Orleans, where my buddy Chris Hannah is *known* for his version, I discovered that if you lick the sugar and let it gently melt on your tongue, the drink is a whole different experience. The key is to only coat half the rim of the glass in sugar so the drinker has the CHOICE of whether they want to make this drink drier or sweeter. Wipe a lemon wedge all the way around the rim, but only sugar half, so one side is sweet and one side is not, and every time you drink, you get one or the other until they both disappear. Flip over to the Sidecar session (page 289) for a specific step-by-step on how to sugar a rim. We do this well ahead of time and store the glass in the freezer so the sugar has time to concentrate on the rim before the cocktail enters the equation.

- **MEASURE.** In your shaker, start with the bitters and simple syrup, then stack the maraschino and curaçao so the total volume does not exceed 1 ounce. Add your three-quarters of lemon. Get that full 2 ounces of Cognac in there, too! Measure each one as precisely as a doctor measures out medications.

- **STRAW TASTE.** To make sure everything is in the tin. Gauge how the maraschino and curaçao and simple syrup are all working together. At this stage it'll taste suuuuper sweet. Register it in your mind, because you will need to pay attention to this again when you do the second straw taste.

- **SHAKE.** Add 5 of the most perfect ice cubes you have to the tin. Throw out the misshapen and mediocre; these will interfere with your consistency. Cap and Coupe Shake (page 45). There's quite a bit of alcohol in this mix so you're gonna need a lot of ice water to get all the ingredients to hush into harmony with one another. It's a bit longer than the shake of a Daiquiri (page 125). Stop shaking when the liquid inside starts to sound real slushy, like the wind blowing through pine trees. Shake for a beat or two more before calling it quits.

- **TASTE, ADJUST, AND STRAIN.** Crack open the tins, tap, and wring (page 45). Straw taste. Look for a big hit of the Cognac with the maraschino as an accent note, not as its own funky presence. If they haven't started holding hands yet, shake more. How is the texture? Does it need a whisper of Demerara syrup to plump up? Do that now! Take a quick beat and remember what you decided to do about the garnish on this drink. If you went the long peel route, you want to add that to the glass before straining. Take the peel, wrap it tight in a circular fashion, and put it into the glass so it will rise when you pour the drink into the coupe. Once it's ready to go, double-strain into the coupe (and sidecar, if needed).

- **GARNISH.** If you chose to keep it simple by using only a regular citrus disk for garnish, now you can express the oils over the top of the drink and discard.

For me, this drink is all about the maraschino. Cognac and other high-quality grape brandies have beautiful stone fruit notes, and the stone fruit-ness of the cherries used in maraschino flow nicely together with those. So to keep that game of footsie at the forefront of the drink, sometimes I drop out the curaçao entirely. I know this is a radical move. Give it a try, if you're up for a fun challenge: 2 ounces of Cognac, 3/4 ounce of lemon juice, 1/4 ounce of maraschino, 1/4 ounce of Demerara syrup, then 2 dashes of orange bitters and 1 dash of Angostura. The addition of the orange bitters keeps the "orange" flavor in play, and the Ango helps make up for the complexity we lose when ditching the curaçao. With this version, garnish with an orange peel to layer on orange aromatics that nod back to the original.

BREAKFAST MARTINI

*A comforting companion
for a Full English*

Most of the time I get prickly when someone describes a drink that's not gin and vermouth and bitters a "martini," but this is an exception to the rule. I get so excited about this cocktail—like, pupils as big as bone China saucers, goosebumps ripping up my arms, the crunch of toast ringing in my ears—because nothing screams "breakfast in London" more than a little dollop of marmalade. The glistening golden jam is SO much more than your average preserve. It's made with the fruit pulp *and* the peels, which brings a lively bitterness to the mix reminiscent of the way Campari brings a bittersweet edge to the Negroni. It's sly, not overt. Pair it with a good English gin, sunny lemon juice, and a hit of candied orange liqueur, and you've got a cocktail fit for a Queen.

Serve:
Shaken,
on the rocks

Tools:
Jigger, shaker,
Hawthorne
strainer,
fine strainer,
paring knife

Glass:
Double Old
Fashioned, chilled

Garnish:
Orange peel

RIYL:
Bramble
(page 93),
Corpse Reviver #2
(page 113),
Sidecar (page 289)

SPEC

London dry gin	2.0 oz
Ferrand dry curaçao	.75 oz
Cocchi Americano	.50 oz
Fresh lemon juice	.75 oz
Orange marmalade	1 Tbsp
Bittercube orange bitters	3 dashes

OUR APPROACH

Maestro bartender Salvatore Calabrese's original spec for this cocktail is very straightforward. In a great way. Its simplicity is one of the many reasons why the drink sticks to the ribs. I encourage you to google it and make one before you try my interpretation. The big thing I'm changing is adding Cocchi Americano to amplify the orange and lemon notes. The aromatized wine has gorgeous citrusy qualities that sync right up with the marmalade. Like drinking a bouquet of yellow and white flowers with bees buzzing around your ankles on a hot summer day, it has a bitterness that comes close enough to sting, but not close enough. It also doesn't change the soul of the cocktail; it just shifts it a bit. Finally, I also change the serve: Putting it on ice gives it a cool narrative arc (page 44) as it mellows over time instead of warming and becoming more intense. If I had to compare this version with Salvatore's, I'd say mine is long and bitter, like a millionaire's divorce, while his is sharp, like the crisp lines of a well-tailored Valentino suit.

CHOOSE YOUR INGREDIENTS

I like using a very soft gin like Fords for the Breakfast Martini, to keep the focus on the cocktail's beautiful orange notes. Alongside the marmalade, the gin tastes borderline comforting. Fords was also formulated specifically to work well in cocktails, is pretty easy to find in every market, and comes at a digestible price point. What more could you ask for? For the aromatized wine, could you use Cocchi's French blonde sister Lillet Blanc here instead? Of course! It'll change the flavor slightly, but there's no harm in giving it a whirl to see which version you prefer. Just don't go cheap on the dry curaçao—a bottom-shelf triple sec will obliterate the elegance of this cocktail faster than the British say "two shakes of a lamb's tail." See page 250 for why I like Ferrand for, well, every single cocktail in this book. Now, I hate jam bands, but I love jams in my cocktails because their flavor remains stalwart and dependable over time and by the batch, unlike fresh fruit, where the flavor, sweetness, and acidity change by the piece, the day, and the season. Jams also last almost forever once sealed in their glass jar tombs. Bonne Maman is a high-quality option, plus the labels come off easily in the dishwasher so you can reuse the jars later. Store your marmalade in the fridge before using, because we are always trying to make our cold drinks as cold as possible. It will take a bit more coaxing to integrate with the other ingredients, but the jam/jelly is worth the stir.

● **PREP THE GARNISH.** Pull your orange peel from the fruit. Set aside.

● **MEASURE.** Bitters into the tin first, to establish good habits. Then the marmalade. Measuring out a jam isn't as easy as measuring out liquid. Obviously. So, if consistency and precision is important to you in this drink (hint: it should be), when you measure the tablespoon of jam, pack it in there, then use the back of your paring knife to level it off. If you want to be really, really geeky, weigh out about 14 grams instead. You have a gram scale to measure your coffee, right? You know what to do. Okay, the marmalade is in the tin, so follow that with the lemon juice, then Cocchi, curaçao, and gin, in that order.

● **STRAW TASTE.** To make sure everything is in the tin. Check: Is the marmalade integrated with the other items? If it's floating around in chunks and you can't taste it at this stage, give it another stir—this also ensures it'll gel properly with the liquid ingredients once ice comes into play and tightens the jam up. You could also cap the tins right now and do a quick Mime Shake (page 45) to get that jam all jammified into the other ingredients before you add ice.

● **SHAKE.** The Breakfast Martini is normally served up in a coupe, but I like mine on the rocks, so we are going to add 5 ice cubes to the tin and do a Rocks Shake (page 46)—shorter than one you'd use for a Whiskey Sour (page 305), but longer than a Bee's Knees (page 81). Jams and jellies are thick, so you'll need to put a little more elbow grease into the motion, like a jackrabbit sprint—tough and muscular, but for about as long as it takes to outrun a tortoise.

● **TASTE, ADJUST, AND STRAIN.** As the cocktail sits on ice in the glass, it'll thin out and dry out a bit, so right now the ideal texture should be kinda thick, and balance should skew a little sweet, so that it ages with grace as it dilutes. (Look to Narrative Arc on page 44 for more on how a cocktail evolves as it sits in the glass, and how you can adjust your shake accordingly.) In other words: The sweetness from the marmalade should be present but not overwhelming—if it's strong and sticky, you just need to shake a bit longer. There are also a lot of sweet ingredients in this drink, so if your second straw taste sticks to the roof of your mouth you can add a splash of more citrus juice. Once you've got the balance where you want it, ice your DOF glass, filling it almost all the way to the top. Double-strain the cocktail into the glass.

● **GARNISH.** Express the orange peel over the top of the drink, then insert.

Breakfast is a personal thing. There are the sweet-toothed folks who want chocolate croissants, pancakes drowning in maple syrup, and cinnamon raisin bagels. Then there are the savory-inclined folks who reach for ham and cheese croissants, omelets with bacon and chives, and everything bagels with lox, capers, and onion. (The third type: folks with the idea that anything other than a cup of black coffee is sacrilege.) It's your druthers, so use those preferences as inspiration for ways to change the drink. I have stirred a wee bit of raspberry jam into my orange marmalade to give the drink a Cosmo Pink vibe and extra-jammy quality. I've split-based the London dry gin with a big, weird gin like the St. George Dry Rye, or even aquavit, when I'm in a savory mood. Hell, have a goblet of sparkling wine to sip on the side like the world's fanciest schmanciest boilermaker!

CLOVER CLUB

*A raspberry cloud laced with
high-altitude botanicals*

As the prettiest pink drink of all time, the Clover Club is so head-scratchingly good, if you order one, it's proof positive that you have excellent taste and complete confidence in your gender identity (no matter what it may be). It's a crowd-pleaser. A lean and ephemeral beauty. A fascinating and surprising sleeper hit that reiterates the old idiom: You can't judge a song by its cover. Drinking one out of a coupe, ideally in a dark bar in the middle of summer with good company in tow, makes it feel as though you will live forever and everything is beautiful. It is also the ideal cocktail for people who think they hate gin, because juniper isn't the star of the show. Instead, the combo of berries and lemon and botanicals shines bright like a diamond.

Serve:
Shaken, up

Tools:
Jigger, shaker,
Hawthorne
strainer,
fine strainer,
paring knife

Glass:
Coupe, chilled

Garnish:
Peychaud's bitters,
lemon disk

RIYL:
Bramble
(page 93),
Hotel Nacional
(page 157),
Pisco Sour
(page 261)

SPEC

London dry gin	. . . .	2.0 oz
Dolin dry vermouth	. . . .	1.0 oz
Fresh lemon juice	. . . .	.75 oz
Raspberry syrup (page 32)	. . . .	1.0 oz
Peychaud's bitters	. . . .	3 dashes
Egg white	. . . .	1

OUR APPROACH

My friend Julie Reiner made history when she took this forgotten classic cocktail, reworked the recipe, and made it glorious at her Brooklyn bar Clover Club. She did this with one simple move: adding dry vermouth. I've always thought it was genius, because it adds complexity and dries out the finish, leaving the palate ready for another sip immediately. It's still a Clover Club, but a much improved version. (Google hers and mix up a round, using Plymouth for the gin and Dolin dry vermouth, as Queen Reiner herself does at the bar.) I am following Julie's lead in this spec by keeping the dry vermouth in play. But I like a stronger punch of juniper in my cocktails, so I add more gin. I also find that dashing a few dashes of Peychaud's, the prettiest pink bitters, into the mix brings a soft vanilla note to the drink, which complements the raspberries nicely and dries out the drink without sacrificing its plush texture. So, in my hubris, I make these adjustments first. Finally, traditionally, the cocktail is garnished with a few raspberries, but I add a slash of Peychaud's across the top of the drink for a little more visual drama and a hint of fennel on the nose. It smells sublime when paired with the wistful aroma of lemon peel oil, which I also suggest expressing over the top of the drink to add bright-ness. Yes, many Clover Clubs were harmed in this experiment, but when both versions are delicious and delightful, just for different reasons, can we really say that's a bad thing?

CHOOSE YOUR INGREDIENTS

The goal is to keep this drink fun and whimsical. The gin and vermouth should both taste bright and herbaceous, but at a flavor volume that's kinda chill. Neither should wrestle the other out of the way, because together they need to hold up the beauty of the raspberry syrup. I can't think of any vermouth that works better than Dolin in a Clover Club, because it has a great balance of sweetness and bright herbaceousness, so try Dolin dry alongside a refined gin like Sipsmith or The Botanist.

- **PREP THE GARNISH.** Cut the lemon disk now, so you don't waste precious time doing it after the drink is ready to drink.

- **MEASURE.** Start with the egg, remembering good eggtiquette (see page 234). Always crack the egg white into the tin you're not using to build the rest of the cocktail, in case you mess up and accidentally plop the whole thing in there and have to start over. Now add the Peychaud's bitters, the raspberry syrup, lemon juice, and dry vermouth into the maw of the eggless side of the shaker. Add the gin last! Be precise in your measurement. No meniscus.

- **STRAW TASTE.** Taste the liquid mixture to make sure everything is in the tin. Now add the egg white to the mix and cap those tins.

- **SHAKE.** As with the Amaretto Sour (page 65) and the Whiskey Sour (page 305), the key to a texturally sound egg white drink is in the shake. Mime Shake (page 45) first, without ice, to infuse air into the proteins of the egg. This is what makes the gooey beast transform into the thick cotton of aerated perfection. After that quick fluttering motion, let the mixture settle for a second; I would recommend you go and put on the Bad Flamingo song "Bottom Shelf Gin" and turn it up to 11. Come back, add 3 cubes and Coupe Shake (page 45) like somebody stole your truck. Use 3 cubes here instead of 5 so you can shake longer without adding a rude amount of water content—this whips up the texture nicely without diluting too much.

- **TASTE, ADJUST, AND STRAIN.** If it's too dry—because egg whites dry out drinks—add a bit of simple syrup to swing it back into balance. Once you've got the flavor nice and tight, tap the tin three times on a solid surface to concentrate the bubbles. Seriously. If it's your first time trying this, you might be inclined to skip ahead, but give it a whirl and marvel at how the small move tightens up the texture. Always double-strain to get rid of ice chips and big bubbles, or "pimples" as they're called when pouring a perfect pint of Guinness. When done right, the whites settle in a thick cap of creamy delight on top of the sour—a visual pleasure and one that has a textural impact, too, because it forces you to dive through that layer of thick tickling froth before getting to the bulk of the cocktail below.

- **GARNISH.** One thing that we didn't mention about working with egg whites in the Amaretto Sour session (page 65) is how egg white drinks need a strong aromatic element in play, because fresh egg whites have a neutral smell, and the frothy spuma masks the aroma of the cocktail below it. So, for the Clover Club, put an odd number of drops or a slash of Peychaud's bitters on the spume, then drag a toothpick or knife straight through the bitters to make a design of your choice. Make it pretty. Express a lemon disk gently from about 4 inches above the drink and discard the disk. This is, objectively, the most beautiful drink in the world: Watch as the bottom of the drink turns pink, and the white puffy cloud solidifies as it sits in the glass.

I've got a fun little alternative approach for cocktails that call for a fruit syrup or liqueur, like this one and the Bramble (page 93). Instead of using said syrup or liqueur, you can muddle fresh fruit and add simple syrup or Demerara syrup for a drink that resembles the original but has bright fresh fruit flavor instead of one that tastes more "baked" or "cooked." For this drink specifically, I have no problem with raspberry syrup, but sometimes I like the berry flavor to taste less like a cobbler, and more like it was picked right off the plant. To do this, omit the raspberry syrup from the recipe and just muddle 5 to 7 raspberries in the shaker before building the rest of the drink. Then swap in simple syrup for the measure of raspberry syrup and you're good to go.

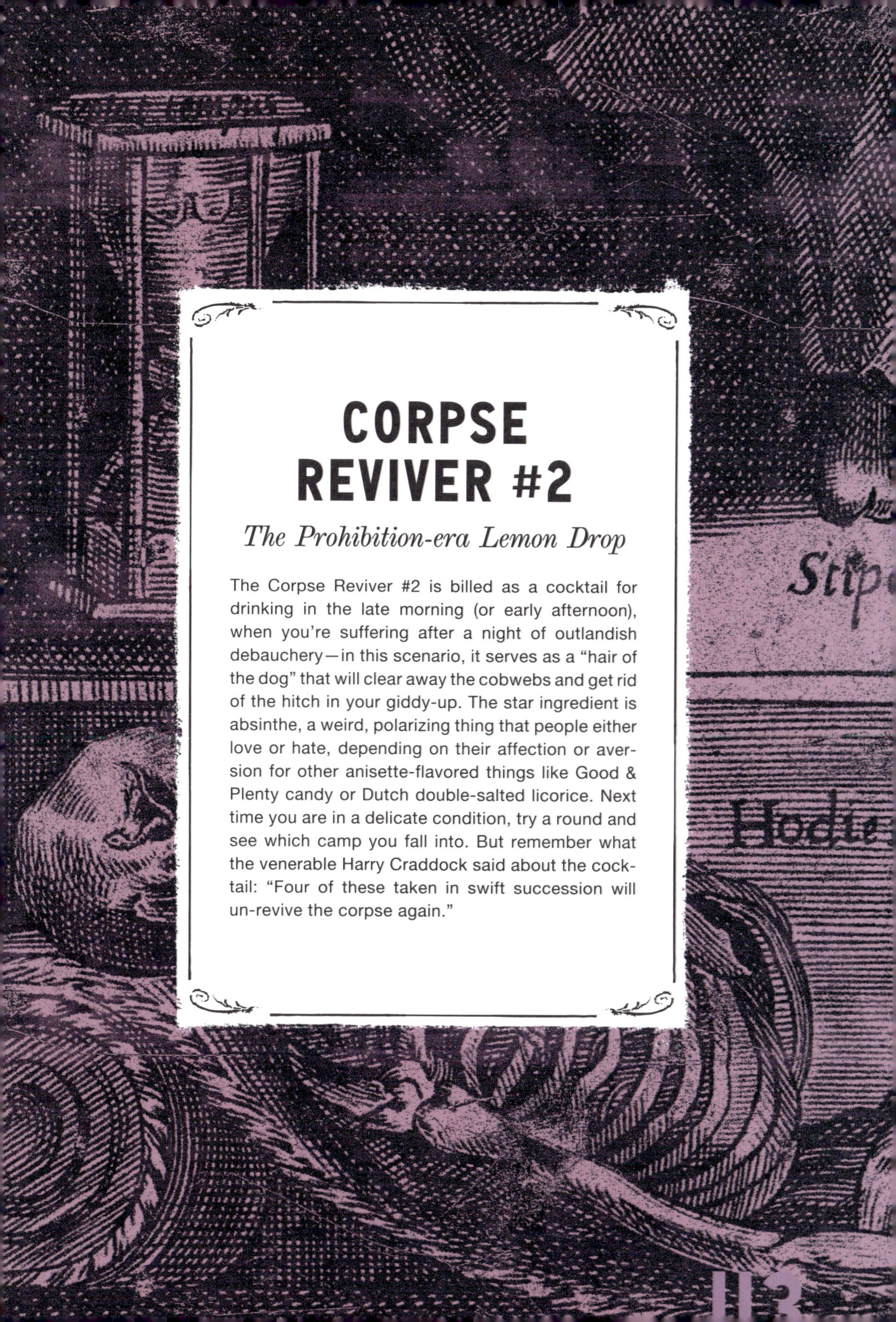

CORPSE REVIVER #2

The Prohibition-era Lemon Drop

The Corpse Reviver #2 is billed as a cocktail for drinking in the late morning (or early afternoon), when you're suffering after a night of outlandish debauchery—in this scenario, it serves as a "hair of the dog" that will clear away the cobwebs and get rid of the hitch in your giddy-up. The star ingredient is absinthe, a weird, polarizing thing that people either love or hate, depending on their affection or aversion for other anisette-flavored things like Good & Plenty candy or Dutch double-salted licorice. Next time you are in a delicate condition, try a round and see which camp you fall into. But remember what the venerable Harry Craddock said about the cocktail: "Four of these taken in swift succession will un-revive the corpse again."

Serve:
Shaken, up

Tools:
Jigger, shaker,
Hawthorne
strainer,
fine strainer,
paring knife

Glass:
Coupe, chilled

Garnish:
Lemon disk

RIYL:
Breakfast Martini
(page 105),
Last Word
(page 185),
Tom Collins
(page 297)

SPEC

London dry gin	2.0 oz
Ferrand dry curaçao	.75 oz
Cocchi Americano	1.0 oz
Fresh lemon juice	.75 oz
Simple syrup (page 29)	.25 oz
Orange bitters	3 dashes
Absinthe, to rinse	.50 oz

OUR APPROACH

When I look at the original recipe for the Corpse Reviver #2 on paper, I want it to taste like a cool gin-and-lemon Margarita, lengthened with a light and slightly bitter aromatized wine. Instead, it sorta resembles an anise-tinged Lemon Drop. Sure, it's zesty and flirty and quaffable, but it's too heavy on the absinthe and lacking in dazzling gin botanicals. I think this is because absinthe overshadows its glassmates, and the recipe originally called for equal parts, so the ingredient is given a disproportionate amount of attention. I want my Corpse Reviver to taste more sophisticated—bright and ginny with an orange note, a lingering bitterness from the aromatized wine, and zippy lemon tying it all together. So, for this updated version we're using a technique I call "rinsing," where we incorporate the "bully" ingredient (see the Aviation on page 73) in a way that's sly instead of overt. By coating the inside of the vessel with absinthe, it is still present in the cocktail, but only in ghostly aromatic fashion. You can still call it a Corpse Reviver; the ingredients are just arranged in a more pleasing composition.

CHOOSE YOUR INGREDIENTS

The Corpse Reviver #2 is usually made with Lillet Blanc, but I like using Cocchi Americano because it has a slight bitterness that brings more complexity to the overall build. The gin you choose really depends on why and when you are downing one of these: If you have a Wobblin' Noggin from a hangover, maybe pick something gentle like Plymouth, Dorothy Parker, or Tanqueray 10. If it's a pre-dinner drink, go with Bluecoat, Copper & Kings The Moons of Juniper, or Hayman's Royal Dock. For most absinthe uses, I like La Muse Verte. It is a super-green, round, sweet faery—made without additional sugars or colorings or additives—coming in right at a hearty 68% ABV. As is the case throughout this book, you really do want to invest in a bottle of Ferrand dry curaçao for all your orange liqueur needs—its steadfast structure and soft elegance is unmatched. I wax poetic about this fine ingredient more on page 250, if you wanna know more details on how it is made.

- **PREP THE GARNISH.** Cut a round disk from the lemon and set it aside. Don't even think about using a cocktail cherry to garnish this drink, which some people mystifyingly do—while that garnish works in a Last Word (because it mirrors the cherry notes of the maraschino liqueur in the build), it does nothing but distract in a cocktail that does not have any other cherry notes in the build.

- **RINSE THE GLASS.** Grab your coupe and fill with ice and ½ ounce of absinthe. Twirl the coupe by its base so the liquid rinses the entire interior of the glass, then dump the ice/water/absinthe mix into the sink. Give it a smell to see if the glass retained enough aromatics. You can add another dash of absinthe if you think it needs more. Or better yet, just use an atomizer—this will spray an even mist over the glass with ease. Before you move on, eyeball the nipple of the coupe to make sure residual absinthe isn't gathering en masse, because you don't want this drink to *taste* like absinthe!

- **MEASURE.** Grab your shaker tin and let's get movin'. Start by dashing the bitters in, then the simple syrup, lemon juice, and Cocchi Americano, followed by the curaçao and the gin. Or, to ensure proper sweetness levels of this drink, stack the syrup and the curaçao instead— the two together make up 1 ounce of sweetener. Any more, and the drink starts to tilt out of balance.

- **STRAW TASTE.** To make sure everything is in the tin.

- **SHAKE.** Add 5 ice cubes and then Coupe Shake (page 45). With all sours, we're listening for the ice to start turning to slush to know the drink is ready for a straw taste—that's the case here, too.

- **TASTE, ADJUST, AND STRAIN.** On this straw taste, check for a balance of sweetness, acidity, bitterness, and booze. If it's too syrupy, try shaking a few more rounds to let the ice mosh with the cocktail. If it's too dry, a barspoon of simple syrup should do the trick. When it tastes good and ready, double-strain into your rinsed coupe, but only fill the glass about two-thirds of the way up so you get the full effect of the absinthe rinse. If you have leftover cocktail in the shaker tin, put it in a sidecar (page 33) so it stays nice and cold until you're ready to top off the drink.

- **GARNISH.** What I love the most about the aromatics of this drink is how you can smell the absinthe and lemon together when you take each sip. (See how this also works in the Sazerac, on page 281.) When you hit it just right with the lemon oil, it becomes more than the sum of its parts. Your absinthe is already in the glass, so now express and discard the lemon disk so those oils coat the surface of the drink, sending rays of lemony sunshine into your face as you sip. The other thing I love about this garnish is it masks the smell of the booze—helpful for those with tummy troubles and when your head is bleary, and innards feel questionable.

If you live on double espressos served out of porcelain demitasse cups standing up, try Salers in this tipple instead of Cocchi Americano. The French liqueur has a bracing bitterness that registers just shy of Malört. I've also heard that some people use Meyer lemon or yuzu instead of regular old grocery store lemons for the citrus component—you might have to adjust your syrup measurement to accommodate for these changes, but it could be a fun personalization to explore. Meyers are typically only available seasonally (December to May), but for the yuzu, Yuzuco sells a cold-pressed yuzu juice from Japan that has an impressive balance of tart to floral qualities. You can buy bottles online.

COSMOPOLITAN

Clean and sharp as a Nagel drawing

When I worked in nightclubs in the late nineties in lower Manhattan, I made gallons of terrible Cosmos every night, slopping together cheap lemon vodka, corn syrup–based triple sec, chemical sour mix off the gun, and shockingly red "cranberry juice cocktail" (which is actually just corn syrup and embarrassment). I added Rose's Lime, a sweet cordial of battery acid and Hulk Sweat, because I didn't know the wonders of fresh lime juice yet. I wasn't the only one making Cosmos this way—this drink has been lowered to the lowest common denominator way too many times—which is probably why it earned such a stigma among respectable barkeeps. It's a shame, though, because every time I bump into a properly made version of this drink, I remember how lovely it tastes when made with high-quality ingredients and a splash of good technique.

Serve:
Shaken, up

Tools:
Jigger, shaker, Hawthorne strainer, fine strainer, Y-peeler, paring knife

Glass:
Coupe + sidecar, chilled

Garnish:
Orange disk

RIYL:
Gimlet (page 145), Jack Rose (page 173), Moscow Mule (page 221)

SPEC

Vodka	2.0 oz
Ferrand dry curaçao	.75 oz
Simple syrup (page 29)	.25 oz
Fresh lime juice	.75 oz
Cranberry juice	.50 oz
Orange bitters	1 dash
Lemon peel	1 to 3 strips

OUR APPROACH

I like to think of the Cosmo as a Margarita riff that's sharp as a straight razor and dry as the Atacama Desert. It looks cute but kicks some serious ass. The original version from the Other Toby—an NYC bartender, last name Cecchini, who wrote a great book called *Cosmopolitan* and invented the cocktail of the same name—is dry. He describes it as "shrill," which I respect, but I need a little more sugar to make the texture bouncier and thus more enjoyable. That's why I add a whisper of simple syrup—it doesn't make the drink "too sweet," it just makes the mouthfeel softer and more supple. My interpretation also features plain vodka shaken with a lemon peel instead of citrus vodka (this is called a "royal" shake), for more of an artisanal version of what Absolut Citron originally brought to the after-party. Then I add orange bitters to complement the dry curaçao and use an orange garnish to complement the bitters and the curaçao. In *Manny*, we call this "echoing," that is, where you look for a single flavor in the drink and find ways to pull it to the forefront by bringing in other versions of that flavor. See how it works with the orange notes here?

CHOOSE YOUR INGREDIENTS

I have tried Cosmos with every kind of cranberry product possible. Ocean Spray cranberry juice cocktail is the best. Hands down. It's balanced, with good sweetness, acidity, and bitterness, and its flavor is what everyone expects when they hear "cranberry." If you must use fancy schmancy real organic cranberry juice, it will be darker and tarter than Ocean Spray, so only use ¼ ounce of juice and then up your simple syrup by ⅛ ounce. The vodka is supposed to be the neutral backbone that allows all of the other ingredients to shine, but if you want to switch the character up a little, try Żubrówka vodka, which has a cinnamon-like note from the inclusion of sweetgrass—that would make the drink a fun little fall-friendly tipple!

HOW TO MIX

• **PREP THE GARNISH.** Cut your orange disk at this time and set it aside for when you need it later. While you're at it, cut the lemon peel that you're going to shake the drink with: Pull a big fat strip of peel with a Y-peeler. If your peels come out puny and frail, make three smaller ones instead of one large one. You don't need to trim the peel, because it's not an ornamental garnish—it will never be seen!

● **MEASURE.** In a serious plot twist, the building of this cocktail starts with the lemon peel you cut for the royal shake. Express it into the empty shaker first: Really squeeze the bejeezus out of the lemon peel, shooting all that oil into the bottom of the tin. Leave the lemon peel inside the tin, so you end up shaking with it. All of this is kind of like making citrus-infused vodka à la minute. Next, into the tin go the bitters. Always bitters first to establish good habits. Then, add the cranberry juice and lime juice. You want this drink to come out barely pink, certainly not red, so DON'T OVERPOUR. Next, hit the three-quarter mark with the simple syrup and stack the orange curaçao on top. Be sure the liquid doesn't peek over the rim (more on stacking in the Measure instructions for Amaretto Sour, page 65). Somersault the jigger and go boldly where many people have been before with the vodka. Let that sit and find your favorite '80s song. My vote would be Modern English's "I'll Stop the World (and Melt with You)," because it'll help you get the vibe right as the citrus melts into the cocktail.

● **STRAW TASTE.** To make sure everything is in the tin.

● **SHAKE.** Add 5 ice cubes and Rocks Shake (page 46). Do this for a little less time than you would a Margarita (page 201), because you have the cranberry juice in the mix, which counts as water content. In other words, this drink already has a bit more dilution than other sours, so you don't have to add the same amount of ice water during the shake. Think of the movement like you are trying to get a drawing off your old, broken Etch A Sketch.

● **TASTE, ADJUST, AND STRAIN.** Crack that shaker open like a geode so you can sneak a straw taste. Remember that this is a dry drink, much drier than a Sidecar (page 289), and decidedly drier than a Margarita. That's a good thing. Look for the vodka in it. It'll be harder to find, but it will be there. This shouldn't taste like a zero-proof cocktail. Could it use a little more brightness and ZING from cranberry or lemon? Add if so. If it's dry to the point of unpleasantness, add a barspoon of simple syrup. I won't tell the other Toby you did this. Taste it again to make sure it's cold as fuck and ready to slurp. Double-strain, so no little ice floes disturb the calm, candied surface.

● **GARNISH.** This drink was designed to be dry as chalk dust and boozy as three bartenders cooking dinner, so the point of the orange oil garnish is to juxtapose that razor-sharp personality with an aroma that's warm and round. The contrast of aroma and contents of the glass makes for splendid complexity. Express the oils of the orange disk over the surface of the drink, to warm up the aromatic entrance to the cocktail. You can flame the orange if you're feeling frisky, just flip to page 175 for how to do this.

You can royal shake with orange or grapefruit peel instead of the prescribed lemon peel, if you want to live dangerously and deliciously. The former will add rich warmth to the drink, while the latter telegraphs a mysterious bittersweet note. You could also pick a different flavor to echo with, like lime bitters or cranberry bitters. Also: Ferrand just came out with a yuzu curaçao in addition to their traditional orange flavor . . . do what you will with that information.

CUBA LIBRE

Waves of molasses with an undertow of baking spice

The Cuba Libre—a rum and Coke with a squeeze of lime—has long been considered a lowbrow highball and not a deep, thoughtful potation. It's usually best suited for mindless fortification in the sticky darkness of a dingy dive bar, or consumed as a no-brainer glass of sheer refreshment on a boat under the sweltering equatorial sun. That doesn't mean the recipe doesn't have any room for improvement, though. In fact, because it has strong, sweet, and bright components (booze, sugar, and acid), it hits a solid bull's-eye for my definition of a proper cocktail. Opportunities abound to make the drink with integrity. You only got one life, why not find a way to make the mundane something special?

Serve:
Built in the glass,
on the rocks

Tools:
Jigger, muddler,
barspoon,
Y-peeler,
paring knife

Glass:
Highball, chilled

Garnish:
Lime peel

RIYL:
Espresso Martini
(page 137),
Old Cuban
(page 237),
Queen's Park
Swizzle (page 269)

Rum	2.0 oz
Angostura bitters	3 dashes
Lime wedges	2 or 3
Coca-Cola, to top	5.0 oz

OUR APPROACH

Think about your average Cuba Libre, free-poured with fervor and recklessly garnished with a lime wedge. Good, right? But maybe not living up to its full potential. Now, imagine a thoughtfully composed version where each element has integrity and is incorporated into the drink with intentionality. A highball with low rumbling molasses notes, angular bitter cheekbones, and a texture so spry you could hear its bubbles POP! all the way from Havana to Hawaii. One so refreshing, your taste buds start to quiver in anticipation of another sip. That's what we're aiming for with this spec, so we're going to upgrade a few of the drink's components, put a careful eye on balance and texture, and tap into the magic of a deliberate aroma. First, Charles H. Baker argues that a few dashes of Angostura bitters turn up the volume on this drink. I agree. There are common elements between the Coke and the bitters—vanilla, cinnamon, nutmeg—that burst forth with zeal when combined, so we're starting with three dashes in this spec. The bitters also help dry out the sweet ingredients and firm up the structure of the cocktail, which improves balance and texture. We're also intentionally introducing more citrus to make it taste more like a cohesive cocktail. Coca-Cola is sweet as hell, and many rums read as sweet, too, so instead of squeezing a wedge over the top of the drink at the end, which does nothing for the balance of the drink, we're going to muddle a few wedges into the glass *before* adding the rum and Coke. This is a cool move because you're inviting both juice and peel oils to the mix, both of which add brightness and counterbalance sweetness. To coax out even more brightness from the drink, I garnish with a citrus peel of the same variety—the way the flavor ends up matching the aroma is marvelous.

CHOOSE YOUR INGREDIENTS

I'll start by saying there are a couple of things that are impossible to make better than the corporate giants: Cola and ketchup are two of them. Sorry, but Coke and Heinz are just better than the bespoke organic, artisanal versions. For this cocktail, ideally you're using Coke from Mexico, because it's made with real sugar instead of corn syrup. Trust me, the difference in flavor and integrity between the cane sugar version and the US version is as vast as the Gulf of Mexico. If you are an RC person, I'm not mad at that. Rumwise, choose your style to match the weather—in the summer a straightforward white rum like Planteray 3-Star keeps the drink coolhanded, while in the winter you could split-base with big bold rums like

Wray & Nephew from Jamaica or Foursquare from Barbados. A dry aged rum from the Dominican Republic, like say, Brugal, would also blow your hair back. If you want to use two rums instead of one, that's another small thing you can do to make this drink your own. Learn more about how rums from around the world differ in the Daiquiri session on page 126, then flip to the session for the Jet Pilot on page 178 for my advice for how to choose multiple rums in a way that tells an interesting story.

HOW TO MIX

● **PREP THE GARNISH.** Just as you would with a lemon or orange peel, use a Y-peeler to pull a swath of peel from the lime. Trim the edges with a paring knife to make them look classy, if you're serving it to someone. First impressions matter! Set aside. Cut the bald-ish lime into the wedges you need for muddling at this time as well.

● **MUDDLE AND MEASURE.** We're going to build this cocktail in the glass. Before you do anything else, make sure your Coke is righteously cold. Like, borderline slushy cold. Why? Good carbonation depends on temperature. Warm soda will have flabby bubbles, which will wreck the texture of the drink post haste. Cold soda has spiky bubs, which is what you want. Throw 3 of the lime wedges into the bottom of your highball glass and muddle them to squeeze out some juice and oils from the peel. You don't need to exert extreme force for this muddle; just lightly smash the wedges until their juices have escaped their vesicles and some of the oils from the skin have cannonballed into the party. The wedges should look a bit shattered, but not completely annihilated. Add the bitters, then add a few ice cubes. Measure out the rum, then top with Cola, using the barspoon technique we use for the Ramos Gin Fizz on page 273. If you need to add a cube or two as you are filling up the drink to make the glass look fuller, do it—a little less mixer in this drink is going to be a good thing, because you will taste the rum more. This move isn't "tuffin' up" a drink by adding extra booze, it's just showing off the spirit.

● **TASTE AND ADJUST.** Give this mix a quick stir, then put a straw in to make sure the ratios of everything in the glass are to your liking. You could dash in another round of bitters if you want to spice things up a touch. Add an extra ice cube or two, to get your wash line looking nice and full.

● **GARNISH.** I'm not sure why I like a lime peel expressed over this drink, because I don't like lime peel as garnish in any other drink, ever. For some reason, it works really well here. Maybe because the Coke does a good job of taming the aggressive bitterness in the lime oil. To garnish: Express the oils of the lime peel over the top of the cocktail and insert into the glass. Use a straw to slurp this drink if you must, but there will be pulp and other obstructions on the bottom from the aftermath of muddling limes, so drinking this straight from the glass is probably best. As an additional benefit, the little bubbles will tickle your nose. This tastes like freedom—Cuba's and yours—so enjoy.

Sometimes I like lemon with my rum and Coke. I realize that in some ways that disqualifies it from being a Cuba Libre, but we aren't about authenticity in this book, we are about deliciousness, so. that's one thing you can try. Who knows, maybe grapefruit wedges will also be delicious? No harm in trying. Or, if you want to get wild with your bitters, neroli oil is one of the components in the formula, so a dash or two of orange bitters teases out a ray of warm sunshine in the drink A dash of Peychaud's will create a Cherry Coke feel, due to its vanilla notes.

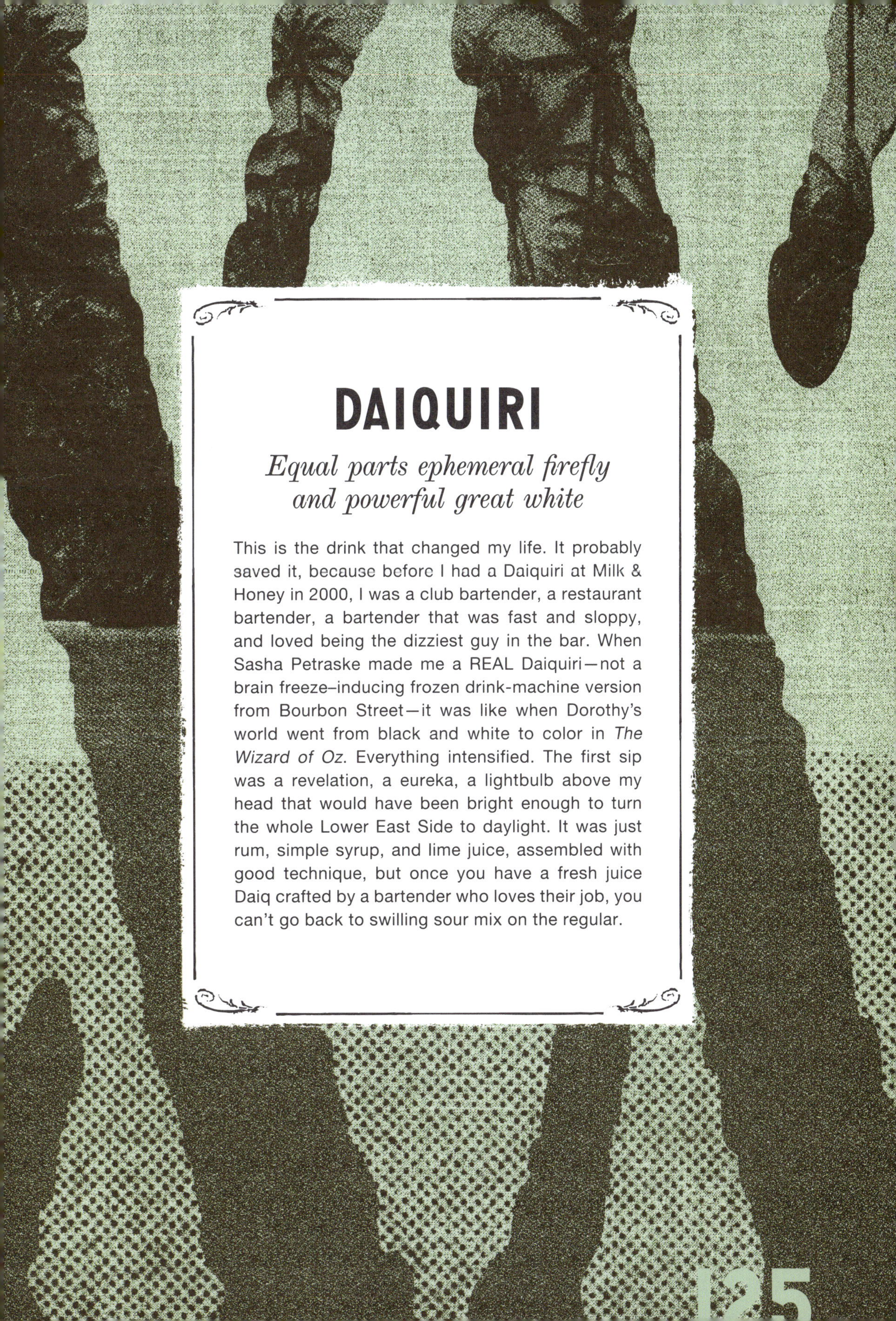

DAIQUIRI

*Equal parts ephemeral firefly
and powerful great white*

This is the drink that changed my life. It probably saved it, because before I had a Daiquiri at Milk & Honey in 2000, I was a club bartender, a restaurant bartender, a bartender that was fast and sloppy, and loved being the dizziest guy in the bar. When Sasha Petraske made me a REAL Daiquiri—not a brain freeze–inducing frozen drink-machine version from Bourbon Street—it was like when Dorothy's world went from black and white to color in *The Wizard of Oz*. Everything intensified. The first sip was a revelation, a eureka, a lightbulb above my head that would have been bright enough to turn the whole Lower East Side to daylight. It was just rum, simple syrup, and lime juice, assembled with good technique, but once you have a fresh juice Daiq crafted by a bartender who loves their job, you can't go back to swilling sour mix on the regular.

Serve:
Shaken, up

Tools:
Jigger, shaker,
Hawthorne
strainer,
fine strainer,
offset serrated
knife (optional)

Glass:
Coupe + sidecar,
chilled

Garnish:
Lime wheel
(optional)

RIYL:
20th Century
(page 57),
Daisy de Santiago
(page 129),
Gimlet (page 145)

SPEC

First rum	1.5 oz
Second rum	.50 oz
Fresh lime juice	.75 oz
Simple syrup (page 29)	.75 oz

OUR APPROACH

A well-balanced Daiquiri is like a French omelet—super simple in construction, and the most perfect thing when done right, but also one of the hardest cocktails to do right. In this session, we're sticking to the classic build of rum, sugar, lime juice, and very cold water (ice), focusing primarily on technique to help teach you how to make the best version possible. The only new-ish thing I'm doing is split-basing the rums. Note how I'm leaving the two rum options vague—this is because I want you to experiment and find what best suits your palate. You can also adjust the ratios, as long as they end up equaling 2 ounces of rum. Go forth and taste a bunch of rums from around the world! A slow night at a tiki bar would be a good place to do this, because you can pick the brain of your bartender when they're not in the weeds.

CHOOSE YOUR INGREDIENTS

With a template this simple—the "two, three-quarter, three-quarter" ounce framework can also be used to make Gimlets (page 145) or Bee's Knees (page 81) cocktails, or any other basic sour you desire—you can use any single rum or combination of rums and it's gonna hit right. Here are some general observations I've learned over the years, in case it's helpful guidance: Clairin from Haiti and aguardiente from Mexico tend to have a quirky grassy personality similar to rhum agricole from Martinique or cachaça from Brazil. Aged rums made from molasses work well in a Daiq if warm vanilla and baking spice notes are your catnip. Jamaican rum is bold and brings a funk in a way Bob Marley himself would appreciate, best suited for the umami hounds out there. A Daiquiri with a single white rum like Probitas from Foursquare is delicious, but I usually want a little more oomph and lingering complexity, which is why I sometimes sneak a bit of Batavia Arrack, a rum from Java, in the build. It has a cool earthy note brought forth by fermented red rice cakes. (Detail-oriented sessioners might notice how I do this in the Mojito too, on page 217.) Whatever you do, just remember to avoid the bottom-shelf swill.

- **PREP THE GARNISH.** Ninety-nine percent of the time you should only use garnishes that add aroma to the drinking experience. Since this cocktail smells great already, you could either go without a garnish, or use a lime wheel, which adds just a touch of fresh lime aroma, but like ten percent of what you'd get from the oils of a peel. Just consider how this drink is often tossed back quickly—a lime wheel floating in the glass can be a choking hazard, so if you go this route, cut a little notch in the bottom of a lime wheel so it sits up on the rim properly instead. Set aside.

- **MEASURE.** This drink can be slammed together and served in less than a minute. But you need to be precise with your measurements for optimal balance. On a related note, remember to taste all of your ingredients before you start to mix; in this instance, you're looking for how fresh the lime juice is (if it's a bit old, the acidity might be lacking), how plump the syrup tastes, and how much sweetness and sharp alcohol your rums have. All of these elements will dictate the balance (and thus the texture) of the drink, so keep this intel in your mind for the straw tastes that follow. Into the tin goes simple syrup, then the lime juice. If you are working in a bar, do not ever pour these together as the viscosity of the two are decidedly different—the simple pours much, much slower, especially if cold, so your ratios are gonna be off from the get-go and then you're fucked all the way to the end. Add the rums.

- **STRAW TASTE.** To make sure everything is in the tin. Scribble down thoughts on the balance, texture, temperature, and aroma in your bartender's notebook. Return to this later, after the second straw taste, to see how ice works its magic on the mix.

- **SHAKE.** Toss 5 ice cubes into the tin and Coupe Shake (page 45) this thing like it owes you money. Remember what I said about how you can use this same "two, three-quarter, three-quarter" ratio to also make a Margarita (page 201) or Gimlet? You totally can, but you have to adjust your shake based on whether the drink is served on ice or not—Gimlets and Daiqs are usually served up, so you'd shake those the same amount of time, whereas a Marg on the rocks you'll shake for LESS time because the ice will further dilute the drink as it sits in the glass. You follow?

- **TASTE, ADJUST, AND STRAIN.** Crack the tins, wring and tap (page 43), and straw taste. Revisit your notes and really give it a beat to ask yourself about the balance between sweet, acid, and booze. Will a whisper more of lime juice help smooth out the sweetness? Or if it's pointy and stabby and dry, a barspoon of simple syrup might make it better. By better, I mean a nicer texture or fuller balance. If so, adjust. Double-strain. Always. I hate the feeling of little ice chips floating in my drink knocking against my lip and teeth.

- **GARNISH.** If you dare.

My favorite thing to do to a Daiquiri in the summer is rip up like three big-ass mint sprigs and toss them in the bottom of the tin. Don't muddle them—just shake like the world is ending in one minute and drink it with the same urgency. In some circles, folks might call this a riff because it's adding something outside the realm of reason—and I know some of you are thinking it's just like a rum-based Southside, or an Old Cuban without the sparkling wine—but it's such a subtle adjustment I think it's within the boundaries of reason for this session.

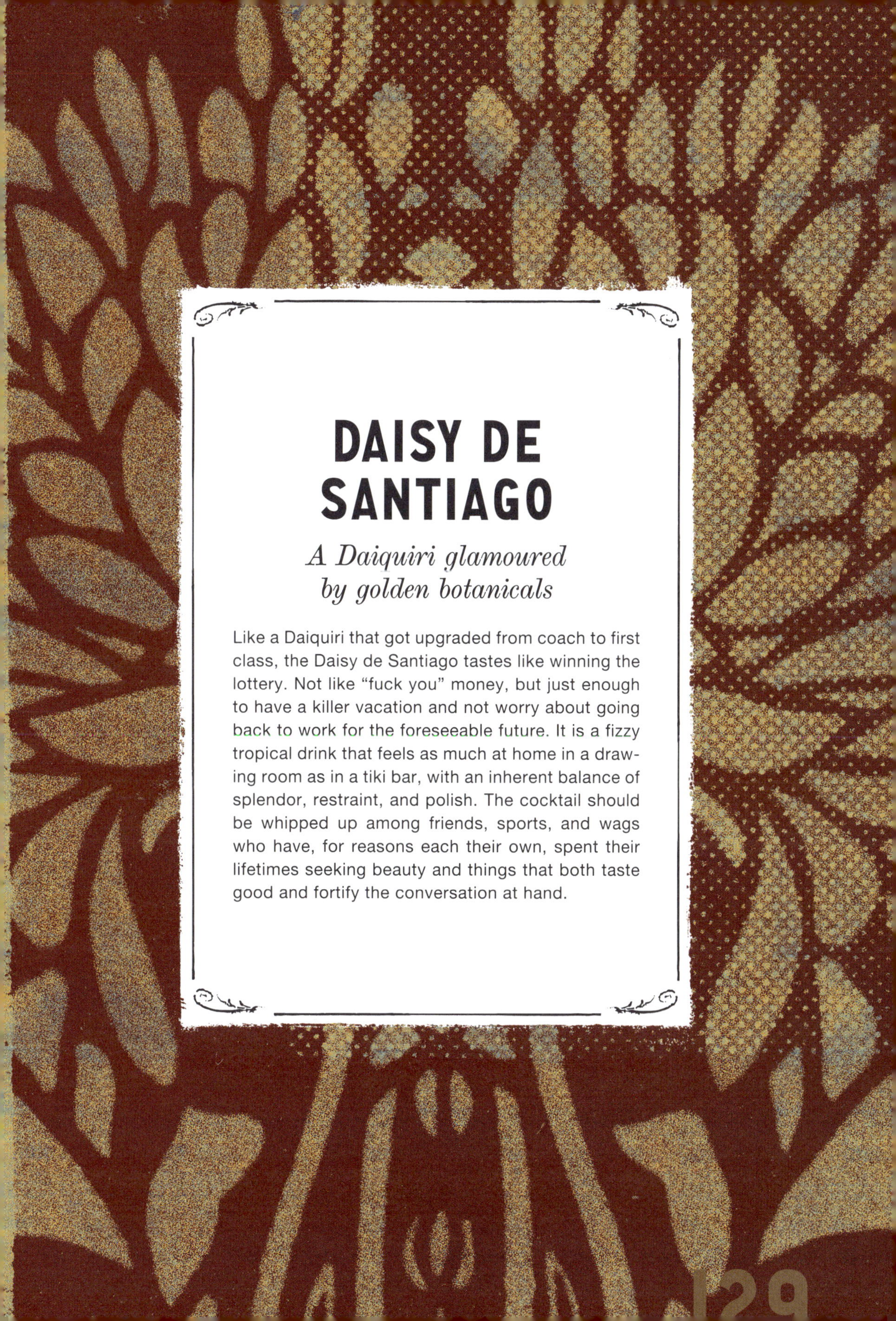

DAISY DE SANTIAGO

*A Daiquiri glamoured
by golden botanicals*

Like a Daiquiri that got upgraded from coach to first class, the Daisy de Santiago tastes like winning the lottery. Not like "fuck you" money, but just enough to have a killer vacation and not worry about going back to work for the foreseeable future. It is a fizzy tropical drink that feels as much at home in a drawing room as in a tiki bar, with an inherent balance of splendor, restraint, and polish. The cocktail should be whipped up among friends, sports, and wags who have, for reasons each their own, spent their lifetimes seeking beauty and things that both taste good and fortify the conversation at hand.

Serve:
Shaken,
on crushed ice

Tools:
Jigger, shaker,
atomizer (optional)

Glass:
Double Old
Fashioned, chilled

Garnish:
Mint bouquets,
Yellow Chartreuse

RIYL:
Airmail (page 61),
Bijou (page 85),
Porn Star Martini
(page 265)

SPEC

White rum	1.5 oz
Aged rum	.50 oz
Yellow Chartreuse	.75 oz
Fresh lime juice	.75 oz
Simple syrup (page 29)	.25 oz
Sparkling water, to bottom	1.5 oz

OUR APPROACH

Many recipes for this cocktail don't include sparkling water, but I like juuust a bit more than an ounce added because it makes the drink feel more spry—not crazy carbonated, mind you, but a touch feistier. Also, usually, the yellow Chartreuse is floated on top, but I wanted to change that drinking experience (ahem, narrative arc, see page 44) so the liqueur's herbaceous beauty fully integrates into the drink. When you use a float, the first few sips have a good aroma, but as you drink, that honeyed smell gets further and further away from the nose, diminishing in impact, and you barely get the flavor until the very end when it's just a big blast of Chartreuse. I'm not saying this is a terrible way to drink the drink, it's just different. For me, I LOVE Chartreuse—there's a special spell enacted when you combine it with weighty aged spirits like Cognac; and when paired with white rum, it spins a ray of gold sunshine—so when the ancient monk-made liqueur gets incorporated into the drink itself instead of floating on top, the whole cocktail becomes gripping and complex.

CHOOSE YOUR INGREDIENTS

Choose a rum that will both tickle your fancy and stand firmly up to the crushed ice that will melt feverishly as you fiddle with the straw; something high-ish proof, like a combination of aged rum (such as El Dorado 3-Year, El Dorado 15-Year, or Planteray 5-Year) paired together with an unaged rum like Banks 5 Island, Ten To One, Probitas, or Planteray 3-Star. The juxtaposition of aged and unaged rums is a shimmering combo, with the white rum serving as an almost "neutral" base, and the vanilla and baking spices of the aged rum echoing and complementing the honeyed botanicals in the yellow Chartreuse. I get chills just thinking about all the different ways you can tap into this magic. See the Aperol Spritz (page 69) for intel on different kinds of bubbly waters.

HOW TO MIX

• **PREP THE GARNISH.** Grab a few big bountiful bouquets of mint, leaves shiny and fresh and aromatic. Treat this bouquet like you are bringing a fistful of wildflowers to your favorite person: assembled with studied nonchalance, leaves beautiful, but not fussy. Set aside. If you're using an atomizer for the spray of yellow Chartreuse, add an ounce or so to the device now.

● **MEASURE.** Stack the simple syrup and yellow Chartreuse to make sure the sum of the two does not exceed even 1 ounce, then add the lime. (If you don't have a jigger with these markings, start with the simple syrup, then jigger out the lime juice, followed by the Chartreuse, so if you fuck up one of the first two measurements and have to start over, you aren't wasting precious, precious Chartreuse.) In the large side of your measurement tool, put the white rum, and stack the aged rum to achieve a level 2 ounces. Set that aside.

● **STRAW TASTE.** To make sure everything is in the tin. Remember, your sparkling water comes into play later, so it will taste "hot" at this time—that means stabby, aggressive, disjointed, unbalanced, etc. Once it hits the sparkling water and crushed ice, it'll all swing into place.

● **BOTTOM THE SPARKLING WATER.** Ditch the ice and water that's melting together in your DOF glass, if you choose to use that chilling technique (more on glassware chilling on page 41). Then fill the glass about one-third up with crushed ice. Now, the bottoming: Hook the lip of your sparkling water on the lip of your glass and drizzle 1½ ounces of bubbles into your glass. If you pour directly into the middle of the ice, it'll bust up a bunch of the bubbles, resulting in a flacid texture. Avoid this! Set that aside.

● **SHAKE.** We're going to Whip Shake (page 46) this fella. Why? There's enough ice in the glass to properly dilute the cocktail so it tastes appealing from start to finish, so you just want to chill it slightly—if you were to not chill at all, you'd melt some of the crushed ice in the glass fast, which ends up in an overdilution situation. Got it? To whip shake this drink: Add 2 ounces of crushed ice to the shaker and shake until the ice is melted and the motion becomes silent, making it appear to your audience that you have transformed from bartender to mime.

● **ROCK AND ROLL.** Roll the contents of the tin gently into the glass with the ice and sparkling water, making sure each precious drop arrives ice-cold. Top with crushed ice: Use your Julep strainer to form the ice into the shape of an Italian Alp. Pack gently, though, so you can insert the garnish without trouble.

● **GARNISH.** To garnish, take a straw and hold it parallel to the surface of the cocktail. Whip a mint sprig against the straw, scattering the essential oils across the jagged surface of the drink. Place the straw and a bouquet of no less than 3 pristine sprigs of mint into the cocktail, near the edge of the glass, so one's inquisitive proboscis is assailed with its summer perfume. If you have an atomizer, spritz on a few kisses of yellow Chartreuse over the top, too. This adds a little extra oomph of alpine aromatics that mirror the aromas of mint.

Instead of only using yellow Chartreuse, you could split-base with Bénédictine so the total sum of both ingredients adds up to ¾ ounce. This brings in a dusty bookish note to the drink and is a great way to stretch your supply of Carthusian Mountain Dew, which is expensive and sometimes hard to find. I know it might seem strange to mix two liqueurs from two different Catholic seminaries, but the result is like Hall and Oates or Simon and Garfunkel—they work well together, creating sweet, sweet harmonies.

DARK AND STORMY

*For toasting to your pirate
crew, telltales flying*

The original Dark and Stormy is like a sea captain's version of a whiskey ginger: one big honking glass of ginger beer with a float of blackstrap rum, garnished with a lime wedge. Cobbled together without much thought to balance and texture and temperature, or how to amplify flavor and dial-in aromatics, it can taste rather one-dimensional. When made with renewed attention to its components and how they work together, though, this drink will transform from ordinary sailing sipper to stormy soliloquy. It can be a deep, contemplative highball that sparks memories and evokes powerful emotions—a cocktail that looks deep into your eyes while strumming a guitar by a beach bonfire and telling you about the philosophies of the universe, or one that brings grandma's gingerbread cookies to mind.

Serve:
Built in the glass,
on the rocks

Tools:
Jigger, shaker,
Hawthorne
strainer, offset
serrated knife,
cocktail pick

Glass:
Collins, chilled

Garnish:
Lime wheel,
candied ginger
(optional)

RIYL:
Espresso Martini
(page 137),
Jungle Bird
(page 181),
Whiskey Sour
(page 305)

SPEC

Aged rum	1.5 oz
Fresh lime juice	.50 oz
Fever-Tree ginger beer, to bottom	3 to 4 oz
Blackstrap rum, to float	1.0 oz

OUR APPROACH

Today we strive to create a version of this highball with dimensions of intrigue that stretch fathoms deep. First, while blackstrap is the norm in this bad boy, we add a sailor's ration of aged rum to the build to amplify the drink's rummy soul and add more nuance. Aged rum has a flavor that is less sweet than blackstrap, with more vanilla and woody elements, and a lighter texture. Those qualities pair well with ginger. We reduce the amount of blackstrap used for the float, too—the dark molasses notes of the rum stay in play but take up less real estate in the full experience. We also raise the citrus ratio to a full ½ ounce, instead of offering a tiny wedge garnish and hoping the drinker squeezes it into the glass. This is how you create further balance and transform this simple highball into a menu-worthy cocktail.

CHOOSE YOUR INGREDIENTS

Think about what the rum in this drink will accomplish: a dry añejo like Brugal (or The Scarlet Ibis, Flor de Caña 4-year, The Real McCoy, or Planteray 5-Year) will dry it out, while a lush rum like Diplomatico (or El Dorado, Santa Teresa 1796, or English Harbour) will plump up the texture. Both are good things; it just depends on what mood you are in. Next, we recommended Fever-Tree for the ginger beer, because its balance of spice to sweet is palatable for a wide range of drinkers. Maine Root is another good middle-of-the-road option; and if you like something really spicy and earthy, Barritt's or Reed's will cut through the depths of the blackstrap with fierce sharpness. Whatever you choose, be sure to taste your ginger beer before mixing. If it's on the terrifically dry side, you might want to have some Demerara syrup nearby to adjust the texture and balance to your likeness down the road.

HOW TO MIX

• PREP THE GARNISH. Cut the lime wheel first, with a notch cut into one part of the rind so it'll sit upright on the rim of the glass. I like a lime wheel in this cocktail because it really adds to the "tropical" vibes of the drink, while adding just a hint of fresh lime aroma—a juicy contrast to the brooding baking spice smells that otherwise set the tone. Then decide if you want to add candied ginger, as I am apt to do. If you do, use crystallized ginger instead of ginger candy. I like ginger cut in cubes, sometimes referred to as "ginger chunks," over slices, because cubes skewer easily. To make the garnish: Skewer the candy through a cocktail pick or two toothpicks, so you can rest the picks on the rim of the glass. This is so the garnish hovers well above the liquid; the ginger candy needs to stay dry. It's not great if the liquid melts the sugar off and makes the drink extra sticky.

● **MEASURE.** In a shaker, combine the lime juice and aged rum. We're not straw tasting at this point because there isn't much to note, and the odds that you forgot to add one ingredient or the other are super slim.

● **BOTTOM THE SODA.** Make sure your ginger beer is ice-fucking-cold, or else the bubbles will fizz out fast and the texture of this cocktail will collapse promptly. You want its personality to be as stormy as possible, not a sad little sprinkle of bubbles. Grab a Collins glass, fill it three-quarters of the way full with chunky ice cubes, and add 3 to 4 ounces of that wicked bubbly ginger beer. Set the Collins aside.

● **SHAKE.** Return to the shaker with the aged rum and lime juice. Add 3 ice cubes and Collins Shake (page 46) just long enough to shout with your best pirate impression: *"It was a dark and stormy night!"* The goal is to add just a slight chill and dilution. Sure, the drink will chill on its own if you skip the shake, but the first two or three sips won't be as cold and refreshing. This is a great example of how every little thing matters when you are making a drink—you want it to taste as cold as possible, and thus nice and balanced from start to finish.

● **STRAIN.** Strain the cocktail, aiming to have the liquid slide down between the ice and the side of the glass, so it flows directly into the ginger beer, incorporating thoroughly, so you won't have to stir and ruin the carbonation.

● **FLOAT THE BLACKSTRAP.** Measure out the blackstrap in a jigger. With two fingers on the bottom of the Collins glass, turn it quickly while gently pouring the blackstrap rum around the inside rim of the glass. This should make for the most intense black float on top of the drink. If you've got an ice cube jutting up above the surface, this can be a great buffer to take advantage of while you do this.

● **GARNISH.** We're using a lime wheel for its large surface area, and because the blackstrap is so rich, molassassy, and funky that you need the zing of lime aroma to balance those aromatic qualities. It's a critical contrast, and one that makes the drink more interesting to smell and subsequently sip. Prop the lime wheel up on the rim using the notch you cut into the fruit earlier. Regarding the optional garnish: I wish the ginger candy added a bite to the aroma, but sadly the candying process coats the aromatic aspect of the ginger. It is a great visual, though, and works as a delicious snack that puts even more emphasis on the ginger aspect of the drink. Nibble on the candy as you sip and see if you get an almost wasabi-like burn all through your head, which is fun. Also, ginger is known to help nausea, so this is a great sipper if you are drinking on a boat on dark and stormy seas.

I would say that your choices here are: Do you want to make your cocktail more Dark? Or more Stormy? If you want the drink to have a more pronounced bitter note, split-basing the blackstrap with an amaro like Averna or Lucano really revs up the darkness and complexity. I would suggest a bit of the Fernet-Vallet, Amaro Ciociaro, or Unicum if you have a bottle banging about. If you want more Storm, grate a bit of fresh ginger into the shaker to give it more pop; it doesn't take much! You could also ditch the commercial ginger beer and make yourself a spicy ginger syrup—combine it with sparkling water and Bob's your uncle. Just BE SURE TO DOUBLE-STRAIN if you have added freshly grated ginger in the syrup or the drink.

ESPRESSO MARTINI

A constellation of caffeine

This drink rattled the mountains of the bar scene when it debuted because it offered two epic promises at once: inebriation and caffeination. It's an upper and a downer. A Red Bull and vodka or Four Loko for people with discerning palates. And unlike the Irish Coffee (page 169) or Spanish Coffee that came before, it is served cold—transforming the drink from a coffee-with-booze to a coffee *cocktail*. One as good for brunch as it is for after-dinner drinking. For some reason this '80s-born babe went out of fashion for a spell, but it's seen a huge resurgence over the last few years—I think this is because as a culture we have started to take coffee more seriously. This is a good thing, for fans of coffee, and for fans of cocktails.

Serve:
Shaken, up

Tools:
Jigger, shaker,
Hawthorne
strainer,
fine strainer,
paring knife

Glass:
Coupe, chilled

Garnish:
Orange disk

RIYL:
Black Manhattan
(page 198),
Clover Club
(page 109),
White Russian
(page 309)

SPEC

Vodka	2.0 oz
Cold-Brew Orange Oleo-Saccharum (recipe follows)	2.0 oz

OUR APPROACH

Dick Bradsell, the drink's creator, insisted that the espresso always be pulled fresh, but the length of time an espresso is good for is a few fleeting minutes, and that's if the person who pulled the shot is great at their job. I like to use a cold-brew orange oleo-saccharum instead. It lends a more pleasing texture to the drink, a more vibrant sense of freshness, and because its temperature is already cold, you don't have to wait for the coffee to cool to add it to the shaker tin, which is great because every minute counts when the promise of deliciousness lies in wait.

CHOOSE YOUR INGREDIENTS

This cocktail is *all* about the coffee component, because vodka's job is to make its surrounding ingredients taste more like themselves. In other words: Choose the vodka you like the most. (If you need guidance, reference the Moscow Mule session on page 222 and the White Russian session on page 310 for some things to think about when picking out a bottle.) But if you have a shitty coffee in play—I'm talking about both the beans and the brewing technique—the drink will taste worse once it's shaken with the neutral spirit. An elegant brew will yield an elegant cocktail. For our version, I recommend an unsweetened cold-brew concentrate, which is easy to find in grocery stores and even easier to find online. The US market is brimming with incredible single-origin options, so don't use the cheap shit. You could also make your own cold brew at home using regular coffee beans or decaf ones. Don't let the haters bring you down: There is NO SHAME in taking the non-caffeinated route—our bodies all react to the drug differently, so do what's right for you.

HOW TO MIX

● **PREP THE GARNISH.** To pull the orange notes of the oleo-saccharum further into focus, we're going to express the oils of an orange disk over the top as garnish. Carve one out of the fruit now and set aside for later.

● **MEASURE.** In the shaker tin, add the oleo-saccharum and the vodka. So simple! So effortless! This is one of the biggest perks of making your oleo ahead of time.

● **STRAW TASTE.** Taste now to see how warm and boozy the drink tastes. It'll be sweet as hell, with the vodka poking out above the sharp, bittersweet angles of the coffee. This is all natural and normal at this stage.

● **SHAKE.** Because this cocktail has no citrus juice—it's just booze and coffee and sugar—cocktail theory states it should be stirred. We break that rule here and shake instead. First, because an Espresso Martini should look like a shot of espresso—that is, dark and velvety on the bottom with a lovely khaki foam on top. Shaking whips up the ingredients into a gloriously soft and spumescent texture, which feels quite pleasing as you guzzle one down. If you were to stir this, the texture would be watery and insipid. Not the vibe you want with your pick-me-up! So add 5 cubes and shake this really hard. Think: a Coupe Shake (page 45) blasting like a train at full speed ahead.

● **TASTE, ADJUST, AND STRAIN.** Straw taste. Make sure that you have tamed the vodka into submission. It's the water content that is drying this out, so if it's too sweet, shake more. Double-strain into a coupe glass—do this immediately after you shake the drink. If you wait a beat or two, you'll lose all of the glorious foamy texture. This would be a terrible waste of all the hard work you put into shaking.

● **GARNISH.** You can add three espresso beans floating on the spuma like everyone else does, but I find them to be just a choking hazard. And they do nothing for the aroma of the drink. Orange oils, on the other hand, add a beautiful warming floral aroma and act as a nice setup for the citrus oleo in the cocktail. To garnish: Hold this disk at least 6 inches above the cocktail and express the oils, making sure you dust the top of the drink evenly, then discard.

If you're a bitters-loving industry type, split-base the vodka with Fernet-Branca or Branca Menta for a cocktail worthy of a late-night Argentinian nightclub. A ratio of 1/4 ounce of Fernet with 1 1/2 ounces of vodka is enough to make it work, but you could go full bore if you please and reverse that ratio. If you do this, take a beat to marvel at how the bitterness of the amaro syncs right up with the edges of the cold brew.

COLD-BREW ORANGE OLEO-SACCHARUM

In the classic Espresso Martini, the coffee and sweetener components are represented by espresso and simple syrup. There's nothing wrong with that combo, but I like using cold brew, which is just as bracing and bitter and acidic as a good espresso, but with more complexity and nuance because the beans weren't scorched during the brewing process. Batching the orange oil–infused sugar (what we call an oleo-saccharum) with the cold brew ahead of time makes this cocktail easier and faster to make on a whim. You don't have to add orange peels to the oleo if a craving for this cocktail strikes unexpectedly and you don't have an orange on hand. It'll still taste competent. But I suggest going the extra mile and trying it out, because adding orange is a wicked cool flex that adds warmth to the drink, echoing the citrusy notes of the world's best coffees. Plus, there's something very Proustian about the early morning combination of coffee and orange juice. **Makes 2 cups-ish**

1 orange
½ cup sugar
2 cups cold-brew concentrate
¼ cup St. George NOLA coffee liqueur
1 teaspoon vanilla extract

If using the orange, pull peels off the orange in strips and bury them in the sugar. Let sit for a few hours at room temperature. Pull the orange peels out of the sugar.

In a blender, combine the sugar and 1 cup of the cold-brew concentrate. Blend on low until smooth, monitoring it closely and reducing the speed if the mix becomes too frothy quickly. If you put the blender on high and walk away, you'll come back to an explosion of froth and sugar all over the counter. Once the sugar is dissolved, let the mixture sit for a few minutes so the foam settles. You'll know it's ready to use when the color turns from light brown to black.

Add the remaining 1 cup concentrate, the coffee liqueur, and vanilla. Store in a resealable container (like a mason jar or similar) in the refrigerator. Should stay good for at least 2 weeks.

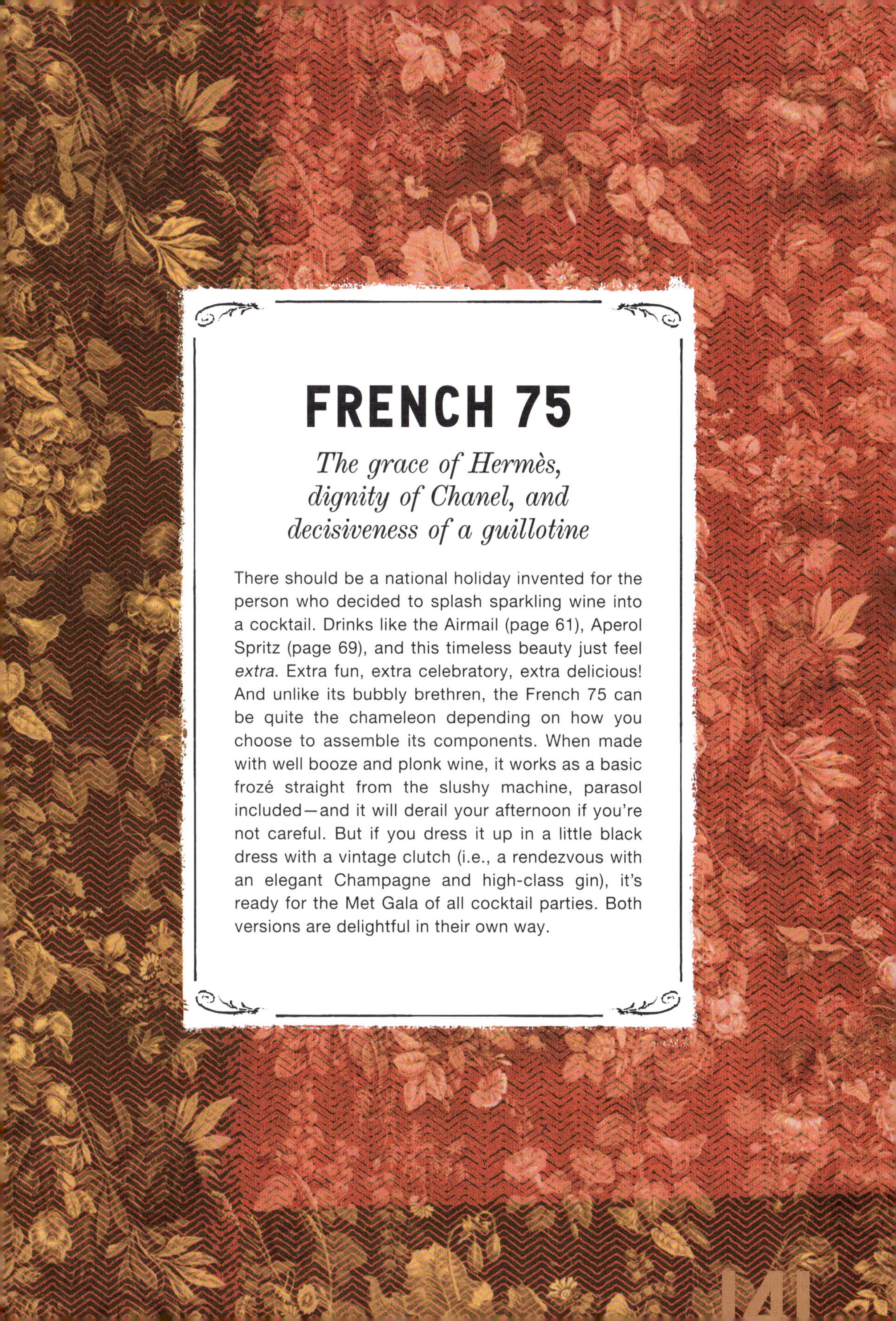

FRENCH 75

*The grace of Hermès,
dignity of Chanel, and
decisiveness of a guillotine*

There should be a national holiday invented for the person who decided to splash sparkling wine into a cocktail. Drinks like the Airmail (page 61), Aperol Spritz (page 69), and this timeless beauty just feel *extra*. Extra fun, extra celebratory, extra delicious! And unlike its bubbly brethren, the French 75 can be quite the chameleon depending on how you choose to assemble its components. When made with well booze and plonk wine, it works as a basic frozé straight from the slushy machine, parasol included—and it will derail your afternoon if you're not careful. But if you dress it up in a little black dress with a vintage clutch (i.e., a rendezvous with an elegant Champagne and high-class gin), it's ready for the Met Gala of all cocktail parties. Both versions are delightful in their own way.

Serve:
Shaken,
on the rocks

Tools:
Jigger, shaker,
Hawthorne
strainer,
channel knife,
Y-peeler,
paring knife

Glass:
Wine glass or
spritz glass, chilled

Garnish:
Lemon disk,
lemon pigtail
or peel

RIYL:
Bee's Knees
(page 81),
Hemingway
Daiquiri
(page 153),
Mai Tai
(page 189)

SPEC

Gin	.50 oz
Cognac	.50 oz
Fresh lemon juice	.75 oz
Simple syrup (page 29)	.75 oz
Champagne, to bottom	3 to 4 oz

OUR APPROACH

I have had, literally, a hundred or more late-night conversations about whether the French 75 is better made with gin or Cognac. No one argues about whether a non-vintage non-Champagne sparkling wine is fair game, or if the drink should really be served in a flute or artillery shell, but so many people will die on the hill of English or French spirit. Luckily, legendary bartender Dale DeGroff, that affable son of a gun, came up with the split-based compromise, which is genius: The gin is mandoline sharp, playing it cool at the poker table, while the brandy is round and cuddly, relaxing in front of a fireplace, indulging in bonhomie and deep conversations. When introduced to one another, you get a cocktail with round, curvy edges and sharp, pointy high notes—a full orchestra of complexity. I'm following his lead with this spec but changing the way you drink it. Sure, a Champagne flute is the de facto option for elegance, but the narrow opening of the glass lacks proper surface area for the aromas to blossom. I prefer serving it like an Aperol Spritz, in a wine glass over ice—this way the cocktail starts all feisty and angular but ends bright and breezy after spending leisurely time with the ice.

CHOOSE YOUR INGREDIENTS

When picking out base spirits, think about what best matches the moment. A New American gin, like St. George Terroir, will make the cocktail stop traffic and give big kisses on the vermillion carpet at the step and repeat. To match the bombasticness of the St. George, I'd reach for the Butchertown American brandy, which is boozy as fuck at 124-proof, with rich fig and dark fruit flavors. If you want more of a wallflower cocktail, pick a soft gin like Plymouth, which'll make for a perfectly sessionable concoction when made with a cute Cava. I make these for friends by the pitcher on my lanai. If you go this route, I would reach for Bas Armagnac instead of Cognac because it has a lighter body due to it usually being made in a column still instead of a pot still. (Go on, google it! You know you want to.)

HOW TO MIX

• **PREP THE GARNISH.** Grab two lemons. Carve a disk from one and set it aside. You have a choice with the visual garnish: If you have a glass that will look good with a pigtail, you can pull one of those to order with a channel knife after straining. If a peel would look better, pull one now using a Y-peeler and set aside. Both will add aromatic flourish to the cocktail.

● **MEASURE.** I know that I've said I like my drinks with a sturdy 2 ounces of spirit for structure, but this is an exception, because we have over half a glass of Champagne swanning in, adding flair to the party. For this reason, we've just got only 1 ounce of spirit in play. Measure and add your simple syrup, fresh lemon juice, and then the Cognac and gin (or one or the other, if you so choose) to one tin.

● **STRAW TASTE.** To make sure everything is in the tin. Set aside for a sec.

● **BOTTOM THE CHAMPAGNE.** Grab your chilled glass and fill it about three-quarters of the way full of ice cubes. Pick up the bottle of Champagne in your nondominant hand and the prepped lemon disk in the other. Then start pouring the wine into the glass slowly. Every time the bubbles puff up too much, squeeze a TINY bit of oil from the lemon disk over the glass and the cascade will shrink back like Gollum in the face of conflict. It'll add a nice ripple of lemon character to the cocktail once it's all integrated. A real Swarovski touch. Once you've added the 3 to 4 ounces of Champagne to the glass, discard that peel.

● **SHAKE.** Add 3 cubes to your shaker, snap it shut, and Rocks Shake (page 46) briefly. This should sound like bamboo swaying in the wind, stalks clacking together. Stop before the breeze dies out and a *sssssssh-hhhh* sound emerges. This shake is just to get the ingredients tied up together quickly and chilled so you aren't adding warm liquids to your sparkling wine. It's also a short shake because there is ice in the glass, which is going to melt and further dilute your drink over time. If you are serving this in a flute, which has no ice, you want to shake the cocktail longer so that it tastes good from start to finish. Trust me here.

● **TASTE, ADJUST, AND STRAIN.** Because this is going over sparkling wine, you want it to taste a bit sharp and edgy and boozy. It should not taste like something you want to drink an entire glass of on its own. If the booze isn't coming through, you can add a splash more of the gin or Cognac, but be super judicious about it. Add by the ¼ ounce. Then double-strain into the glass prepped with the sparkling wine—go slowly! The wine might bubble up as it eagerly meets the cocktail, and you don't want overflow.

● **GARNISH.** If you pulled a peel for this, express the oils of the peel over the surface of the cocktail and insert the peel into the glass. To make a pigtail garnish, grab your lemon and channel knife and hold the citrusy orb 6 or 7 inches above the surface of the cocktail. Pull a thin spiral of peel off the citrus, allowing the oils from the peel to gently waft down onto the drink. Insert the pigtail.

When you're sessioning this drink, try it three ways to see how the drink changes with each different base spirit option. First, mix it with just gin. Next, with only Cognac. For the third time, use the 50/50 split as we detailed. I'm not saying find your favorite and then only drink the cocktail that way forever, but learn to appreciate what virtues each version has, so you can mix each up according to the location, time of year, guest list, weather, etc. Emma has also approached this drink using a seasonal framework, flavoring the simple syrup with subtle additions to match the occasion: A little bit of cinnamon is a small but mighty flex for Cognac-based iterations during cold-weather months, and she's also had success with inviting floral flavors like marigold and dandelion into the mix during gin-fueled summer sessions.

GIMLET

*Sitting on the bow of a
sailboat, sea spray flying*

The Gimlet is a contender for my best go-to drink,
alongside its doppelganger the Daiquiri (page 125).
It can be made with vodka or gin or any other spirit
you deem worthy, so it's more like a formula than
a rule. It's also a concise lesson in the virtues of
brevity and tastes refreshing as hell, like running
ice-cold water over your wrists after a long, hot
bike ride in the summer. I like one as an amuse-
bouche—the drink to drink while you look at the
drinks menu—because it's as fast to mix as an
Olympic ski jump, and offers an uncomplicated hit
of razor-sharp refreshment that sets up the palate
for more complex cocktails to follow. According
to the Royal British Navy, the vitamin C in the lime
juice also helps ward off the dreaded scurvy, so
there's that, too.

Serve:
Shaken, up

Tools:
Jigger, shaker, Hawthorne strainer, fine strainer, Y-peeler, offset serrated knife (optional)

Glass:
Nick & Nora, chilled

Garnish:
Lime wheel (optional)

RIYL:
20th Century (page 57), Old Cuban (page 237), Sherry Cobbler (page 285)

SPEC

Fords gin	2.0 oz
Fresh lime juice	.75 oz
Simple syrup (page 29)	.75 oz
Lime peels	2

OUR APPROACH

The original Gimlet features lime cordial, a sweetener with bright citrus oils and acidic tartness both present and accounted for. That version of the drink can taste a bit muddied to me, though, like the gin and the cordial are competing for the mic. It also tends to veer to the sweet side. So, nine times out of ten, I am NOT making a sherbet or a cordial for my Gimlets, or using Rose's Lime, because it tastes like green, sweet car battery acid. Ick. Instead, I make it like a fresh Daiquiri (page 125) using a royal shake (see the Cosmo, page 117) with lime peels. This imitates the interesting aspects of a lime cordial without fussing with an oleo-saccharum, which takes a few hours to make. Royal shakes don't demand more effort: you just express some bright oil into the cocktail as you shake, easy-peasy, lime skin squeezy. Some people will argue this isn't a Gimlet, but to that I say, listen up: It's easier. It puts more of a singular spotlight on the distillate, and the lime peel oils round out the flavor with ripples of lime flavor. For a weeknight toss-back, it tastes great! Take the easy route, take the win.

CHOOSE YOUR INGREDIENTS

I call for Fords in this drink because it is a fantastic weeknight go-to London dry–style gin, beloved by barkeeps everywhere for its deft balance of botanicals and cocktail-worthy proof. For occasions where you're feeling fancy and want to upgrade the character of your Gimlet, there are dozens of other great gins on the market that'll layer distinct personalities onto the blank slate of lime and simple syrup. For example, these days gin distillers everywhere use local botanicals to bottle up the flavor of their region. So, a fun way to shake up routine is to make a round with a gin that reflects the terroir of where it's made. Emma loves doing this with a Gimlet when she's feeling wanderlusty—for her, whipping up a round that's reminiscent of springtime in Japan (Nikka Coffey gin) or the dry sweeping desert of New Mexico (Los Poblanos Western Dry) is the next best thing to hopping on a plane. One of her all-time favorites is St. George Terroir, whose flavors were inspired by the bay leaf and Douglas fir–filled woods of Northern California. Give it a whirl and see what you think.

- **PREP THE GARNISH.** Pull two lime peels to use in the royal shake. Set aside. You don't need a garnish for this drink, because its aroma is spectacular as is, but you could use a freshly cut fragrant lime wheel on the rim if you are feeling fancy. Cut a notch in the bottom so the wheel sits on the rim instead of bobbing around in the glass.

- **MEASURE.** Squeeze the oils from the lime peels into the shaker tin, then drop them in. Next, the humble simple syrup. Squeeze the lime juice to order. Add your gin of choice. Measure each so that there is no meniscus bubbling up over the rim of the jigger. Precision matters more than anything else with this drink.

- **STRAW TASTE.** To make sure everything is in the tin. This should taste like your seven-year-old nephew tried to make limeade and forgot the ice and water, or like a key lime pie served at room temp.

- **SHAKE.** Contribute 5 ice cubes to the mix. Cap your tins and channel your inner sailor (scurvy-free is the way to be) as you Coupe Shake (page 45) the living daylights out of the drink. The Fords gin is 90-proof, so listen for the ice breaking down and getting a little slushy—that's when you know it's time to stop and twist open those tins for a straw taste. Don't worry too much about overshaking—it's hard to do with this gin that's higher-proof, plus you'll have a chance to fix the balance during the adjustment period. In the event you chose a gin of lower proof, stop shaking a few beats before you would with the Fords. This is a nebulous concept, I know. When I'm teaching new bartenders, I have them make one Gimlet with 80-proof gin and one with 90-proof gin, shaken the same amount of time, to illustrate how dilution works. The 80-proof one might taste just right, whereas the 90-proof one will taste a bit bold on the booze, because it needs those extra shakes of dilution to come into balance. With time and practice, this will eventually come naturally to you.

- **TASTE, ADJUST, AND STRAIN.** Do a quick straw taste. If it howls with too much high-pitched acidity, you might need to recap the tins and shake for a few more seconds to get more water into the mix; if the texture is thin and the acidity is searing, add a touch more syrup. This will help the balance and the texture of the drink without adding noticeable sweetness. It should feel light enough to giggle but heavy enough to hit the bottom of your gums. If you did in fact overshake, you can sneak ¼ ounce more gin into the tin, give it a suuuper short shake just to work into the mix, then proceed. Double-strain, quickly and with gusto. As with the Daiquiri, you want this drink to still be "laughing" with bubbles when you take that first sip (to sorta paraphrase the late great Harry Craddock).

- **GARNISH.** Only garnish with a lime wheel if you want this drink to look cute.

Like the Margarita (page 201), you could try serving this one on the rocks if you shorten the shake a touch. I've heard Tom Macy (Clover Club in NYC) muddles lime wedges into the syrup as he builds the drink to get some of those oils that get lost by not using a cordial back into the equation. This is also a fun idea worth playing with. Also, and yes, this isn't really a personalization, but more of a fun insider tip: If you make this Gimlet with mint added to the shaker tin, you've got a Southside on your hands! Look at the Mojito (page 217) and Mint Julep (page 213) for tips on working with this vivacious herb.

GRASSHOPPER

Mint chocolate chip
ice cream for grown-ups

Back in the day when we only had mass-produced liqueurs at our disposal, this cocktail tasted like being mugged with a candy cane or a York Peppermint Patty. Thankfully, now we have elegant liqueurs to work with instead of industrial facsimiles of flavor, so you don't have to completely change this drink to make a version that begs for another round. The key is treating it like a *dessert* cocktail! It's built for drinking after gorging on a meal at a midcentury-style supper club. You should lean IN to the over-the-top components, not try to bury them. I really dig how the cacao serves as the vibrating bass notes of the build, while crème de menthe soars in like a wintery palate cleanser—that juxtaposition of high and low notes, amplified by a blanket of soft cream, makes for a charming liquid last course.

Serve:
Shaken, up

Tools:
Jigger, shaker,
Hawthorne
strainer,
fine strainer

Glass:
Coupe, chilled

Garnish:
Mint leaf

RIYL:
Daisy de Santiago
(page 129),
Stinger
(page 293),
White Russian
(page 309)

SPEC

Tempus Fugit white crème de menthe	1.0 oz
Tempus Fugit crème de cacao	.75 oz
Fernet-Branca	.25 oz
Heavy cream	1.0 oz

OUR APPROACH

For us, the grasshopper is ultimately all about the mint. The chocolate notes from the crème de cacao should serve as mysterious sidekick to the herb, like Robin to Batman. Think: 80 percent mint, 20 percent chocolate. To this end, I'm skewing the ratios to best achieve that personality. I'm also taking a note from Jeffrey Morgenthaler again (see his genius flex in the Amaretto Sour on page 65), following the way he injects a bit of bittersweet Fernet-Branca to the build. The minty Italian amaro strengthens the mint flavors and contributes dark tangles of complexity in the same way adding Angostura cocoa bitters to the Brandy Alexander (page 97) does.

CHOOSE YOUR INGREDIENTS

Despite the campy reputation the Grasshopper has earned over the decades, I fully believe the cocktail can taste decadent as fuck while still maintaining its integrity. To strike a balance between the two ideas, we reach for the liqueurs made by Tempus Fugit. Both the menthe and the cacao have a texture registering just shy of syrup, but with good sturdy backbones and great waves of complexity. Giffard makes good versions as well, though they are quite different in flavor, proof, and character—their crème de menthe especially is much brighter and bouncier. If these qualities sound more appealing to you, try 'em out! Either way, this is a reminder to taste your ingredients before you mix with them, to remind yourself of how small nuances will change a drink faster than you can say lickety-split. One more note before we dive in: Did you know that Fernet is actually a category of Italian amari and not just a singluar product? Fernet-Branca is the most widely known and consumed version, beloved by barkeeps the world over for its aggressive attack of medicinal bitterness, but there are other Fernets you could audition in a Grasshopper if you want to shift the herbaceous quality of the drink. Branca Menta is a sweeter, more minty version; Fernet Leopold from Denver has a cocoa reverb that plays splendidly with the chocolate liqueur in the build; and Fernet-Vallet from Mexico has a sinister dark dry allspice quality that moves the narrative into more dramatic territory. Bonus points if you can score some Fernet-Branca from Argentina, where the recipe is bone dry to accommodate the way the locals drink it with Coca-Cola—its earthy qualities sync up with the liqueurs in wondrous ways.

- **PREP THE GARNISH.** Pluck the prettiest mint leaf from your crop, for garnish.

- **MEASURE.** Did you smell and/or taste your heavy cream first, as per our suggestion on pages 40 and 41? If not, do that now, because shitty cream will fuck this drink up in the blink of an eye. If your spidey senses detect even a skosh of funk on the nose, put heavy cream on the grocery list and find another session to do in the meantime. If it smells good to go, toss the heavy cream into the tin. Then the Fernet. The crèmes come last. Rinse the jigger immediately, because now it's somehow both sticky and slippery, and messy to boot. If you let it sit, it'll get gross quick.

- **STRAW TASTE.** To make sure everything is in the tin. Notice how thickkkk the texture is right now, and how sweet the drink tastes. It will thin out and dry up a bit after you shake, at which point it should taste like a palatable cocktail.

- **SHAKE.** Add 3 cubes to the tin—not 5, because this is a low-proof drink, so it does not need as much dilution as one with 80-proof gin or vodka or whiskey. Then Rocks Shake it (page 46) like a paint mixer at Lowe's. The key to this is trying to get as much "fluff" into the drink as quickly as possible. (Read more about shaking with heavy cream in the Shake section of the Brandy Alexander session on page 99.) All the ingredients are low-proof, so just get after it with vim and vigor to incorporate air and then strain it into the glass.

- **TASTE, ADJUST, AND STRAIN.** Straw taste. Look for how the texture has changed since the first taste. Is it spumescent or does it need more vigorous shaking to fluff up into a pleasing cloud of dairy? Is it tasting a bit thin and wimpy for you? You could add a bit more Fernet to bulk up the proof and complexity, but remember how that will change the flavor, too. If you want the flavor to stay the same but the texture to improve, add a little Demerara syrup to pump it up into something plusher. This is inspired by a thing chefs do called monter au beurre when you are finishing a sauce and you whisk a few pats of cold butter in to make it silky, shiny, and sumptuous. It doesn't change the balance or flavor of the sauce; it just makes it richer. Shake more if you need to, but check on it every few shakes because, again, this is a low-proof drink, so you don't want to overdo it. Double-strain.

- **GARNISH.** The aroma of this cocktail should smell so good you just can't wait to take that first sip, but you should add a garnish anyway. A mint leaf, floating softly on top of the drink, is a nice visual touch. It will have a small amount of aroma, but it's mostly just for looks.

In addition to Fernet-Branca, Morgenthaler also uses ice cream in his build and runs the drink through a blender. Emma revives this version every year for the first Midwestern snowfall. If you wanna do that, add ½ cup of crushed ice to the blender with one scoop of ice cream plus the rest of the cocktail and go to town. For the garnish, sometimes she adds Bittermens Mole bitters for a spicy chocolatey aroma that echoes the crème de cacao in the drink, shifting the focus away from the mint and toward the cocoa notes. If mole isn't your thing, try Angostura cocoa bitters for a more confection-like chocolate quality, or the Chipotle-Cacao bitters from Bittercube, which bring a little chile pepper heat to the mix.

HEMINGWAY DAIQUIRI

A sandy beach bar at noon-thirty,
a cool breeze off the ocean

The Hemingway is a classic Daiquiri (page 125) injected wlth grapefruit juice and maraschino liqueur. These ingredients propel the cocktail into celestial territory, lifting rum and lime and bringing a certain lively je ne sais quoi to the combo. I love watching the bartenders whip batches together at El Floridita in Havana, where the cocktail was born. They bang them out with precision and speed, without blinking, using a few ounces of crushed ice in hand-cranked milkshake tower machines. This is a great way to make the drink if history matters to you, but you could serve one in almost any fashion— swizzled over crushed ice, blended together in a Vitamix with 2 ounces of crushed ice, on the rocks in a Double Old Fashioned glass, or, as we will do here: shaken and strained up in a coupe, because it makes for a wonderfully melodious experience. Gracefully mix up a pitcher of these, sit down at your typewriter, and wax poetic.

Serve:
Shaken, up

Tools:
Jigger, shaker, Hawthorne strainer, fine strainer, Y-peeler, paring knife

Glass:
Coupe, chilled

Garnish:
Grapefruit peel, Luxardo maraschino cherry

RIYL:
Brandy Crusta (page 101), Last Word (page 185), Jet Pilot (page 177)

SPEC

White rum	1.5 oz
Aged rum	.50 oz
Grapefruit juice	1.5 oz
Fresh lime juice	.75 oz
Luxardo maraschino liqueur	.25 oz
Simple syrup (page 29)	.50 oz

OUR APPROACH

This is an uncomplicated Hemingway Daiq featuring two rums instead of one for a little extra panache. I've also adjusted the ratios to temper the overpowering floral notes of the maraschino (a bully) and get the liqueur meshing together harmoniously with the grapefruit, lime, syrup, and rums. We've talked about bully ingredients a few times in previous sessions—see the Aviation on page 73 and the Corpse Reviver #2 on page 113—that is, liqueurs and liquors that push their way to the frontlines of flavor in a cocktail, eclipsing the others in the glass. In this drink, that's the maraschino liqueur by a mile or two. Most recipes have either too much or too little. It's taken me many, many trials to get this recipe close to right. In this case, my sweet spot turned out to be 1½ ounces grapefruit and a small ¼ ounce of maraschino, because the wet leaf flavors of the latter peek through the curtains just slightly, letting the perkiness of the grapefruit airlift the darker notes into something divine. I add a little bit of simple syrup, too, because otherwise it comes out too dry. You can adjust that to fit your palate—start with ¼ ounce and then add more on the second straw taste if you find it's necessary.

CHOOSE YOUR INGREDIENTS

Most Hemingway recipes call for a single rum, but I use two to create a more sturdy canvas for the grapefruit and the maraschino to waltz upon. Grapefruit is a super-complex citrus, with sweetness, acid, and bitterness, and the maraschino has a "rainforest floor, rotting tropical fruit" flavor going on, so you need to choose rums that have enough substance to grab the mic and leave it all on stage, but quiet enough in rumminess so that they don't overshadow the other ingredients. Jamaican rum can form too much of an allegiance with the maraschino and come off as overwhelming, for example. Something super molasses-y also will ruin this drink because those dark sugars aren't complementing the brightness of the other ingredients. I'd personally go with Planteray 3-Star, Probitas, or Banks 5 Island as the base—both have complexity but aren't spotlight stealers. For the aged rum, something dry and demure, like Brugal, will send a shiver of woody electricity up and down the spine of the cocktail.

- **PREP THE GARNISH.** Pull your grapefruit peel for garnishing later. Trim the edges with a paring knife to look appealing, because the peel will end up in the glass. Skewer your cherry if that's how you are going to roll. If not, you can plop it into the bottom of your chilled glass before pouring the cocktail in.

- **MEASURE.** Stack the simple syrup and maraschino together, because they both have sweetness, and you want to make sure you don't accidentally add too much of either to the cocktail. The full measure of sweetener in this drink is ¾ ounce. Then add the lime juice and grapefruit juice. Stack the aged rum and white rum to make a solid 2 ounces. Do not let surface tension make it look like a dome. (For more on stacking, see the Measure instructions for the Amaretto Sour, page 65.)

- **STRAW TASTE.** To make sure everything is in the tin. Note the volume of the maraschino at this stage; that flavor will soften and sink deeper into the grapefruit juice after you shake, so wait until the second straw taste to fiddle with that measurement.

- **SHAKE.** If you haven't pretempered your ice, put on some música Cubana and let those cubes sweat a bit before you start mixing. You want the cubes to temper and chill *before* you shake, otherwise your dilution won't be sufficient, and your balance will suck. Add 5 sweaty cubes. Coupe Shake it (page 45), gently for the first 10 or so gallops, then really intensely for the rest of the time. Try to do this as quickly as you can read Papa Doble's six-word story—shake until it sounds like slush.

- **TASTE, ADJUST, AND STRAIN.** Straw taste. If it's on the dry side, and you want a bit more of that floral maraschino in the mix, add a barspoon of maraschino and a barspoon of simple in the drink then shake it again briefly. If it's on the dry side, but you *don't* want more maraschino flavor, just add simple syrup by the barspoon. The texture should feel like a whirlpool of sea foam and the acidity should be bright and bouncy—if the cocktail feels insipid or flat, or tastes a bit muddy or too sweet, add ⅛ ounce of lime juice to perk up the mix. Straw taste again to make sure it's sitting where you like it. If you made adjustments, cap the tins and give this one last super-fast hard shake to rile up the juices and rums again; just like with the Gimlet (page 145), you want this drink to be buzzing with energy when it hits the glass. Double-strain that tropical wonderland into your chilled glass.

- **GARNISH.** Take your peel, hit the surface of the cocktail with a liberal amount of grapefruit oils, then insert the peel! Add the cherry, either skewered or not. Drink deeply or give it to the person who's about to be transported to the Caribbean.

Angostura bitters and grapefruit fuse together magnificently, so sometimes I add five dashes to this build. The structure and slight bitter bite it brings to the glass are quite pleasing. It does push the drink slightly into riffs territory, but we won't snitch on ya if you want to go that route. When adding bitters to a cocktail that doesn't normally call for the ingredient, I always suggest starting with one or two dashes and adding more on the second straw taste if you want.

HOTEL NACIONAL

A passport stamped with memories of humid nights in a lover's arms

The Hotel Nacional is one of Cuba's lesser-celebrated classics, which is a shame because it is one of the most sophisticated and restrained tropical cocktails known to humanity, with layers of flavor that dance on the tongue and a texture that reminds me of how it feels to catch a killer wave. It's what I mix for people who say they don't like tropical cocktails. I get it! Many tropical drinks are too bombastic and hyperbolic in their flavors and presentation. The Piña Colada (page 257) is a peacock. The Zombie can be frightfully overwrought. The Hotel Nacional, on the other hand, will draw you in like the Hotel California. No matter your locale, the intriguing combination of apricot and pineapple keeps you coming back for more.

Serve:
Shaken, up

Tools:
Jigger, shaker,
Hawthorne
strainer,
fine strainer

Glass:
Coupe, chilled

Garnish:
Peychaud's bitters

RIYL:
Airmail (page 61),
Porn Star Martini
(page 265),
Sidecar (page 289)

SPEC

White rum	1.5 oz
Aged rum	.50 oz
Fresh lime juice	.50 oz
Pineapple juice	1.0 oz
Rothman & Winter apricot liqueur	.50 oz
Simple syrup (page 29)	.25 oz

OUR APPROACH

I often talk about drinks that require exacting assembly to make well, like the Daiquiri (page 125) or Martini (page 205), because they are hard to balance perfectly with so few players in the glass. Drinks with liqueurs and juices are a little more forgiving, and the Hotel Nacional especially is hard to fuck up because all the ingredients taste delicious. Sure, you can lean too hard on the sugar or not shake hard enough—both will end up with a drink that teeters on the edge of being too sweet—but this is a GREAT drink for people who are just getting into bartending because you can err here or there, and it'll still taste pretty damn good. This spec is standard for that reason, though I do split-base the rums for some extra reverb, and add Peychaud's as a garnish instead of Ango, for a little tickle of fun.

CHOOSE YOUR INGREDIENTS

If you need a refresher on when and why we split-base cocktails, flip back to the Amaretto Sour to see our approach, on page 65. In this drink, for the white rum, I find Probitas by Foursquare reliably sturdy in tropical drinks. Banks 5 Island, which is a blend of different batches, also has a cenote's worth of complexity. The aged rum works as a support beam in the cocktail, adding underlying structure while still putting the apricot and pineapple on a pedestal, so it should taste dry and not toooo aged because that will make the cocktail read sweet; Planteray Barbados 5-Year is a killer companion to the 3-Star, but you could also try to get a rum that's as close to Havana Club 3-year or 7-year as you can find, because those flavor profiles work so well in this cocktail. Flor de Caña 7-year or Planteray Grand Añejo are no-brainers. For the liqueur, I like the Rothman & Winter apricot from Haus Alpenz, because its flavor comes across more like cooked apricot than candied apricot. Let's talk about pineapple juice for a quick sec. It isn't the star of this show, but rather the stage on which the rum and the apricot interact, but it still needs to be as fresh as possible and not poured out of a grubby can, because the gossamer texture of fresh pineapple juice just can't be beat. At Manolito, a sweet little Cuban cocktail bar in New Orleans, they liquefy pineapple in a Vitamix instead of running the fruit through a juicer, which creates this magnificent frothy texture, so that's an option if you have a blender. Either way, taste your pineapple juice and clock how sweet and acidic it is before you mix—bookmark this in your brain for when you take the second straw taste, because you might have to adjust your sweeteners and citrus to support the pineapple.

- ● **MEASURE.** Start by stacking the simple syrup and apricot liqueur, so the total measurement of the two comes out to ¾ ounce. Like a baker would, make sure the surface of that measurement is even with the rim of the jigger and not at risk of overflowing. Precision is key. Once that's in the tin, add the pineapple and lime juice (you could stack these, too, if you want). If you're using fresh pineapple juice, or Vitamixed pineapple juice, give it a moment to settle before you jigger so what's hitting the vessel is mostly juice and not just pineapple foam. Then stack and add the rums.

- ● **STRAW TASTE.** To make sure everything is in the tin.

- ● **SHAKE.** Add 5 uniform ice cubes and give this a vigorous Coupe Shake (page 45)! Start slowly, listening to the ice bash against the corners of the tin, learning its rhythms. Then increase your speed when you hear the corners of the cubes starting to chip, tuning in for the electrifying moment when the drink starts to sound like sludging through snowy slush on a shivery midwinter's night. Shake a bit longer for this drink, then stop and crack open those tins for the second straw taste.

- ● **TASTE, ADJUST, AND STRAIN.** When you straw taste, check to see what happened when water was introduced to the pineapple. Did it whimper out into wateriness? The cocktail could need ¼ ounce of simple syrup to smooth the edges and make the tropical part of the drink pop. Did the shaking tamper down the brightness and acidity too much? Add ⅛ ounce of lime to brighten it up. If you are adding tiny amounts to tweak you probably don't need to reshake, just swirl, and straw taste to make sure the improvements improve it. Double-strain.

- ● **GARNISH.** Peychaud's adds a lovely vanilla aroma to this drink, which makes me grin because pineapple and vanilla tango so well together. It's also cool because there are no Peychaud's inside the drink, so its sole purpose is to spark curiosity and surprise in the nostrils before the mouth gets the first and second sips. Take a peek at the Pisco Sour garnish on page 263 for another example of how this amusing technique works. To garnish: Hold a napkin up underneath the lip of the glass on the left (if you are a righty) to stop your bitters garnish from splashing all over the surface where you are making the drink. Hit the napkin with the beginning dash of bitters and drag the bottle above the whole cocktail surface. You don't want to start the dash IN the cocktails because the initial velocity will push the bitters into the body of the drink. This won't really make the same pretty visual as it would with a cocktail made with egg white, but it changes the aroma dramatically, so it's worth the 30 seconds it takes to go the extra mile.

This recipe is as close to perfect that I wouldn't do much, if anything, to change it. The only thing I'd do is throw a dash of Peychaud's into the mix to up the vanilla note in the aged rum. You could also experiment with citrus oil garnishes; lemon really brightens up the mix. If you come up with a more interesting idea, dear reader, drop us a line and let us know.

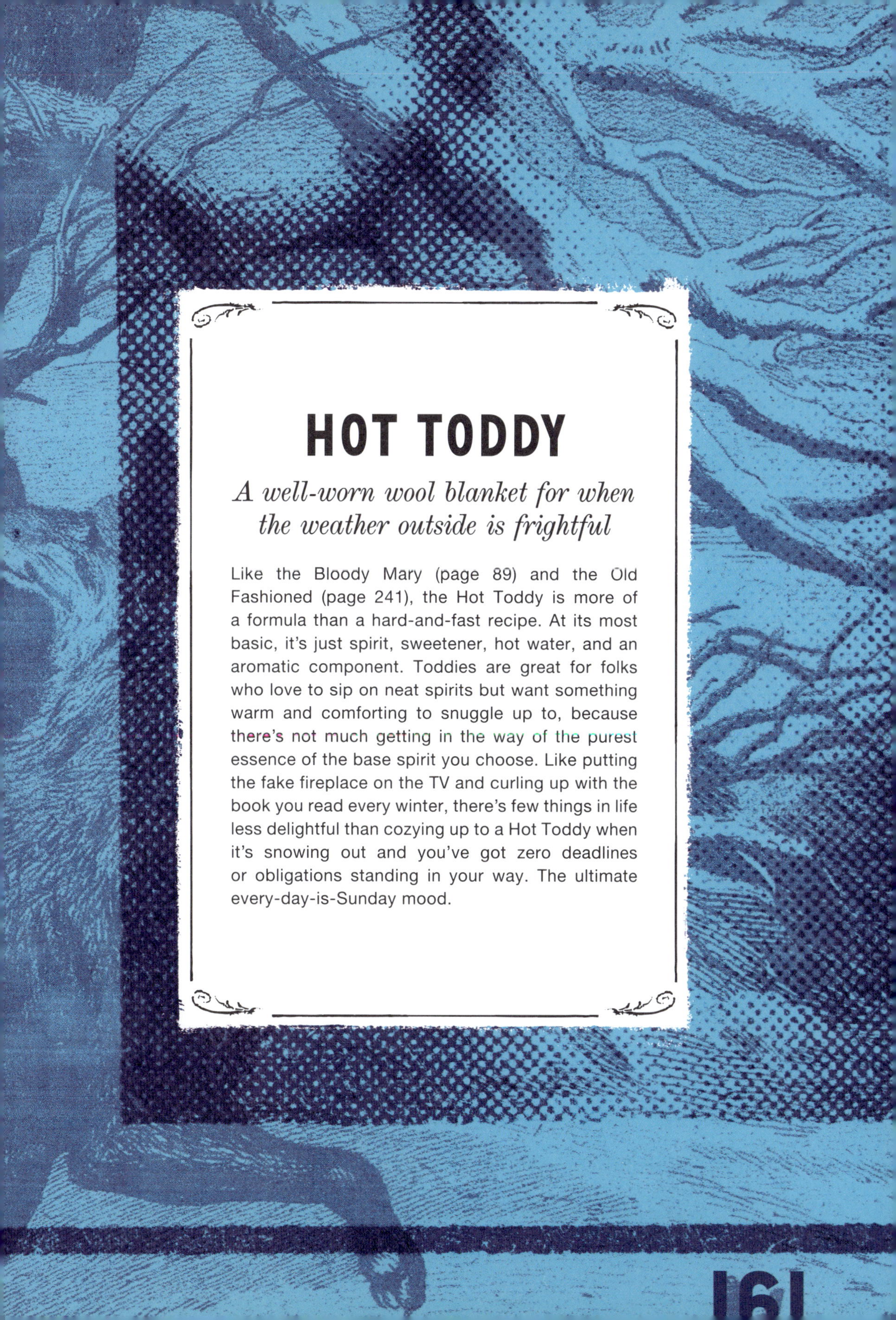

HOT TODDY

A well-worn wool blanket for when the weather outside is frightful

Like the Bloody Mary (page 89) and the Old Fashioned (page 241), the Hot Toddy is more of a formula than a hard-and-fast recipe. At its most basic, it's just spirit, sweetener, hot water, and an aromatic component. Toddies are great for folks who love to sip on neat spirits but want something warm and comforting to snuggle up to, because there's not much getting in the way of the purest essence of the base spirit you choose. Like putting the fake fireplace on the TV and curling up with the book you read every winter, there's few things in life less delightful than cozying up to a Hot Toddy when it's snowing out and you've got zero deadlines or obligations standing in your way. The ultimate every-day-is-Sunday mood.

Serve:
Built in the glass, hot

Tools:
Jigger, barspoon, paring knife

Glass:
Stemmed, flared tulip (à la Irish Coffee glass) or mug

Garnish:
Citrus disks

RIYL:
Amaretto Sour (page 65), Sazerac (page 281), Vieux Carré (page 301)

SPEC

Base spirit of choice	2.0 oz
Syrup of choice	.75 oz
Bitters of choice	1 dash
Hot water	6 to 7 oz

OUR APPROACH

This is a pretty classic build for a Hot Toddy. I am only tweaking two things. First, I believe to be a proper cocktail, the toddy must have some bitters included for complexity. The cocktail is, after all, just a hot version of the Old Fashioned. I also always add an aromatic element to help a hot drink come alive. In fact, I often do two rounds of citrus peel expression here: one express and discard in the tin as the liquid ingredients are tempering, and another once the cocktail has been poured into its mug, which is also an express and discard. Hot drinks typically don't involve a citrus juice component, but this bit of acidity in the aroma is as integral as the aromatic garnish in the Old Fashioned. The one moment you can bring brightness and complexity to the drink before it is consumed.

CHOOSE YOUR INGREDIENTS

I am a HUGE fan of rum and brandy toddies, because they heat up in a way that highlights their best qualities and dims their worst. Plenty of people also dig whiskey. I personally don't like the way most grain-based spirits transform when hot—often they smell like the sodden, unkempt back of a barn. If you like that kind of thing, go for it! For me, rye is the worst. Scotch is the best. Bourbon is neutral. Irish is passable. My absolute favorite is hot gin. If that sounds outlandish, start with barrel-aged gins like Kyrö Koskue from Finland or St. George Dry Rye Reposado from California. The vanilla and baking spice notes from the oak are reminiscent of whiskey or rum, while the underlying botanicals bob merrily around in the background for a fun secondary melody you wouldn't normally find in a hot cocktail. And maybe it doesn't need to be said but I also wouldn't make a vodka Hot Toddy for the same reason I wouldn't make a vodka Old Fashioned: The vodka adds nothing to the party but the dizzy. For the syrup, Demerara is an obvious choice for any aged spirit (and especially bourbon) because it is traditional and will keep the spirit of the cocktail "old-fashioned," if you will. Think about what spirit you are using and make a choice that supports it—grenadine would work well with aged tequila, while cinnamon or vanilla bring out the stone fruit notes of a good brandy. Ginger is my favorite with whiskey. Do this with restraint: Something like Fassionola (page 32), which has a ton of ingredients, might redefine the cocktail as a riff. Use the same judicious approach for the bitters: Angostura is a classic companion for aged spirits. If you want less of those deep spices, go with orange.

• PREP THE GARNISH. Get two citrus disks at the ready: one for expressing into the tin and one for expressing over the top of the drink. You will discard both, so they don't have to look like a work of modern art. I use lemon disks to create a bright and lively aromatic first impression of the cocktail, and orange disks when it's extra-cold outside and I want to feel extra cozy. You could also use one of each if you want to bring the best of both worlds to the first sip.

• BOIL THE WATER. To get the right temperature we use a Zojirushi machine, which boils water and then keeps it at the right temperature all night (great for use at the bar). We aim for 210°F (that's 98°Celsius), which is as hot as can be without reaching boiling. If you don't have a way of measuring temperatures, listen for the water to rise to almost a fever pitch, then remove from the heat before it starts to boil.

• TEMPER THE SHAKER TIN AND THE GLASS. Everything about this drink has to be HOT, not warm, to the touch, to make an outstanding toddy. Place your toddy mug on a tray and fill it halfway with hot water. Gently ease the smaller side of your shaker tin (a super-clean one, for god's sake) into the mug. A little water may overflow, which is why you had the foresight to place the mug on the plate or tray to catch the spillage. The metal tin will heat up lightning fast when sitting in hot water.

• MEASURE. Remove the tin from the hot water and express one of the citrus disks into the tin for aroma, then discard. Add the bitters, syrup, and booze.

• STRAW TASTE. To make sure you didn't forget anything, and to determine whether you like the balance of sweet:booze:bitter. Adjust now, to taste. When the bitters, syrup, and whiskey meet the hot water, their intensity will dilute a little, so adding a bit of extra syrup (for texture) or bitters (for complexity) right now could set you up for a successful first sip. If you're not confident trying this at this stage, you can always adjust after you've added the water.

• STIR. Give that a good stir, to make sure the syrup has dissolved into the mix.

• ROCK AND ROLL. Carefully dump the priming water out of the mug. Pour the cocktail in and top with hot water (near boiling!). Start with 6 ounces, then taste and add more by the ounce if it tastes too rich for your liking.

• GARNISH. Express the second citrus disk over the top of the drink, and discard.

I've given you plenty of ingredient choices in this session, but you can take your Hot Toddy to the next level by using a different hot liquid and sweetener for the "water" and "syrup" components. Try hot apple cider with Calvados, ginger syrup, and Angostura; or hot black tea with aged rum, Demerara syrup, and Bittermens Elemakule Tiki bitters. Cognac with Dem, Tempus Fugit crème de banane, and Angostura is a killer mix. You could also think about different beverage traditions from around the world: Would a soft gyokuro green tea pair well with kome shochu, simple syrup, and Japanese yuzu bitters? You betcha! When all else fails, use The Flavor Bible by Karen Page and Andrew Dornenburg to see what flavors they think pair well together.

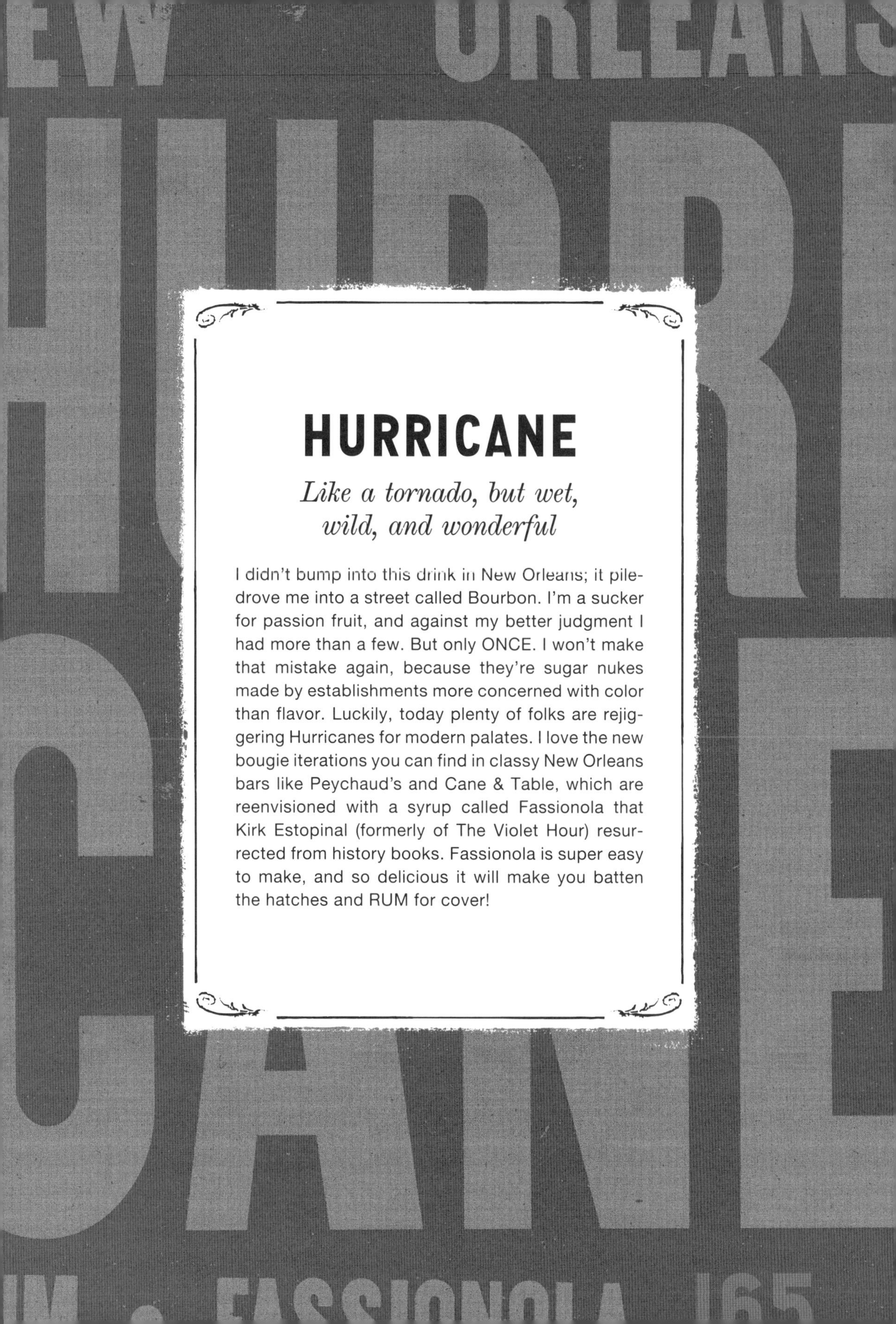

HURRICANE

*Like a tornado, but wet,
wild, and wonderful*

I didn't bump into this drink in New Orleans; it pile-drove me into a street called Bourbon. I'm a sucker for passion fruit, and against my better judgment I had more than a few. But only ONCE. I won't make that mistake again, because they're sugar nukes made by establishments more concerned with color than flavor. Luckily, today plenty of folks are rejiggering Hurricanes for modern palates. I love the new bougie iterations you can find in classy New Orleans bars like Peychaud's and Cane & Table, which are reenvisioned with a syrup called Fassionola that Kirk Estopinal (formerly of The Violet Hour) resurrected from history books. Fassionola is super easy to make, and so delicious it will make you batten the hatches and RUM for cover!

Serve:
Shaken,
on crushed ice

Tools:
Jigger, shaker,
small knife

Glass:
Hurricane, chilled

Garnish:
Pineapple leaf,
pineapple wedge

RIYL:
Breakfast Martini
(page 105),
Hemingway
Daiquiri
(page 153),
Jet Pilot
(page 177)

SPEC

Aged rum	1.5 oz
Different aged rum	.50 oz
Fassionola (page 31) or Chinola passion fruit liqueur	.75 oz
Fresh lime juice	.75 oz

OUR APPROACH

The coolest thing about this drink is that it's super simple—just like a classic Daiquiri (page 125) it's only got rum, lime, and a sweetener in the game—but it still has a wellspring of nuance thanks to the use of this wondrous syrup called Fassionola. With his state-of-the-art Fassionola, Kirk restored balance and sophistication to a drink that for a long time didn't deserve such titles. The syrup has hibiscus in the build, which changes the perceived sweetness of the historically "sweet" cocktail. You know that feeling in your mouth when you have a big chewy Cabernet Sauvignon? That's the tannic acid of the wine. Hibiscus has a similar texture—it's grippy as hell and makes the cocktail a red so bright it stains your white shirt just looking at it. Fassionola also includes Goya guava jam—the fruity notes nod back to the passion fruit liqueur used in the original recipe, while its pectin makes the texture lovely and round. All of that said, I know many of you just want to buy a bottle of liqueur instead of making your own syrup, so if that's the case, I'm giving you the option here to just use Chinola, a phenomenal liqueur that tastes kinda like your tongue is getting pelted by fresh passion fruits. When built with this spec, it's still a much more palatable Hurricane versus the ones you get on Bourbon Street. Like an actual cocktail and not a sugar smoothie!

CHOOSE YOUR INGREDIENTS

The easiest way to upgrade your Hurricane from one you'd find in a shitty Daiq shop to one worthy of menu placement in a fancy cocktail bar is to pick out a seaworthy rum combo. No bottom-shelf rot! I personally like Hamilton 86 Demerara as the primary rum, because it has lots of caramel, molasses, and vanilla notes, but any quality aged rum will shine in this drink. For the second rum, I'd look at any of the "signature blends" by Planteray and be prepared to pay in the $25 to $30+ range for the good shit. If you want to go really wild and use more than two rums, go forth and chase that horizon—check out the Jet Pilot session (page 177) for some hot tips on using Survivorship Bias to curate your own personal rum blend. As usual, if you don't want to split-base your spirits in this version, you don't have to. Just make sure you're using 2 ounces of your most steadfast rum instead of using two different rums.

● **PREP THE GARNISH.** Cut a notch in the bottom of the pineapple leaf, so that it'll sit on the rim of the glass. You might think this looks ridiculous at first, but you want the height so you don't poke yourself in the eye when diving in for a drink. Cut a pineapple wedge with a notch etched into the bottom as well, so it too will sit on the rim of the glass.

● **MEASURE.** This is a two, three-quarter, three-quarter cocktail—the same ratio I use for Daiquiris (page 125), Gimlets (page 145), and other simple sours (see how the total ounces of rum add up to two?). So funny how a drink that seems very complicated in one's mind's eye can be so beautiful in its simplicity. Keep that in mind as you build the drink: With so few ingredients in the drink, precision is of the utmost importance for achieving balance. Lime first. Then, in the small shaker tin, slowly, because that's the only way it comes out, measure out the Fassionola syrup (or the liqueur, if you're subbing that in). You could recite a Shakespearean soliloquy during this time. Hold that above the tin for a bit, making sure it all drips into the shaker. Then the aged rums, stacked to make sure you've got a crisp 2 ounces in the tin. Over the gangplank and into the tin with this pirate's mixture.

● **STRAW TASTE.** To make sure everything is in the tin. The drink will taste like a storm of sugar and booze at this stage.

● **SHAKE.** Add 2 ounces of crushed ice and Whip Shake (page 46) until the shaker is silenced. The goal is not to add a ton of water content to the cocktail, because it's about to hit a mountain of crushed ice and absorb plenty of dilution in the glass. You just want it to chill slightly so it matches the coolness of the ice it's about to meet.

● **TASTE, ADJUST, THEN ROCK AND ROLL.** Reinvigorate the contents of the shaker tin with a quick swirl. Taste. It won't taste too different than your first straw taste at this stage, just slightly colder. So what are you looking for? Remember how I said this is basically just a more complicated version of a Daiquiri? Think about the same acid to sweet to booze balance as you're contemplating whether or not you need to adjust anything in this moment. It'll differ based on what rums you chose, and whether or not you use Fassionola or passion fruit liqueur. If you think the mix will get better with a little more acid, because it reads a little dull or muddy, squeeze a barspoon or more into the tin now. If you chose really dry rums and Fassionola, it could taste a bit thin, so you could plump up the texture by adding some simple syrup or Demerara, which'll thicken things up without changing the flavor of the drink. Fill your Hurricane glass up three-quarters of the way full with crushed ice, then roll the entirety of the shaker tin mixture into your glass.

● **GARNISH.** Add more crushed ice, creating a dome the shape of the blue churches of Santorini. Garnish with the pineapple leaf and wedge.

If I'm feeling precious, and rollin' in it, I'll muddle a few Luxardo maraschino cherries into the tin. I love how this adds a deep rich sweetness to the drink. Or, if I want a version that's a touch more sessionable, I'll sneak 1/2 ounce of grapefruit juice into the mix and bring down the rum by 1/2 ounce. You could call this version of the drink a modest tempest vs. a full-blown hurricane.

IRISH COFFEE

A cup of ambition with a splash of zero fucks

The thing about the Irish Coffee cocktail, and what makes it different from a basic cup of sweet coffee spiked with booze, is the ritual layering of cold, slightly frothy cream on top. The white, chilled stratum cools the coffee—not enough to chug, but enough to make the sensation unique in the cocktail world. If you ever get the chance to visit its place of birth, The Buena Vista café, I highly recommend it as one of the most entertaining things to do while in San Francisco. I always go there for "one quick one" and then end up staying for another round, because the old-school way they line up the glass mugs in a long row, plop the sugar cubes in unceremoniously, then splash the hot coffee followed by the Tullamore Dew and cold whipped cream is truly a spectacle. The show hasn't changed in forever, and that nostalgia is something to hold dear.

Serve:
Built in the glass,
hot

Tools:
Jigger, barspoon,
paring knife

Glass:
Stemmed,
flared tulip,
Irish Coffee
glass, or mug

Garnish:
Orange disks

RIYL:
Brandy Alexander
(page 97),
Dark and Stormy
(page 133),
Manhattan
(page 193)

Hot coffee	4.0 oz
Irish whiskey	1.0 oz
Demerara syrup (page 29)	.25 oz
Heavy cream, to float	2.0 oz

OUR APPROACH

I'm keeping the spec basic as the day it was born, so we can zero-in on a few technique things that'll make the cocktail a bit more *Swan Lake*. First, I love the showmanship involved in stirring the sugar cubes into the coffee as they do at The Buena Vista, but the resulting texture isn't as pleasing in the long run, so I use Demerara syrup, which contributes a little oomph to the watery texture of the coffee. Dem also bolsters the woody aged notes of the whiskey in a way I dig. Time for the whiskey: Think about how *really* cold things, like slushies, barely taste like alcohol, while cold-ish things taste a bit more like booze, and hot things taste like BOOOOOZE. This prompted me to drop the amount of whiskey in the glass to 1 ounce instead of 2. At 1 ounce you still get the bump of booze, but it's not punching you in the throat. Finally, I'm hitting the drink with two rounds of orange oil because I love coffee and oranges together. The aromas make the entryway particularly beautiful.

CHOOSE YOUR INGREDIENTS

There is so much java in this cocktail, and its flavor profile is such a bully, it's arguably the ingredient you want to spend the most money, attention, and time with to make sure the cocktail turns out delicious. Use something nicer than what you throw into your morning cup (see the Espresso Martini session for more deets on coffee, page 137). Some baristas might scoff at this suggestion, but why not try something extravagant like Ethiopian Geisha? You only live once! For the whiskey, there are loads of great Irish whiskey brands on the market—you could grab something easy to find like Jameson or Powers, or you could do a little liquor store spelunking for a more stylish or avant-garde one like Connemara Peated Single Malt or Knappogue Castle Single Malt. Emma likes the Glendalough line, which sometimes features whiskey aged in a cool barrel like ex-Calvados, ex-Madeira, or Mizunara oak; or if you can find a bottle of the cask-strength High N' Wicked Wild Rover, that'll take your Irish Coffee into a new stratosphere—just be sure your coffee quality matches the prestige of the whiskey.

HOW TO MIX

● **PREP THE GARNISH.** Using a paring knife, cut two orange disks. Why two? You're going to use one to add orange oils to the body of the drink in addition to the garnish, which adds echoes of orange personality throughout the entire sipping experience. A super-cool flex we sometimes use in cold cocktails (like the Cosmo, page 117) but that works even better in hot ones. Set aside.

● **WARM UP A MUG.** Just as you'd use a cold glass when you are making cold cocktails, you need to make your hot drink glass is *hot*. You can just fill up your mug with boiling water and let it sit while you make the coffee. If your Dem is in the fridge, now is a good time to pull this out as well, so it has a few minutes to inch closer to room temp. Cold syrup won't ruin the drink entirely, but room temp syrup will earn you a gold star for attention to detail.

● **BREW YOUR COFFEE.** Your coffee shouldn't be anywhere near the boiling point (212°F or 100°C) because it will scorch the mouth. Brew to about 195°F (90°C) instead, which is enough for the drink to feel hot and brings out cool floral and nutty notes in the coffee, preventing that "burned" element from coming through. Drip is fine, but if you can do a fancy pour-over you'll see a marked improvement in the coffee. Just start this step sooner if you do, because that takes more time to gracefully enact this act. If I were a barista, I'd give you more detailed instructions on how to brew coffee here, but I'm a bartender, and I don't want to step too far into someone else's arena, so go seek out the writing of James Hoffmann of Square Mile Coffee Roasters, or Michelle R. Johnson aka The Chocolate Barista, who both have a wealth of knowledge and can give you far better advice than I on this front. You could also check out *The Bartender's Pantry*, which Emma coauthored with Jim Meehan. She hates to pull the shameless plug, but the book has an entire chapter on how to best source, store, brew, and work with coffee in cocktails, so it's worth checking out if you love the Irish Coffee (or Espresso Martini, page 137) and want to reeeallly up your coffee cocktail game.

● **MEASURE.** Discard the hot water from the tempered glass, then add the Demerara syrup, followed by the whiskey. Express a little bit of one orange disk into the mix at this point for extra brightness, and discard. Give these things a stir so they start mingling nicely. Then add the coffee. By adding the hot ingredient to the room temperature ingredients, it creates a gorgeous aroma that stimulates your thirst complex as you mix. It also integrates all the components well without having to pick up your barspoon again.

● **TOP WITH CREAM.** Snag your cream from the fridge. Flip over to the White Russian session on page 311 for instructions on whipping heavy cream for a cocktail. Follow those now. Gently donate 2 ounces to the top of the cocktail.

● **GARNISH.** The flavor of coffee and orange are inextricably linked in my head because of working a million brunch shifts where all we'd serve is coffee by the gallon and OJ, either in its pure form or adulterated with Champagne. This is what Saturday and Sunday mornings smell like to me, so I find the combination both comforting and delicious. To channel this vibe into your Irish Coffee, express the second orange disk over the top and discard.

Three ideas for y'all: First, sometimes Emma likes to whip the dairy with a 1/4 ounce of amaro, like Fernet-Branca, Averna, or Zucca, to change the flavor of the cream and the aroma of the cocktail. Or you could add a dash or two of bitters (chocolate, orange, or Ango) to the build, to create a more thoughtful structure and add warm baking spice notes to the mix. You could also grate fresh nutmeg or cinnamon or clove on top of the cream after you've floated it on top of the hot cocktail, to add more flair to its fragrance.

JACK ROSE

Cicadas chirping in the breeze,
Spanish moss dangling from trees

I'm always on the lookout for the underrated, under-promised drinks that overdeliver in the glass. The Jack Rose is one of those. Like finding a perfect 1970s Halston sunbeam yellow tie or high-waisted gray patterned pants with suspender buttons already installed, it's a drink that may seem a bit ordinary on paper, but once you taste one that's perfectly fresh and frothy, it will light up your eyes. The way apple brandy knocks around in the glass against the orange bitters—apples and oranges are very cool together—is marvelous. Perky lemon juice lifts the darker boozy notes, and when the warm hug of pomegranate swoops in via the grenadine, the whole outfit becomes spectacular. It is complex but easy; boozy and fruity; worthy of serious contemplation; and perfect to knock back without a care in the world, 'cause it's just plain delicious.

Serve:
Shaken, up

Tools:
Jigger, shaker, Hawthorne strainer, fine strainer paring knife

Glass:
Coupe, chilled

Garnish:
Orange or lemon disk

RIYL:
Aperol Spritz (page 69), Hurricane (page 165), Whiskey Sour (page 305)

SPEC

Laird's Bottled-in-Bond apple brandy	2.0 oz
Fresh lemon juice	.75 oz
Grenadine (page 30)	.75 oz
Orange bitters	1 to 2 dashes

OUR APPROACH

There are many things bartenders argue about, like the base spirit in a French 75 (page 141) or the perfect Mai Tai spec (page 189), but the debate that's gotten me closest to fisticuffs is whether the Jack Rose tastes better with lemon or lime. In the beginning of my bartending career I thought the citruses were interchangeable—probably because I was used to the sweet-and-sour mix off the gun—but while working at Milk & Honey, where we juiced à la minute, I learned the vivid difference between the two and developed theories about which juice went best with which spirit and in which cocktail. For the Jack Rose, die-hard originalists say lime, but I'm in the lemon camp. Lemon buddies up to the spirit. Laughs at their jokes and becomes part of the entourage. The synergy between the citrus and apple brandy sparks electricity in a way that I just don't get with lime. So we're going with lemon. I also add orange bitters, because apples and oranges work well in tandem. I'm not sure if it's the saying about comparing "apples to oranges" that made it seem like they shouldn't go together, but it might be a reason I was so surprised that they did.

CHOOSE YOUR INGREDIENTS

Sometimes I'll improvise with this recipe by adjusting the base spirit in terms of seasonality. Say you are serving it in deep fall or during a blizzard, in which case you could use Calvados instead of Jersey's finest apple brandy (Laird's) for the French spirit's warm baked apple pie notes. If you make this swap, I'd use Angostura instead of orange bitters, because its deep cinnamon and clove flavors also evoke the comforting vibes of the holidays. Just note that most Calvados brands come in at 80-proof, compared with Laird's scrappy 100-proof, so you will shake the French version for less time. For your everyday apple brandy, look at the label and make sure it says Bottled-in-Bond. That means the spirit was made by one distiller at a single distillery in one season, aged for at least four years in a bonded warehouse, and bottled at 50% ABV. Because it's high-proof but isn't diluted with neutral grain spirits (as some apple brandies are), it brings the most brilliantly robust "apple" flavor to the drink. For the grenadine, you could buy a commercial bottle, but the custom recipe we give you on page 30 has some seriously divine flourishes that contribute extra pizzazz to this cocktail, so I'd advise you to follow our lead if you want an extra memorable Jack Rose session.

- **PREP THE GARNISH.** For the garnish, you have three options. If the drink needs a little extra brightness because the grenadine presents as extra rich and sweet (this will usually be in the summer when the lemons are thin and watery), I will echo the lemon juice with lemon disk oils. Alternatively, I love how apples and oranges work together, so an orange disk, expressed and discarded, is always a good call. If it is autumn and I want to be fancy as all get out, I use a *flamed* orange disk. This just reminds me of leaves being burned, Irish knit sweaters coming out of storage, and the sun setting during dinner. Cut the disk from the fruit of your choice and set within arm's reach.

- **MEASURE.** Bitters first. Then, into the tin goes the grenadine. Now, put in the lemon juice, followed by the Laird's. Exacting, level measurements, please.

- **STRAW TASTE.** To make sure everything is in the tin.

- **SHAKE.** Add your 5 cubes and Coupe Shake (page 45) the drink, giving it a few more walloping gallops than you would normally because of the 50% ABV of the distillate. Listen for the *whooosshhhhh* of ice turning into slush and carry on for a few more beats before tasting.

- **TASTE, ADJUST, AND STRAIN.** Straw taste. If the contents of the tin taste slightly dull or weak, add a little squeeze more of lemon juice. If it's too thin and needs textural improvement, you could add a bit of simple or Demerara syrup here, to bring heft to the drink without adding more grenadine flavor. If you loooooove grenadine and want more of that element in play, go for it! Just remember how grenadine has sweetness and acidity, and in the case of our recipe on page 30, bitter qualities also, so if you add more, you're changing the balance of those other elements in the cocktail as well, which might throw the drink into a wild tailspin that needs further adjustment. If you're new to cocktail making, I'd keep it simple and just add simple or Dem until you get the hang of adjusting a component with so much complexity. Double-strain.

- **GARNISH.** Express the oils of a citrus disk over the drink and discard. If you want to flame the peel: Grab your orange disk. Make sure it's dry and at about room temperature. Hold the circular peel with your index finger, middle finger, and thumb, with the skin side pointing toward the top of the drink. Light a flame and hold it about an inch away from the disk, hovering just above the rim of the glass. Light the flame and quickly move the peel 3 inches above the flame, making sure not to blacken it, just warming the skin. Pull the disk back 8 to 10 inches from the flame. Move your hand briskly toward the flame and squeeze the disk when you are 1 to 2 inches from the fire. This will send flamed oils over the top of the drink. Discard the disk after squeezing.

As I mentioned before, I prefer lemon in this recipe, so I tailored the spec accordingly, but you could go with lime, or head completely "off book" and make one with an equal pour of each type of citrus to make up the 3/4 ounce. Could be a worthy dalliance. There is also a lot of room to play with bitters. Consider the theories of complementing and juxtaposition as you do. I personally love the Bittercube line, so I'd reach for their Grapefruit Hibiscus (formerly Jamaican No. 2) or the Cherry Bark bitters. The grapefruit notes in the former mirror the aspects of the grenadine in the drink, and the Cherry Bark will sidle up to the pomegranate and make it taste more like itself. Both bulletproof options.

JET PILOT

*Buckle up and get ready
to kiss the sky*

For a long time, I didn't realize how the Jet Pilot recipe skews SO close to the classic Zombie. They might as well be brothers from different mothers. The primary difference is the amount of rum used, and how the Zombie also includes grenadine. Emma and I both prefer Jet Pilots, so that's the session we've given you in this book. (If you want a good Zombie, seek out Jeff "Beachbum" Berry's recipe.) The Jet Pilot is so luscious and juicy, my eyebrows almost always end up on top of my head when I take that first sip. The combination of rum, lime, cinnamon, and grapefruit makes me crazy. It's one of those pairings where the individual components come together to become this whole different thing. So good. Now I order these all the time when I am in a bar with fishing nets on the walls and aloha shirts sashaying behind the bar.

Serve:
Shaken,
on crushed ice

Tools:
Jigger, shaker,
offset serrated
knife

Glass:
Hurricane glass,
chilled

Garnish:
Ango-soaked
grapefruit wedge,
Peychaud's bitters

RIYL:
Jungle Bird
(page 181),
New York Sour
(page 233),
Paloma (page 245)

SPEC

High-proof Jamaican rum	1.0 oz
High-proof rum of another origin	.75 oz
Aged rum	.75 oz
Grapefruit juice	1.5 oz
Fresh lime juice	.75 oz
John D. Taylor's Velvet Falernum	.75 oz
Cinnamon syrup (page 30)	.50 oz
Angostura bitters	3 dashes
Absinthe	1 dash

OUR APPROACH

Compared to the same old, same old Jet Pilot, I'm upping both the acid and the bitterness and making the drink longer and juicier because I always want my drinks to push the envelope of booze/sweet/acid. When I was a cook, I wanted my sauces to taste as if there was one more goddamn grain of salt it would be too salty, one more knob of butter and the thing would break, one more squeeze of lemon or hit of vinegar, and your face would pucker and your eyes would tear up and your salivary glands would go off like golf course sprinklers. I like extremes in most things, so my ratios reflect that. Don't be shy picking out the big boozy rums! It's a bombastic drink that'll keep its sea legs, even when served on crushed ice, as we do here. Also, the original recipe does not call for a Peychaud's float, but I love the way the fennel notes of the bitters chirp alongside the anise notes of the absinthe.

CHOOSE YOUR INGREDIENTS

In this recipe, you are looking for three rums that are very, very different, so when they come together you get as full a "rum flavor" as possible. I do this by using Survivorship-Bias: When I'm tasting my first rum, I think . . . what is missing from this? Not what's good about the rum. And then I reach for a rum that has that missing element. Then I add those two rums together and taste them to see what is missing. So, for example, in Planteray 5-Year aged rum I get a nice woody vanilla note, but not many fruity notes; so for the second high-proof rum I bring in The Scarlet Ibis from Trinidad, which has a pineapple quality. For the Jamaican, Hamilton's brings the funk that the other two lack. See what I'm getting at? Together, all three create a very interesting chord of "rum" for the other ingredients to bounce around on. A bit more advice to make this process easy for you: Don't pick rums made in the same place because they will often taste rather similar. Next, get rums aged for very different numbers of years, because the influence of the barrel will vary depending on whether the liquid has been in contact with wood for, say, five versus fifteen years. Finally, get rums that are very different proofs, because different flavors come out at different ABVs.

- **PREP THE GARNISH.** I like using an Angostura-soaked grapefruit wedge as the garnish because it echoes and complements the components of the cocktail: The grapefruit matches the juice and the baking spices in the bitters pull out the cinnamon in the syrup. There is also a classic cinnamon and grapefruit tiki syrup called Donn's Mix, named after Don the Beachcomber, that's long been a tried-and-true combo, so this is not just me making things up. The garnish is also pretty and adds nice aromatics. To prep one: Slice a wedge of grapefruit and make a "courtesy cut" into it—that's the little cut that makes it easy to slide onto the rim. Place it on a small plate and dash enough Angostura bitters until the whole side, pith included, is soaked. Flip it over and repeat. Make sure your Peychaud's bitters are within arm's reach—you'll be garnishing with that later, too.

- **MEASURE.** Into the tin go the dashes of absinthe and Angostura. Stack the cinnamon syrup and falernum. Follow with the lime and grapefruit juices, then all of the rums. Be precise; there are so many ingredients in here, a little overpour here or underpour there will throw off your balance.

- **STRAW TASTE.** Give this a straw taste. Is the grapefruit standing up to the rum and all of the sugar? You are going to shake this a lot, so adding ½ ounce of extra grapefruit juice now to give it more of a firm footing isn't a bad idea. It's up to your palate. Prep the glass by filling it three-quarters of the way full with crushed ice and set that aside before you shake.

- **SHAKE.** Add about 4 ounces of crushed ice and shake until silent. This is called a Whip Shake (page 46) because it's just a few quick whips of the wrist to get the ingredients cold enough so they don't spark immediate ice melt when the mixture gets strained into the glass. Normally we whip shake with 2 ounces of crushed ice, but in the case of the Jet Pilot we double the amount to compensate for the high volume of high-proof rum.

- **TASTE, ADJUST, AND ROLL.** Pour the drink directly into the dimple of crushed ice in the glass. Stick a straw into the glass and give it a quick taste. Extrapolate what this drink is going to do over time as it sits on ice. It should be a bit sweet, and pretty "hot," right now, but both things will mellow over time, especially with the fiddling of the crushed ice that everyone inevitably does when presented with the drink. On tiki menus around the world, the Jet Pilot is often marked with the most number of skull icons to indicate it's high alcohol content—seriously, it's the most boozy drink in the book—so resist the urge to add more rum at this stage. If the flavor profile and texture need a boost of complexity, reach for the Ango instead. One dash at a time. Trust.

- **GARNISH.** Slide the Ango-soaked grapefruit wedge onto the rim. Gently dash Peychaud's on top so the liquid rests on the surface of the drink; you want those pretty aromas to speak loudly!

This drink is almost un-fuckwith-able. Refreshing and dry and bitter, also easy to toss together—a solid above-deck cocktail once the boat is moored. Just what you need after sailing. I think it's the optimal drink for folks who like a Hemingway Daiquiri but are in the mood for something a bit more complex. You could make a honey-cinnamon syrup instead of just a plain ol' cinnamon syrup—I dig the way the honey plays with the grapefruit juice and the nutmeg notes of the falernum—for a different shade of sweetness. Or if you really like absinthe and want to amplify that quality, rinse the glass with the ingredient first, or use an atomizer to spray a mist over the surface of the drink as garnish. Tiny tweaks, big results.

JUNGLE BIRD

*Blackbeard's take on
Italian aperitivo hour*

The Jungle Bird is one of the weirdest drinks in the tropical canon. A conundrum of a cocktail that brings three powerhouse ingredients together in confounding harmony. Blackstrap rum is as funky and dark as the flop sweat of Beelzebub. Pineapple juice telegraphs vacation vibes: whimsy, rustling palm fronds, and gently swaying hammocks. Sure, there are other tropical flavors like mango or guava that have a similar feeling, but they aren't as ubiquitous in drinks. Then you have Campari, a petulant teenager full of angst. And Italian! In a tropical cocktail! But damn, you put these things together (in the right ratio) and it is a thrilling roller coaster ride. Like a liquid mullet: party in the front, mixology in the back. Tiki through-and-through but outfitted in a way that sends a siren signal out to fans of bittersweet Italian aperitifs as much as it does to tropical shirt–clad rum nerds.

Serve:
Shaken, large
cube or sphere

Tools:
Jigger, shaker,
Hawthorne
strainer, fine
strainer

Glass:
Double Old
Fashioned, chilled

Garnish:
Pineapple leaf,
pineapple wedge
(optional)

RIYL:
Kingston Negroni
(page 230),
Last Word
(page 185),
Mai Tai (page 189)

SPEC

Interesting rum	. . . .	1.5 oz
Blackstrap rum	. . . .	.50 oz
Campari	. . . .	.75 oz
Fresh lime juice	. . . .	.75 oz
Pineapple juice	. . . .	1.5 oz
Demerara syrup (page 29)	. . . .	.50 oz

OUR APPROACH

The first time I had this drink my only thought was "What the actual fuck?" It was my introduction to blackstrap rum, which gave me a Proustian memory of my mom's gingerbread cookies. I loved the juxtaposition of round rum and sharp lime. And the Campari and pineapple were having an actual MMA fight on my tongue, like a mixologist and a lifeguard were roughhousing to the death. This is all to say that this spec is relatively straightforward—not throwing you any curveballs—because the balance of these contrasting flavors is hard to get right, so we're just focusing on nailing that, and coaxing out the best texture of the drink. It should taste light and fluffy from the pineapple juice, with an undercurrent of bitterness.

CHOOSE YOUR INGREDIENTS

Finding the right "interesting" rum for a Jungle Bird can be tricky, because it must hold up against the bitterness of Campari and the spiky corners of blackstrap. The Scarlet Ibis is a surprising winner in this build, dry as a dusty desert highway but with a round vanilla note that clings to the pineapple juice without dragging its brightness down. Other young-ish rums with a middle-ground personality should also work well. Two James Spirits Doctor Bird is a funky option if you like Jamaican-style rums. We also talked a little bit about the blackstrap rum in the Dark and Stormy (page 133); mostly about how I find the ingredient to be rather one-dimensional. I hold fast to that assessment. I just don't get as much heart and soul as many other better crafted rums. But I will say Cruzan blackstrap has a bit more complexity than Goslings, so that's my rec, and I'm sticking to it. For intel on pineapple juice, see the Hotel Nacional on page 157.

HOW TO MIX

● **PREP THE GARNISH.** If you want to use a pineapple leaf and wedge, prep those now. First, cut a leaf from the pineapple. One that doesn't have any blemishes or dry edges. Unlike in the Hurricane (page 165), where the leaf will sit on the rim of the glass, this leaf will submerge into the cocktail itself, so it doesn't need a courtesy cut etched into the bottom. Set aside. Some folks also appreciate finishing a bitter-sweet Jungle Bird with a bite of juicy pineapple, so if you want to do that, cut a wedge now, with a notch in the tip so it sits on the rim of the glass.

● **MEASURE.** Start by measuring and pouring the Demerara syrup into the tin. Follow that with the pineapple juice, then lime juice. Campari comes next. Stack the rums so they equal a sharp 2 ounces, and into the tin they go. Here is where stacking can be really cool: Sure, the spec says 1½ ounces of the first rum and ½ ounce of the second, but if you know you really like the molasses notes of blackstrap, you can pour a shy half on the first rum, and bold on the blackstrap—as long as the full measure equals 2 ounces, the balance of the whole drink will remain intact. (See page 42 for more on "shy" and "bold" measurements when jiggering.)

● **STRAW TASTE.** To make sure everything is in the tin, and to see if you like the balance of sweetness to bitterness you've created. When you do this, notice how the Campari has both sweetness and bitterness, while the pineapple has both sweetness and acidity, and the blackstrap has a touch of bitterness baked into its rough sweetness as well. No ingredient is one singular thing. When you go to adjust the balance on the second straw taste, this information will be helpful.

● **SHAKE.** Add 5 ice cubes, cap, and Rocks Shake (page 46). Remember that pineapple juice is like 90-something-percent water, so soften this motion a little to account for how much dilution the fruit juice is already adding to the drink. Think: the pace of a slow ambling Amtrak versus a rockin' roller coaster.

● **TASTE, ADJUST, AND STRAIN.** Straw taste. Take a beat and think about how the lime juice and pineapple acid stand up to the gingerbread notes of the blackstrap and sugar in the Demerara syrup and the Campari. It should taste kind of sweet and boozy right now because it will soften over ice in the glass, but it should taste good and not too jammy, so you might want a skosh more lime or pineapple. Take another beat to see what happens on the finish. How long is the bitterness hang-ing around? Is it pleasing, or does it maybe need a dash of bitters (try Bittercube Blackstrap or Angostura) to ramp up the complexity? Recall what I said about how each ingredient has multiple characteristics. If you add more pineapple juice, you're adding acidity and sweetness, not just fruity flavor, for example. Once you've got it where you want it, add ice to the DOF and double-strain the cocktail into the cold embrace of the chilled glass over a large ice cube or sphere.

● **GARNISH.** This is one of the few drinks in this book that doesn't have an aromatic garnish. The cocktail smells weird as hell (in a cool way) as is, and you don't want to get in the way of that. If you want the visual appeal, you could garnish with a pineapple leaf, even though it is somewhat of a threat to one's eyeballs, or a wedge of fresh pineapple for a tasty denouement. Your call.

If you want this to taste really, super, uber pineapple-y, use Planteray Stiggins' Fancy pineapple rum and pineapple syrup. Add xanthan gum to make a gomme syrup (or buy the pineapple gum syrup from Liber & Co.) and get the benefits of a smooth, slick texture. I like playing around with Campari alternatives, too: Try splitting the measure with ½ ounce of Cynar and ¼ ounce of Aperol. Cynar swings in with dry bitterness, while the Aperol is softer and gentler than Campari—the way it cuddles up against the sweeter parts of Cynar is capital "A" awesome. Yes, this could almost be considered a different drink, but not crazy different. More like twins that look exactly alike but act very differently.

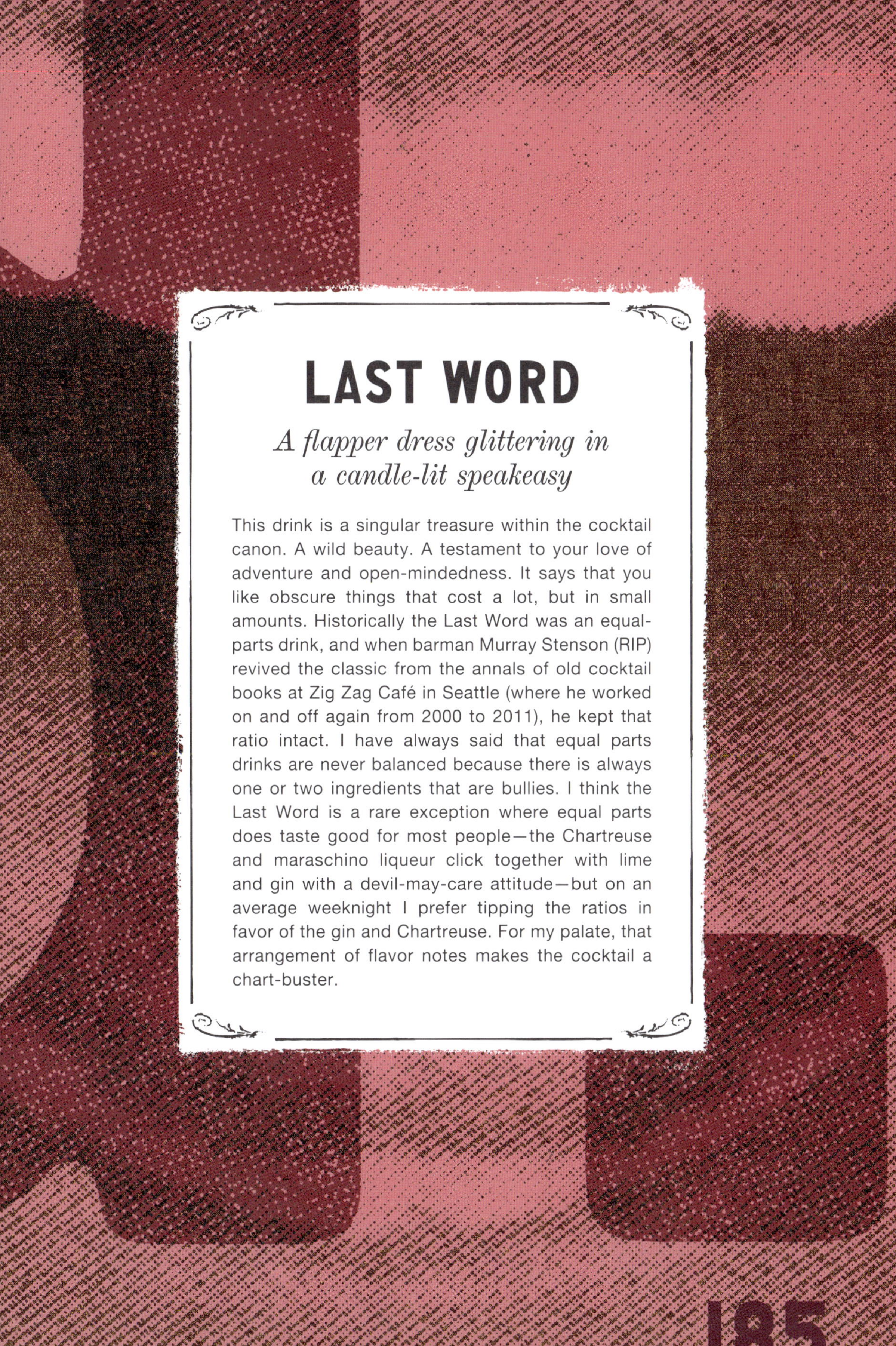

LAST WORD

*A flapper dress glittering in
a candle-lit speakeasy*

This drink is a singular treasure within the cocktail
canon. A wild beauty. A testament to your love of
adventure and open-mindedness. It says that you
like obscure things that cost a lot, but in small
amounts. Historically the Last Word was an equal-
parts drink, and when barman Murray Stenson (RIP)
revived the classic from the annals of old cocktail
books at Zig Zag Café in Seattle (where he worked
on and off again from 2000 to 2011), he kept that
ratio intact. I have always said that equal parts
drinks are never balanced because there is always
one or two ingredients that are bullies. I think the
Last Word is a rare exception where equal parts
does taste good for most people—the Chartreuse
and maraschino liqueur click together with lime
and gin with a devil-may-care attitude—but on an
average weeknight I prefer tipping the ratios in
favor of the gin and Chartreuse. For my palate, that
arrangement of flavor notes makes the cocktail a
chart-buster.

Serve:
Shaken, up

Tools:
Jigger, shaker,
Hawthorne
strainer,
fine strainer,
paring knife

Glass:
Coupe, chilled

Garnish:
Luxardo
maraschino
cherry,
grapefruit disk

RIYL:
Aviation (page 73),
Cosmopolitan
(page 117),
Martini (page 205)

Fords gin	1.5 oz
Green Chartreuse	.75 oz
Luxardo maraschino liqueur	.50 oz
Fresh lime juice	.75 oz
Simple syrup (page 29)	.25 oz

OUR APPROACH

My favorite version of the Last Word recalibrates the ratios of the classic equal parts model, because I fucking love gin, and I like Chartreuse more than maraschino—it is a holy concoction that comes in like a squall and out like a cyclone. We used to call adding green Chartreuse to a cocktail "cheating" because it makes almost all drinks immediately more delicious. I love how it bludgeons the palate with booze while simultaneously coddling it with sugar *and* mystifying it with complexity. That's why I've dropped the amount of maraschino down and added a bit of simple syrup to bulk up the texture of the drink. The simple also makes up for the sweetness that gets lost with the cherry liqueur subtraction. Like when Alice takes that fateful swig of magical elixir that transports her into Wonderland, this version screams: "Drink Me!"

CHOOSE YOUR INGREDIENTS

All the ingredients in the glass are LOUD, so you need a gin with formidable grit and resolve to match their intensity, like Fords or Beefeater or Hayman's London Dry. You for sure don't want a shrinking violet gin trying to soft snuggle with the green Chartreuse and maraschino because it'll get lost in the mix faster than a hungover bartender tossing together Snaquiris for a "safety meeting." For the maraschino, my friend Maranda Howell, the Tipsy Librarian in Baton Rouge, swears by the liqueur made in Croatia, going by the name Maraska, over the better-known Luxardo from Italy. I love both, for different reasons. The Luxardo has a thrumming cherrystone attack so appealing, bees and hornets would swarm for a sample. The Maraska is lighter, more floral, and less sweet.

- **PREP THE GARNISH.** Use a barspoon to fish out a nice plump maraschino cherry from the Luxardo jar. Let it rest on the spoon while you mix the drink. Or you might want to put it on a cutting board or napkin so you don't accidentally stain your countertops. Cut a grapefruit disk now, if you think you want to use its oils as a final aromatic touch. I love how grapefruit and maraschino go together—like potato chips with caviar and crème fraiche—but you can check out the Hemingway Daiquiri (page 153) for more thoughts on that.

- **MEASURE.** First, the simple syrup. Then, the lime. Follow those with the maraschino, then Chartreuse. Be especially precise with those last two measurements—they both have a LOT of sweetness. Finish with the gin.

- **STRAW TASTE.** To make sure everything is in the tin.

- **SHAKE.** Because this cocktail has more sweetness and proof than others, it becomes a train wreck if not shaken long and hard enough. See, the dilution from the ice tamps down the sugar in the liqueurs and lifts up the lime juice to a volume that meets the sweetness on equal footing. The gin ties it all together. If you aren't getting enough water in there, the Chartreuse and gin and maraschino and lime cage-fight. So add 5 cubes and engage with a long, fervent Coupe Shake (page 45). Even longer than you'd shake the equal-parts version.

- **TASTE, ADJUST, AND STRAIN.** Straw taste. Now is the time to goose one of the flavors if need be. Do you want your cocktail a wee bit heavy on the green Chartreuse because you just love that taste? Add ⅛ ounce. You could also do this if the cocktail is reading maraschino-heavy to you, and that's not something you were aiming for with your spec. Just remember Chartreuse has a lot of syrupy sweetness in addition to its wondrous botanical profile, so adding more will further sweeten the cocktail. You could alternatively add more maraschino if you want more "adult cherry" personality in play (see page 102 for more on how Luxardo maraschino cherry liqueur is made), but it is also a sweetening agent, so proceed with caution. I'm not saying more sweetness is a bad thing, just that these decisions are up to you and your palate. Finally, because there are three sweeteners in this drink, the odds of it reading too sweet are pretty high, so if the second straw taste proves that to be true, throw in a little more lime juice to chew up some of that sugar and put a better spotlight on the gin. Swirl in the tweaks and double-strain into your chilled coupe.

- **GARNISH.** Drop a Luxardo maraschino cherry in the bottom of the coupe, unskewered. You want it to soak for as long as possible before it's picked out with greedy little fingers. If you want to add grapefruit disk oils to this, be my guest.

If you want the drink to reverberate with an even bigger reference to the Carthusian monks who make Chartreuse, stack green and yellow versions for a tornado of alpine herbs. The saffron notes of the yellow add a cool Mark Hoppus–style bass riff to the background. I just wouldn't sub in yellow for green entirely, because that'll taste like a totally different cocktail vs. a slightly unusual Last Word.

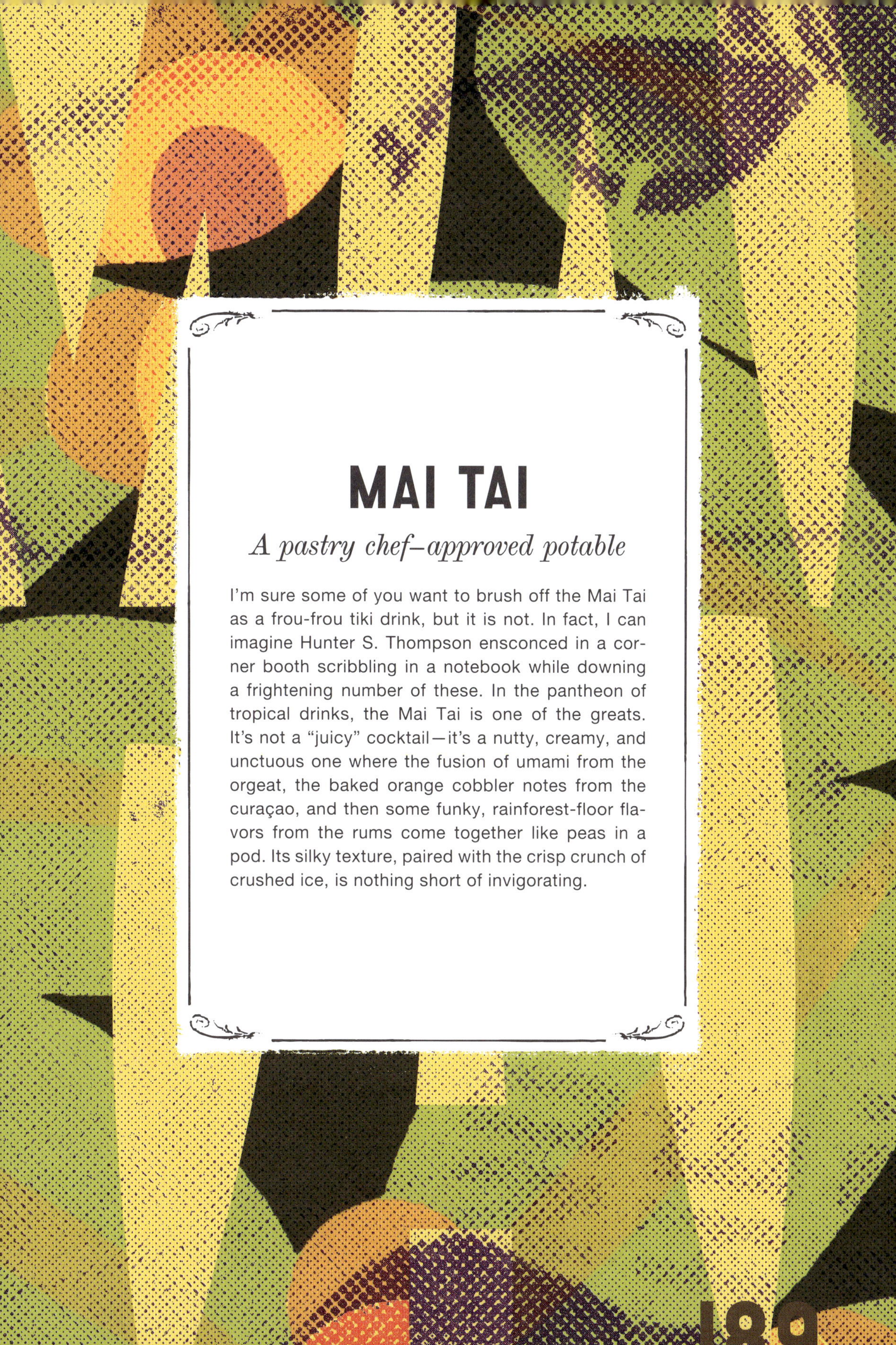

MAI TAI

A pastry chef–approved potable

I'm sure some of you want to brush off the Mai Tai as a frou-frou tiki drink, but it is not. In fact, I can imagine Hunter S. Thompson ensconced in a corner booth scribbling in a notebook while downing a frightening number of these. In the pantheon of tropical drinks, the Mai Tai is one of the greats. It's not a "juicy" cocktail—it's a nutty, creamy, and unctuous one where the fusion of umami from the orgeat, the baked orange cobbler notes from the curaçao, and then some funky, rainforest-floor flavors from the rums come together like peas in a pod. Its silky texture, paired with the crisp crunch of crushed ice, is nothing short of invigorating.

Serve:
Shaken,
on crushed ice

Tools:
Jigger, shaker,
Y-peeler, paring
knife (optional)

Glass:
Double Old
Fashioned, chilled,
or a cool tiki mug
that holds about
12 ounces

Garnish:
Mint bouquet,
orange peel

RIYL:
Brandy Crusta
(page 101),
Pisco Sour
(page 261),
Whiskey Sour
(page 305)

SPEC

Jamaican rum	....	1.0 oz
Second rum	....	1.0 oz
Fresh lime juice	....	.75 oz
Orgeat (page 31)	....	.50+ oz
Ferrand dry curaçao	....	.50+ oz
Orange bitters	....	3 dashes

OUR APPROACH

This spec skews very close to the original, because only fools fuck with a good thing without a compelling reason. All I do is split-base the rums to multiply the rumminess (see the Amaretto Sour approach on page 65 for more on split-base theory) and then add some orange bitters to tease out the orange qualities of the orange flower water in the orgeat. While this cocktail should always have a fresh mint sprig nestled atop for garnish—like a lone palm tree on a deserted beach—I feel that an orange peel, expressed and inserted, is also a bitchin' accent that brings a third echo of orange to the glass. I also like how the peel looks like a surfboard stuck in the sand. Surf's up, bro! Let's get mixing.

CHOOSE YOUR INGREDIENTS

I like a big bombastic rum in the Mai Tai, because the orgeat is a heavy blanket that gobbles up a lot of the real estate in the cocktail. The warm spice of the curaçao, which has a good amount of sweetness, latches on to this heaviness, creating a dynamic duo that is apt to stage a coup (not a coupe) against the rum if allowed. But at its core, it's a RUM drink—you want those round, sweet notes to poke through the veil of sweetness. I like Saint James aged rum 100-proof, and Smith & Cross is never a bad idea because it's a brawny and distinctive beast. Hamilton 86 from Demerara is also a good bet because it's got a nice tannin quality that balances out sweetness. I've also seen some intrepid bartenders split-base with rhum agricole from Martinique to weave in the grassy personality of fresh cane with the darker notes of barrel-aged rum. Could be worth trying if agricoles float your boat.

● **PREP THE GARNISH.** One big fresh mint bouquet, with no dehydrated brown edges or jagged tears in the leaves, is a picture-perfect—and aromatically intense—requisite for this drink. The orange peel will be inserted, so make sure it also has no tarnished disfigurements. For extra points, take a beat and trim the edges with a paring knife so they look intentionally curated, like an exhibit at the Kon-Tiki Museum in Oslo.

● **MEASURE.** Dash the bitters in first. In your jigger, measure the curaçao. Normally I would tell you to aim for a clean, zero-meniscus pour here to keep the balance of the drink as precise as possible, but I'm calling for a bold ½ ounce pour instead, because I like a bit of extra sweetness to buffer the rums in this cocktail. (More on bold and shy pours on page 42.) Same deal goes for the orgeat; measure boldly, so the amount of liquid in the jigger blooms above the rim just slightly. All good? Then toss in the fresh lime juice. Flip the script and in the big side stack your 2 ounces of rum.

● **STRAW TASTE.** To make sure all the ingredients made it into the tin. Notice how thiiiiiiick the texture is right now—that's because of the orgeat, which has protein and fat from the nuts. The texture will settle down after it encounters enough ice melt. The ice will also eat up some of the sugar and dry out its extreme round edges, so don't worry about how intensely sweet the drink tastes right now as well. This is all normal.

● **SHAKE.** Get 2 ounces of crushed ice, toss it in the shaker, and Whip Shake (page 46). You do this just to lend a kiss of chill to the contents of the tin, so the cocktail doesn't melt all the ice in the glass when the two meet. Shake until you can't hear the pebbles bouncing around inside the tin anymore.

● **TASTE, ADJUST, AND ROLL.** The texture of the orgeat should feel less overwhelming than it did on the first straw taste, but still intense, because as this drink sits on crushed ice the sweetness will fade. If your rums aren't clicking with the other ingredients seamlessly, you could add a dash of Angostura to help connect the dots. I don't know the science behind why bitters help tie disparate ingredients together, but I am so grateful they do. Fill your Mai Tai glass three-quarters of the way full of crushed ice, then roll the contents of your tin gently into the glass. Add more ice to make it pretty, if you please.

● **GARNISH.** Let's hit the gas on our one-two punch of aromatic flourish. Grab your mint sprigs and your straw. Hold the straw horizontally about 1 inch above the ice. Spank the straw with the mint. This motion will send a shower of invisible mint oils onto the surface of the drink. Use the straw to make a divot in the ice for the mint bouquet and then insert the straw next to the mint for best aroma. Express the oils of your orange peel over the top of the drink and insert the peel next to the mint plume.

One fun thing modern barkeeps do with orgeat is look beyond the almond for new flavor horizons. I've had dazzling Mai Tais made with orgeat that swap in pistachios, or cashews, or sunflower seeds— even birdseed! Yes, that happened once. It was a bit weird. The point is, you can fiddle around with your orgeat base if you want to bring something subtle and different to the cocktail. Just sub in your nut of choice to the recipe on page 31.

MANHATTAN

A hearty handshake to seal a good deal

It is impossible to say there is one Queen of cocktails, one drink that reigns above all others. Most folks with a can of PBR to their head and an uncapped Bic pen in their fist would probably blurt out MARTINI, but there is also an argument to be made for a Manhattan. When you really take your time with a round, the cocktail opens like a Kansas highway, every sip becoming more breathtaking as time leaves its fingerprints on the glass. It is also the quintessential comfort drink. One that's complex and enjoyable, without the attitude. A profound cocktail, served with little fuss.

Serve:
Stirred, up

Tools:
Jigger, mixing glass, barspoon, Julep strainer, paring knife

Glass:
Coupe, chilled

Garnish:
Luxardo maraschino cherry, lemon or orange disk

RIYL:
Bijou (page 85), Mint Julep (page 213), Vieux Carré (page 301)

SPEC

Rye whiskey	. . . .	1.0 oz
Bourbon whiskey	. . . .	1.0 oz
First sweet vermouth	. . . .	.50 oz
Second sweet vermouth	. . . .	.50 oz
Angostura bitters	. . . .	2 dashes

OUR APPROACH

My modern Manhattan is the ultimate lesson in stacking ingredients, which is when you get to play with different expressions of the same spirit and the ratios in which they come together, to create a more complex version of the original drink without really changing the spec itself. In this case, you choose the brands you want to work with. Just keep the booze at 2 ounces, the vermouths at 1 ounce in total, and go with your gut. Taste all four of your ingredients before you mix, so your memory of them is as fresh as your vermouth, then decide how much of each you want in the mix. Play in the shadows—this balancing act of a little more of this-vs.-that can help you dial in a completely unique spec that only you can re-create. It's not always a precise science. Sometimes it's more like getting a recipe from your grandmother who never picked up a measuring cup or a set of tablespoons or teaspoons. Like adding five cloves of garlic to a marinara instead of two. The magic lies in the finesse and your intuition.

CHOOSE YOUR INGREDIENTS

A Manhattan is like a steak doused with pan sauce—the purpose of the sauce is to complement and showcase the protein with a chorus of complex accompanying characters: herbs and garlic, red wine and maybe a bit of brandy, butter, and more butter, then a bit more butter. What you end up with is a simple dish so delicious, it's iconic. In the cocktail, this is all about putting the whiskey on a pedestal and getting the vermouth and the bitters to maypole around it. To get started, pick ingredients that have qualities you enjoy the most. Rye is dry, bourbon a touch sweeter. Both have vanilla and baking spice notes. High-proof whiskey will bring a heftier punch to the mix, whereas an 80-proof will settle in faster. Then figure out which vermouth is going to shimmy up to the whiskey in a pleasing way. Carpano Antica sweet vermouth WOWS me with its thick texture and studious vanilla notes—it works splendiferously with high-proof whiskeys that need a bold counterpart. Cocchi di Torino, on the other hand, has a lighter body and big jammy cherry flavors, so it softens the rough edges of a raggedy rye. Dolin has dusty dried herb undercurrents, which can buff up a bourbon in no time.

● PREP THE GARNISH. Ideally, your cocktail cherries are in a cold place, so you don't warm up the drink when you plop one into the glass. This isn't mandatory; I have cried havoc and let loose the dogs of war about my disdain for room-temperature olives in a Martini, but a room-temp cherry doesn't mess with the narrative arc of a Manhattan as much, because sweet vermouth and whiskey tend to taste better together as they warm, instead of worse. You can get away with it if you really want to. Pick out a good-looking cherry and set aside for later. Then cut a disk of lemon or orange using a paring knife. I like orange peel in the colder months because it tricks the mind into thinking the drink tastes lusher and sweeter. Lemon creates the perception of dryness, which I dig juxtaposed against the richness of whiskey and vermouth in the summer. A little flutter of sunshine is a super-cool sleight of hand. Set the disk aside for later.

● MEASURE. Fill the mixing glass three-quarters of the way with ice, then add the bitters. I like to dash them down the side of the glass, so they don't sit on top of the ice where they'll stay disjointed from the other ingredients. You need your first straw tasting to be fully informed, so the bitters need to be fused to the other liquids. Add the business part of the cocktail next. Stack the vermouths first, then the whiskeys. Do not go into the positive meniscus. Balance is in the micro-details.

● STRAW TASTE. Give the contents of the mixing glass a quick stir to make sure they're all incorporated, then straw taste to make sure everything is in the glass.

● STIR. Give the cocktail a good Coupe Stir (page 47) until the ice has settled well into the liquid. If you're new to this, straw taste occasionally to see how the drink sighs into place as it dilutes. The more attention you pay to the way a drink comes into balance as it absorbs water content from the ice, the more your palate will sharpen, and your technique will blossom. For my Manhattans and Martinis, I tend to stir until it looks like the volume of liquid in the mixing glass has almost doubled.

● TASTE, ADJUST, AND STRAIN. At this point you want to be looking at texture, temperature, and balance. IGNORE FLAVOR. Instead, ask yourself: How boozy is it? If it's tasting a bit wimpy, add another dash of bitters. Too harsh? Stir longer. Is it cold enough? I find that picturing the previous state of the drink (i.e., the first straw taste) is helpful as I ask myself these questions. Once it's tasting good to you—strong enough to stay cold enough for a while but not a murderous stab of booze—strain into your coupe.

● GARNISH. First, skewer the cherry. Then express the oils of your citrus disk of choice over the top and discard.

Adding a bit of your favorite amaro into the ratio of aromatized wine will make this drink pop. (Some intrepid barkeeps have been known to eliminate the vermouth altogether in favor of Averna, which is called a Black Manhattan.) Wanna make a Perfect Manhattan? Divide the sweet vermouth 50/50 with dry vermouth. Another relative, the Rob Roy, features Scotch. And the Boothby, by addition of a bit of effervescence, makes the Manhattan a cocktail that would laugh giddily on a carousel, ignoring the brass ring. You can find our ratios for some of these on the following pages.

MANHATTAN FRIENDS & FAMILY

German architect Mies van der Rohe argued that "less is more" when it comes to designing timeless buildings, and while that sentiment also applies to the classic Manhattan, restrained tweaks to the standard ratio have yet to ruin the integrity of the drink. When exploring these variations—both modern and vintage—use the same mixing techniques we lay out in the Manhattan session at large, then bask in the glory of how the three ingredients come together to create something more wondrous than the sums of their parts. And don't forget the garnish! A Manhattan without a citrus garnish is as unbalanced as a two-legged stool. With that bright flare of oil to balance out the drink's depths, the cocktail becomes downright poetic.

BLACK MANHATTAN

The invention of Bourbon & Branch bartender Todd Smith, back in 2005. To me, it's like an Espresso Martini, both in metaphor and simile. I often make this drink for people's first Manhattan experience, because it, somewhat improbably, feels gentler and more comforting than the sweet vermouth version.

Rye whiskey	2.0 oz
Averna	1.0 oz
Angostura bitters	1 dash
Bittercube orange bitters	2 dashes

Serve: Stirred, up
Glass: Nick & Nora, chilled
Garnish: Cherry, orange disk

BOBBY BURNS

If you want a Vieux Carré in a kilt, this is for you. It takes a brave heart (I know, I KNOW, different Scottish guy) to make this with Islay Scotch. If you want to soften its brutishness a touch, sneaking in a bit of Highland is your prerogative.

Blended Scotch	2.0 oz
Sweet vermouth	1.0 oz
Bénédictine	.25 oz
Regans' orange bitters	1 dash

Serve: Stirred, up
Glass: Nick & Nora, chilled
Garnish: Lemon pigtail

BOOTHBY COCKTAIL

You don't need a celebration to add bubbles to your Manhattan—this is a great tipple for work-a-day imbibing, too. The sparkling wine does a great job of stretching out a spirituous drink without taking its chutzpah. This recipe comes from Robert Simonson's book *The Encyclopedia of Cocktails*. Mazel.

Bottled-in-Bond rye whiskey	2.0 oz
Sweet vermouth	1.0 oz
Angostura bitters	3 dashes
Prosecco	1 to 2 oz

Serve: Stirred, up
Glass: Coupe, chilled
Garnish: Lemon peel, Luxardo maraschino cherry

BROOKLYN

There is a reason why the "dry" Manhattan isn't as iconic as the classic version—the latter rose higher in the ranks of popularity over the years because sweet vermouth rolls out the rough edges of the whiskey, whereas dry vermouth tends to scuffle with the spirit. The Brooklyn works because the dry vermouth and intense amaro (you can use Ramazzotti if you can't find Picon) combine to kind of create their own version of sweet vermouth; there's enough sugar and complexity in that combo to complement the whiskey.

Rye whiskey	2.0 oz
Dry vermouth	.75 oz
Amer Picon	.25 oz
Maraska liqueur	.25 oz
Orange bitters	3 dashes

Serve: Stirred, up
Glass: Nick & Nora, chilled
Garnish: Lemon pigtail

CREOLE COCKTAIL

Everyone seems to have their own hot take on this very old New Orleans classic. This is the "family-friendly" version that Emma served at her NOLA wedding—the way the orange notes of the Ramazzotti (you can use Amer Picon if you can find it) sync up with the dusty herbs in the Bénédictine makes it a real stunner.

Bourbon	2.0 oz
Carpano Antica sweet vermouth	.75 oz
Ramazzotti amaro	.50 oz
Bénédictine	.25 oz

Serve: Stirred, up, or stirred, large cube
Glass: Coupe or DOF, chilled
Garnish: Orange peel, Luxardo maraschino cherry

LITTLE ITALY

Audrey Saunders, in her infinite genius, created this beauty in addition to her other modern classics in this book (see Old Cuban on page 237). The drink has ragged edges, like the rocky cliffs of a gorge. Instead of sweet vermouth, I like using Punt e Mes because it adds some surprising chocolate bittersweet notes. So fucking good.

Bottled-in-Bond rye whiskey	2.0 oz
Punt e Mes	1.0 oz
Cynar	.50 oz

Serve: Stirred, up, or stirred, large cube
Glass: Coupe or DOF, chilled
Garnish: Lemon peel, Luxardo maraschino cherry

RED HOOK

Created by bartender Enzo Errico at Milk & Honey in NYC back in the heyday of this cocktail revival thing, the Red Hook tastes kind of like a whiskey-fueled version of the Martinez. If you don't like maraschino liqueur very much, either find another drink to make or lower the measure to ⅛ ounce (about halfway toward the ¼-ounce mark of the jigger) and bump a barspoon of Demerara syrup into the mix to keep the texture nice and sexy.

Bottled-in-Bond rye whiskey	2.0 oz
Punt e Mes	1.0 oz
Luxardo maraschino liqueur	.25 oz

Serve: Stirred, up
Glass: Nick & Nora, chilled
Garnish: Orange peel, Luxardo maraschino cherry

ROB ROY

This cocktail and the Bobby Burns are fun ones to make side by side to see how the smallest of changes in a drink make a massive difference in its flavor. Of the two drinks, the Rob Roy skews closer to the original Manhattan recipe—think of it as the smoky uncle in the schema of the classic's family tree.

Blended Scotch	2.0 oz
Sweet vermouth	1.0 oz
Angostura bitters	3 dashes

Serve: Stirred, up
Glass: Nick & Nora, chilled
Garnish: Orange peel, Luxardo maraschino cherry

TORONTO

Canadian whisky and maple syrup are a perfect example of how "what grows together goes together." The fernet's brightness shines through the combo like a sled dog's eyes at night. Need I say more?

Canadian rye whisky	1.75 oz
Fernet-Branca	.25 oz
Maple syrup	.25 oz
Angostura bitters	3 dashes

Serve: Stirred, up
Glass: Coupe, chilled
Garnish: Orange peel, Luxardo maraschino cherry

HER.

MARGARITA

Like jumping into a cool
Texas swimming hole

You probably don't need me to tell you how the Margarita is one of the most fan-fucking-tastic cocktails ever created. The Prom King of tequila drinks. Satisfying in the morning, noon, or night. Delicious when served in coupes with high-class, traditionally crafted agave spirits in cold cocktail bars made with bottom-shelf triple sec, on the rocks at casual neighborhood taquerias along-side bottomless chips and salsa, or blended to a brain-freeze chill and served alongside melt-in-your-mouth brisket. All of these versions do the spec justice. And I hold fast to the point that it's the only classic cocktail that works well with food. Margaritas and tacos go together like sherry and jamón. Like shepherd's pie and Guinness. Like sashimi and nihonshu! One just begs for the other.

Serve:
Shaken,
on the rocks

Tools:
Jigger, shaker,
offset serrated
knife, Hawthorne
strainer

Glass:
Double Old
Fashioned, chilled

Garnish:
Half salt rim,
lime wheel
(optional)

RIYL:
Airmail
(page 61),
Last Word
(page 185),
Paloma
(page 245)

SPEC

Tequila blanco	1.5 oz
Mezcal	.50 oz
Fresh lime juice	.75 oz
Simple syrup (page 29)	.75 oz

OUR APPROACH

We're going with Emma's favorite spec here. It takes inspiration from the Tommy's Margarita, which features agave nectar instead of curaçao, so the spirits in the glass shine brightest. Most commercially available agave nectar options are not great quality (to give you the short version), though, so she uses simple syrup instead for better quality control and consistency. She also sneaks a little mezcal into the build—not too much, because the good stuff is hard to come by and expensive to boot—to give the drink a studied nonchalance. Served on the rocks, it's like the Margarita we all know and love, just with a shimmering new architecture.

CHOOSE YOUR INGREDIENTS

Spirits-wise, Emma likes to split-base with two types of agave, ideally ones that are made in line with traditional heritage practices that cost more than 30-ish bucks; if a bottle costs less than that, chances are some contract worker in the supply chain is getting paid subpar pesos for long hours of grueling physical labor. For the tequila, her everyday picks are Siete Leguas, Tapatio, and El Tesoro, because they all have digestible price points and offer a wellspring of complexity. If she's feeling fancy or needs a spiritual pick-me-up, she might use a bit of Tequila Ocho or Cascahuín instead. Always blanco, because wood-aging covers up all the gorgeous herbaceous and vegetal notes of the agave, and those qualities should shine bright in a marg. For the mezcal, something with a brawny attitude and good structure punches up the complexity of the drink. Try Banhez or Tosba as solid beginner options.

HOW TO MIX

● **PREP YOUR GARNISH.** Because there's so much going on in the glass aromatically, the Margarita doesn't need an aromatic garnish like many other cocktails do. You could add a lime wheel if you want a little flourish; if so, cut a nice thin slice right now, with a notch etched into the wheel so it'll stand upright on the rim of the glass. A floating lime wheel does nothing but impede the drinking process. Most people also opt for a salted rim, because a little lick of saline in between sips is akin to catching the perfect breeze on a hot summer's day in the middle of the desert. BUT most people overdo this—instead of smothering the glass in salt, only prepare half the rim so the drinker can have the option of enjoying that extra layer of flavor experience or not. Plain old sea salt—find one that's coarse like brown sugar instead of flaky like Maldon—is a solid everyday pick. Try sal de gusano (worm salt), Tajín, or celery salt mixed with coarse sea salt, for fancy occasions. To rim: Run a lime wedge or wheel around half the rim, then dip that rim in salt. Do this now so the salt has a chance to dry as you mix the drink.

- **MEASURE.** A Margarita should come together as easy as homemade queso made with Velveeta. Add the simple syrup to the shaker tin, followed by the lime juice. You really want to keep these two right at the lip with no positive meniscus because there are so few ingredients in this drink, even a tiny twist over or under can impact your balance. Stack your spirits for precision.

- **STRAW TASTE.** To make sure everything is in the tin. I know, it sounds dumb, but TRUST. Forgetting to put an ingredient in the tin is as common as a mixologist correcting you when you say mezcal is tequila's smoky cousin.

- **SHAKE.** The quality of this cocktail—like all sours—hinges entirely on getting enough dilution in play to keep the citrus, spirit, and sugar in alignment. Ice your shaker with 5 cubes and Rocks Shake (page 46) it with a pace of the early punks like The Clash and the Sex Pistols. Stop shaking when you hear the ice starting to turn to slush.

- **TASTE, ADJUST, AND STRAIN.** Stick that straw in the cocktail for a taste. Is it too dry or pointy from the lime acids? Give it a bump of simple syrup. Shake briefly again, to wake up the cocktail. Look in your shaker after you've finished shaking; if the drink doesn't look like that grand moment where the sea hits cliffside rocks, all bubbles and froth, you didn't give it enough oomph. Try again. You want that frothy liveliness! Throw some cold ice cubes into your chilled glass, then strain the cocktail in.

- **GARNISH.** If you chose to prep a lime wheel earlier, prop that up on the rim right now. If not, don't waste any time taking that first sip.

We all know Margaritas are historically a vessel for tequila, but the agave spirits category is one of the most diverse in the world—no two tequilas, mezcals, bacanoras, or raicillas will taste the same—which is why you can quickly but profoundly change the character of your Marg based entirely upon your spirits selection. Understanding that detail alone will up the ante on your Margaritas for the rest of your days. Sotol, a spirit from Northern Mexico that's made in a way like mezcal, but from the Dasylirion plant instead of agave, is another great alternative; sotol flavors can range from mushroomy and earthy to singing with bright sweetgrass. Emma is also apt to add bitters to switch up the mood: A dash or two of Scrappy's celery makes the drink screamingly herbaceous, while Bittercube Chipotle Cacao offers an earthy warmth and wink of spice. Orange bitters could be useful in bringing the orange note one might expect from orange curaçao back into play. All of these options will lock eyes with agave spirits and lime with gusto.

MARTINI

*A glistening glass of
golden gumption*

It's impossible to imagine a world without the Martini. It is arguably the most classic classic of all time—a drink of such mythical status, and so woven into our culture, that the universal symbol for a bar is often a martini glass. The cocktail has endured countless shifts in what's considered fashionable since its invention. You want it up? On the rocks? 50/50? 2:1? Twist or no twist? You are the boss. When I first started bartending, the call was shaken with vodka, don't even think vermouth, and add as many olives as possible. If you had blue cheese–stuffed ones, all the better. Everyone wanted it cold as a winter night in Siberia, with slush floating on top. Now trends skew closer back to the drink's original form: a glowing glass of frosty gin, supported by bracing dry vermouth, a few dashes of bitters, and a proper garnish. It's elegant. Sophisticated. Timeless. That's the vision we're chasing in this session, albeit with a few touches that make it really pleasing to my palate.

Serve:
Stirred, up

Tools:
Jigger, mixing glass, barspoon, Julep strainer, channel knife, or paring knife

Glass:
Coupe, chilled

Garnish:
Lemon pigtail or grapefruit disk

RIYL:
Bamboo (page 77), Corpse Reviver #2 (page 113), Ramos Gin Fizz (page 273)

Navy Strength gin	2.0 oz
Blanc vermouth	1.0 oz
Grapefruit bitters	2 dashes

OUR APPROACH

I like boozy, sweet drinks. That shouldn't come as a surprise to anyone. Also, I like gin to a ridiculous degree. So, my superlative Martini harnesses the spirit of these two things and ties them up in a big car-size bow. It's BIG and wily and verbose. Not quite a "beginner's" Martini, but definitely a memorable one. The first thing I do is upgrade 80-proof gin to a high-proof one that would test the mettle of sailors in the Royal British Navy. At over 100-proof, gunpowder will literally light up if soaked with this liquid. From there, I swap in a blanc vermouth for dry. Blanc doesn't seem to ever get the attention it deserves in the martini conversation—dry and extra dry always suck the air out of the room—but I love blanc vermouth because it's swankier in its texture. It's so good, I'll happily drink Dolin blanc on the rocks with a twist, everywhere, anytime. Finally, grapefruit bitters splash into the mix instead of orange, because they add an unexpected point of interest while connecting the dots between the gin and vermouth.

CHOOSE YOUR INGREDIENTS

Figuring out your preferred gin and vermouth combo will take practice, like finding a life partner, or the right tattoo artist. I like Perry's Tot from New York Distilling Company, followed by Hayman's Royal Dock. Both are great options that will cure the boredom and trepidation of a life before the mast. You might prefer the brash juniper-ness of something lower-proof like Beefeater, whereas other styles like Plymouth or New Western open Pandora's box of new flavor adventures. Try lots of different gins and see which one gives you a wink and a nod. For the vermouth, I mentioned I like Dolin blanc for this, but Emma likes to split Dolin blanc with Dolin dry for a nice mix-and-match of dusty herbaceous notes and softly sweet floral ones. You could probably try a different combination of glassmates every day for the rest of your life and discover something new every time. It's a wonderful endless journey where there are no right or wrong answers because at the end of every session, you've at the very least had a pretty tasty glass of dopamine.

- **PREP THE GARNISH.** Choose which citrus you want to use: A lemon pigtail is traditional and will brighten up the contents of the glass in a singsong-y way, but I also like the way the shiny musk of grapefruit oils echoes the bitters in the build. If you're using a lemon pigtail, grab your channel knife and lemon and set aside for later, because you'll add this at the very end. If you choose grapefruit disk, cut a nice thick one now and set aside.

- **MEASURE.** Start by filling the mixing glass three-quarters of the way full with ice, then slide the bitters down the sides of the cubes so they will fuse thoroughly into the liquid when you start stirring. Gently contribute the blanc vermouth, then the gin. With only three ingredients coming together, it's of the utmost importance that your measurements be precise as hell. Be surgical about it. Give this mix a quick stir to get all of the ingredients cohesive before the first straw taste.

- **STRAW TASTE.** To make sure everything is in the glass.

- **STIR.** A technically proficient Martini is all about creating the right texture and temperature. The drink should bear an exquisite opulence with a toothsome chill. To get to that point it takes more than good technique—it takes a ritual as enigmatic and complicated as Sunday Catholic Mass. You can slam together a jack and Coke; you *finesse* a Martini with a practiced stir (never shake) to get its components to align and become something bigger and more impressive than its list of ingredients. Revisit how to do a Coupe Stir (page 47) and get stirring. Straw taste as you go, to see how the ingredients relax and align as cold water enters the mix. Don't flail about or you will chip the ice. If you start with 3 ounces of components, by the time you are done stirring you should have a 6-ish-ounce Martini.

- **TASTE, ADJUST, AND STRAIN.** Taste. Does the temperature make your teeth chatter yet? If not, keep stirring. Stir and stir until the gin has melted together with the vermouth and the bitters whisper; it should be bracing and elegant at the same time. Strain. Don't showboat this movement from on high because that will introduce unwanted bubbles. Instead, deftly pour its ribbons into the frosty coupe with gentle grace.

- **GARNISH.** Lemon oils spritzed above a Martini's viscous body maintains harmony in all respects. If you love this idea, grab the lemon and hold it about 6 inches above the cocktail, then pull a long, winding ribbon of skin off with a channel knife. This should send sunny oils cascading over the surface of the drink. Wind up the pigtail and place it on the side of the glass. If you choose to garnish with grapefruit oils to add a fresh shade of grapefruit aroma to the subdued grapefruit flavor of the bitters, hold the disk with the skin side facing the drink, pinch it to let the oils fly free over the cocktail, then disk-card the disk.

The thing about the Martini is that there are a thousand ways to personalize the cocktail. The gin choice, the vermouth choice, how you split-base one or both ingredients, the aromatics, the garnish—the sky's the limit. Have a look at the Martini family tree on the next pages for more specific ideas. I personally like to make Martinis in batches and keep them in the freezer, so I've got a bottle available at a moment's notice. My "Freezer-Door Martini" is 25 ounces of gin (about one 750ml bottle), plus just shy of 7 ounces of vermouth, and a bit more than 1 ounce of water, plus ½ ounce of orange bitters. Put it all in a 1-liter bottle and store in the freezer, at least for one night, before pouring into an ice-cold glass. Garnish with a lemon twist.

MARTINI FRIENDS & FAMILY

The Martini has evolved in all sorts of directions since the drink was first invented, but ask any modern barkeep worth their salt for a definition and the smart ones will hold firm that the drink must contain gin and vermouth, plus bitters. (Okay, sometimes vodka, but that's called a Vodka Martini, like if you order a hamburger made with turkey it's not a hamburger anymore.) Sometimes there's a secondary modifier in the mix, like a liqueur, but that can't be the main ingredient. (To this end, the Espresso Martini [page 137] and Porn Star Martini [page 265] are delicious, but they aren't true Martinis.) As one of the most customizable cocktails in the canon, there's no right or wrong ratio with the Martini variations that follow—the most important thing is that the drink be calibrated to your liking. The specs in this collection are calibrated to ours. Use the mixing instructions presented in the main Martini sesh as your main squeeze guide for how to mix the following recipes.

ALASKA

Chartreuse bears all the same complexity and sweetness as a good vermouth, which makes this outlier a honeyed marvel. Many specs feature an entire ounce of yellow Chartreuse, but that can be a cloying combo for modern palates. With less Chartreuse in the mix, and a little blanc vermouth in play to keep balance intact, this is a dignified and fashionable take on the original, perfect for palates that skew dry.

London dry gin	. . . .	1.5 oz
Old Tom gin	. . . .	.50 oz
Yellow Chartreuse	. . . .	.25 oz
Dolin blanc vermouth	. . . .	.25 oz
Bittercube orange bitters	. . . . . .	3 dashes

Serve: Stirred, up
Glass: Nick & Nora, chilled
Garnish: Orange disk

DIRTY MARTINI

Sometimes you want something that's not citrusy, bubbly, bitter, or a slug of booze. The landscape for savory cocktails is sparse, though, so I understand that the Dirty Martini fills a need. You could think about it like a minimalist Bloody Mary, I guess. Great for if you are a reincarnated deer who misses salt licks.

Vodka	. . . .	2.0 oz
Olive brine	. . . .	.50 oz

Serve: Stirred, up
Glass: V-shaped Martini glass, chilled
Garnish: Lemon pigtail, 3 olives

FITTY-FITTY

Martinis aren't meant to be sessionable; just ask Dorothy Parker. But this witty little ditty—born in the hallowed halls of Pegu Club—is one you can have more than two of, because the gin portion is dialed down and the vermouth dialed up. Pure, balanced genius on the part of its creator, Audrey Saunders.

Tanqueray gin	. . . .	1.5 oz
Noilly Prat extra-dry vermouth	. . . .	1.5 oz
Orange bitters	. . . .	2 dashes

Serve: Stirred, up
Glass: Coupe, chilled
Garnish: Lemon peel

GIBSON

If you're the kind of Martini drinker who tends to skew toward the classic dry gin style but has enough self-confidence to unabashedly revel in the occasional round of Dirty Martinis, the Gibson might be the Bonnie to your Clyde. The pickling vinegar used to make the cocktail onion—the traditional accoutrement—adds a lively aspect to the drink, similar to the salty savory brine of an olive, but with more pizzazz. There's nothing wrong with a messy Dirty Martini, but the Gibson is a more sophisticated call. This version is a Sasha Petraske recipe from the John Dory Oyster Bar when it was the bar at the Ace Hotel in NYC. I love how he sidesteps the traditional pickled onion and reaches for a spring onion or ramp instead. Gently muddle the spring onion in the bottom of the mixing glass before adding the vermouth and gin, and garnish with a second onion.

Gin	. . . .	2.0 oz
Dry vermouth	. . . .	1.0 oz
Spring onion or ramp, to muddle		

Serve: Stirred, up
Glass: Coupe, chilled
Garnish: Cold spring onion bulb

GIN BLOSSOM

Invented by the magnificent Julie Reiner of Clover Club in Brooklyn, this modern classic teeters on the edge of not being a Martini, because of the inclusion of eau-de-vie. But Toby loves this drink, and he is the captain now. This is her spec for the drink—just be sure you use apricot eau-de-vie and not sweetened apricot brandy—an easy mistake to make if you aren't paying close attention—because the devil is in the details.

Plymouth gin	1.5 oz
Martini & Rossi bianco vermouth	1.5 oz
Apricot eau-de-vie	.75 oz
Orange bitters	2 dashes

Serve: Stirred, up
Glass: Nick & Nora, chilled
Garnish: Orange disk

HANKY PANKY

Adding amaro to a Martini is an epic middle finger to tradition, which makes this drink even more audacious when you consider it was invented by Ada Coleman at the American Bar at the Savoy at the turn of the twentieth century. Today it's no less fierce, thanks to that cheeky dose of Fernet-Branca. Kinda like drinking and brushing your teeth at the same time, that little nip of bitter chocolate and mint notes from the amaro is a great way to start the day.

London dry gin	2.0 oz
Cinzano sweet vermouth	1.0 oz
Fernet-Branca	.125 oz
(about halfway toward the .25-ounce mark of the jigger)	
Bittercube orange bitters	3 dashes

Serve: Stirred, up
Glass: Nick & Nora, chilled
Garnish: Orange disk

MARTINEZ

Historian types will tell you this recipe came before the dry gin Martini. That's worth knowing because the drink was traditionally made with Old Tom gin. For modern palates, that combo skews a bit too sweet, so to pull it into this century, we recommend splitting the Old Tom with something sharper, like Fords. We also ditch the Angostura, because it makes the drink taste more like a gin Manhattan, which is weird. When the right ratios come into play, it's like a Martini that has done a somersault and gets up grinning with grass in its hair.

London dry gin	.75 oz
Old Tom gin	.75 oz
Sweet vermouth	1.5 oz

Luxardo maraschino liqueur	.125 oz
(about halfway toward the .25-ounce mark of the jigger)	
Orange bitters	1 dash

Serve: Stirred, up
Glass: Nick & Nora, chilled
Garnish: Lemon pigtail

TUXEDO #2

If the Martinez is too rich, and it's too early for a Brooklyn (page 198), this threads the needle between the two. Think of it like a Fifty-Fifty with a bit of ripe fruit in the mix.

London dry gin	1.0 oz
Noilly Prat dry vermouth	1.0 oz
Luxardo maraschino liqueur	.125 oz
(about halfway toward the .25-ounce mark of the jigger)	
Bittercube orange bitters	3 dashes

Serve: Stirred, up
Glass: Nick & Nora, chilled
Garnish: Lemon pigtail, spray of absinthe

VESPER

One of the most notorious Martinis of all time, thanks to the famous words uttered by James Bond. I'll say that Ian Fleming was a wonderful author, but a crappy mixologist. The drink shouldn't be shaken. I like to think of this spec as what Dashiell Hammet would have created. If you've got lemon bitters on hand, try those instead of orange—it turns the lights up on the brightness of the Cocchi.

Navy Strength gin	1.5 oz
Vodka	.50 oz
Cocchi Americano	.50 oz
Orange bitters	1 dash

Serve: Stirred, up
Glass: Nick & Nora, chilled
Garnish: Lemon pigtail

MINT JULEP

Derby bound and feeling soigné

I have a love-hate relationship with this cocktail. It took me a long time to realize it's just an Old Fashioned on crushed ice, which made me like it more than before, but probably not enough to favor one over a Whiskey Smash. I do see its virtues as a good "dressing drink," though, as a Brooklyn roommate once described it. He hailed from well below the Mason-Dixon line, and his mother would always have a leisurely sipper while selecting an ensemble for the evening, putting on makeup, finding the right brooch, doing her hair, and so on. Because it's swizzled with crushed ice down to below zero, served in a metal tin so that it melts very slowly, it should absolutely sit on a glass coaster in a boudoir while you "put your face on."

Serve:
Built in the glass,
on crushed ice

Tools:
Jigger,
swizzle stick,
Julep strainer

Glass:
Julep cup

Garnish:
Mint

RIYL:
French 75
(page 141),
Old Cuban
(page 237),
Stinger (page 293)

SPEC

Whiskey	2.0 oz
Demerara syrup (page 29)	.25 oz
Angostura bitters	1 dash

OUR APPROACH

For this version of the Julep, we're aiming for a spirit-forward cocktail with a light cloak of fresh mint flavor and a sharp, complex backbone that doesn't wimp out over crushed ice too quickly. To achieve this, we deviate ever so slightly from the original build by adding bitters and changing the traditional choice of simple syrup to Dem. My rule is if the spirit is clear, use simple syrup; if it's aged, use Demerara syrup, because Dem is darker and richer, which aligns righteously with the wood and vanilla notes of spirits like whiskey and Cognac and rum. Why the bitters? The inspiration for this came from a story I heard many years ago, when I was in my cups, three sheets to the wind. It goes: A guy making whiskey in Tennessee used to make his Juleps with tansy root instead of mint, which is decidedly more bitter than spearmint. I was intrigued by how the mint does the double-duty of adding freshness *and* bitterness. So since then I've thrown some Ango in my Juleps to get that extra bit of complexity. I find it really ties things up properly. I'm also switching up the traditional technique in this session, using a Caribbean swizzle to create proper water content and get the cocktail cold as the Cherokee Park Holler in January. Done right, there will be a frighteningly cold sheet of ice on the outside of the tin when you are done. This is a good thing.

CHOOSE YOUR INGREDIENTS

Bourbon is a common A-list selection for a Mint Julep, and while I get that—it has a nice big texture that holds up well on ice—I like a gentler wheat-forward whiskey in mine because it has more of that Southern drawl effect. It vibrates at a frequency that's lovely, low and slow. With all cocktails, I start with the good stuff first because after a couple of rounds your palate isn't as sharp as it was before you started, and you can get away with drinking something cheaper. For this drink, maybe start with the Weller 12-year, then move on to something like Old Fitzgerald 80-proof, or Maker's Mark. All dignified selections.

HOW TO MIX

• **PREP THE JULEP CUP AND GARNISH.** You want to use mint as fresh as possible, which is a somewhat relative concept—I've had mint that had been picked in Israel and shipped to Minnesota, so I don't think it needs to be picked and used immediately. But once you have it, mint doesn't like to be super cold, so I wrap it in a clean cotton towel and then put it in a zip-seal bag and keep it in the warmest part of the fridge. Gather an obnoxious amount of mint, like 20 leaves, off the stem. Insert them into the Julep cup, but DO NOT MUDDLE THEM. Instead, you are going to use a cocktail spoon to pull the mint up the sides, rubbing the oils all over everything to get their aroma into the mix. (Read more about the Sasha Petraske mint method in the Mint and Measure section of the Queen's Park Swizzle sesh on page 271.) Gently tamp the mint down at the bottom of the glass, just to soften it a bit. Gather a second bouquet of mint and set aside for garnish.

● **MEASURE.** A Julep cannot be rushed. A Julep takes a while to make, and a while to drink. Get this tempo in your head before you do anything else. In fact, put on "Georgia" by Ray Charles, or "Summertime" by Ella Fitzgerald, to get in the right frame of mind. Then, to your prepared Julep cup, add the bitters, followed by the Demerara syrup and the whiskey. Give it a gentle stir, say something Southern like "well shucks, aren't you just as pretty as an Easter bonnet." Walk away. Come back after 3 to 5 minutes. The alcohol in the whiskey will have pulled the flavor from the oil in the mint during this marinating time.

● **SWIZZLE.** Add crushed ice about one-third of the way up. Stick the swizzle stick into the ice so that it hovers just above any mint on the bottom of the Julep cup: Place the shaft of the stick between your palms with your hands in prayer mode. Now rub your hands together, like you are plotting an evil scheme. Move your hands up and down a bit as you do this, making sure you are churning all the ice in the glass. You don't have to go crazy; you just want to get the first blast of water and chill into the liquid. Gently pull the stick out of the glass. Walk away for another few minutes, so the drink takes on some of the slush from the ice.

● **TASTE AND ADJUST.** Give it a straw taste—if it's too dry for you, now is the time to add another ¼ ounce of Demerara syrup and swizzle again to incorporate. The cocktail will dilute further over the mountain of crushed ice, so for me, at this moment, I want the whiskey to stand confidently at the forefront of the drink, with the bitters adding just a suspicion of baking spice. If you need to top off with a touch more whiskey in this moment, I'm giving you permission to do so now. Got it where you like it? Add a final mound of crushed ice; I like using a Julep strainer for this, because it creates a lovely dome that prevents your hot hand from melting the ice.

● **GARNISH.** A huge mint bouquet is best. You want the mint to overwhelm the senses, in a good way, before sweet whiskey hits the palate. Stick it in the ice, near the rim of the glass. Now, you need a straw. You will probably have to cut a 7½-inch one down a bit or use one of your cool short metal ones.

Play with bitter alternatives: I like a dash of the Bittercube Cherry Bark bitters as I find the big juicy cherry flavor bounces off the mint beautifully. Their Root Beer bitters also do a very interesting thing because wintergreen, a mint flavor, is part of the "root beer flavor compound," adding a spearmint note that dovetails with the fresh mint so nicely. If you've only had access to basic grocery store mint—no harm, no foul—I'm going to give you a super-cool tip here: Just as with other types of herbs, mint comes in many different varieties, each with its own slightly different flavor personality. So, if you want to get super geeky with your personalized Mint Julep, seek out some pineapple mint or chocolate mint for the garnish—the former, as its name suggests, does have a bit of a fruity note, while the latter nails that after-dinner mint vibe.

MOJITO

For sparkling conversations
under late-summer skies

There was a point at the dark depths of the '90s when the Mojito was so popular people ordered it everywhere—restaurant bars and dive bars and beach bars and hotel bars and nightclubs—literally no bartender was spared the order. There was much gnashing of teeth and rending of garments as the trend ramped up, because the drink took longer to make than a Long Island Iced Tea, and we often got stiffed on the tip. At the time, none of us were making a GOOD version, either, which is probably why it ended up earning a somewhat shitty reputation among the fancy mixologists who would follow that dark era. It makes sense, though. Very, VERY few bars had good mint or fresh lime juice back then, and most of us who didn't know any better were muddling the mint into a paste so thick and vegetal we might as well have been adding crabgrass to cocktails. Truth is, a well-made Mojito has the same prowess as a proper Tom Collins (page 297) or upscale Pimm's Cup (page 253). Seriously! When made with top-shelf rum and fresh mint, it's a tall glass of "ahhhhhh, delicious."

Serve:
Shaken,
on crushed ice

Tools:
Jigger, barspoon,
shaker, Hawthorne
strainer, fine
strainer

Glass:
Collins, chilled

Garnish:
Mint, loads of it

RIYL:
Bamboo
(page 77),
Daisy de Santiago
(page 129),
Last Word
(page 185)

SPEC

White rum	2.0 oz
Fresh lime juice	.75 oz
Simple syrup (page 29)	.75 oz
Sparkling water, to bottom	4 to 5 oz

OUR APPROACH

One sticky summer afternoon in Chicago at The Violet Hour, we decided to see who could make a better Mojito. We set some ground rules for the competition: The mint had to be the star of the show, with the rum melting into the background. The drink needed to be long and refreshing—like walking into an air-conditioned movie theater in the middle of August—and the lime wedge was an affront to all the old, cool gods, so a new garnish had to be employed. Many rounds were made, and in the end, what we came up with is that it's impossible to add too much mint to a Mojito. It's best when you get mint in three places: dragged up the sides of the serving glass, pushed gently with your muddler in the bottom of the shaker to release the oils, letting it marinate in rum, and then a shameless, unabashed bouquet of mint, serenely thrashed, as a come-hither garnish. That's exactly what we're doing in this session. The spec is pretty standard, but we go absolutely batshit crazy with the herb.

CHOOSE YOUR INGREDIENTS

In the Mint Julep (page 213), the herb plays a secondary role to the whiskey, but the Mojito is all about how much mint flavor and aroma you can jam-pack into the glass. Because of this, I like to use a middle-of-the-road rum—something not too audacious, funky, or weird. It should be servile and attentive to the mint, so think about using something like Planteray 3-Star, which has a bit of vanilla but not so much that it shoulders its way to the front of the drink. If you want something a little more adventurous, try The Scarlet Ibis, which is dry as a fucking Bolivian desert. I recommend the latter for a winter Mojito because Ibis is aged, so you get the same drink but a different outcome—like going downhill on a mountain bike vs. on skis over fresh powder. See the Tom Collins (page 297) for my two cents on how to choose sparkling water for a cocktail, if you want—just keep the bubbles SUPER COLD for this drink, because cold bubbles keep their fizzy texture longer, which is especially important when the cocktail is served on crushed ice.

HOW TO MIX

● **PREP THE GARNISH.** Grab a ludicrously full bouquet of mint for garnish. The leaves should look nice enough to admire in a vase on your desk for a week, like a thoughtfully arranged bouquet of flowers. Set aside.

- **MINT AND MEASURE.** In your shaker tin, add an amount of mint that would get you sent to prison if it was *"hierba buena"* confiscated from your pocket at a Grateful Dead show. Now push that down to the bottom of the tin with a muddler so it's a green pillow that will soak in the liquid you are about to toss in. Don't muddle it, just use the tool to arrange the leaves. (Refer back to the Queen's Park Swizzle session on page 271 for more insight into why we follow this procedure with mint.) Add the rum. Wait a minute or two before proceeding, to give the mint oils time to bleed into the rum. Add the lime juice and the simple syrup.

- **STRAW TASTE.** Notice how intense the mint flavor is at this stage. Is it pronounced enough, or do you want even more? Remember there will be mint in your Collins glass, too.

- **BOTTOM WITH MINT AND SPARKLING WATER.** Grab your Collins glass and fill it halfway full of mint leaves. Make a little raft with them, then press on the mint GENTLY and pull it up the sides of the glass, slathering oil over every inch of the inside of the vessel. I like to do this dry; my compatriot likes to add simple syrup to the mint, so it slides more easily up and down the glass. Try both ways and decide for yourself which you prefer. Add crushed ice, three-quarters of the way up. If you need to use your spoon to move the straggling mint below the ice, do that. Now add your sparkling water. Set aside.

- **SHAKE.** Pick out 5 cubes for this Collins Shake (page 46) to take the edge off the room temperature of the ingredients and add a bit of water content to the mix, because most of your H_2O (necessary to smooth out the rough edges of the acid and booze and reduce the sweetness of the syrup) will get added to the drink when it meets the sparkling water and ice. Set a timer in the back of your mind: This shake only lasts as long as it takes for the ice to sound like it's about to turn to slush.

- **TASTE, ADJUST, AND STRAIN.** When tasting this cocktail again, it should taste almost the same before and after the shake, just a modicum colder. The sparkling water is going to eat up the alcohol and the sweetness, leaving the cocktail dry in its wake—does it need a little bump of simple syrup to accommodate this? Add it now. Be sure to double-strain into the glass, because little mint flecks will do their best to wend their way into this cocktail and, subsequently, into the crevices of your choppers. If you haven't made many of these before, nab a quick straw taste out of the glass, too, to see how it all comes together. Pay attention to how all that sparkling water really affects the rum and the sugar but doesn't dilute the lime juice as much. Add a bit more crushed ice to the top of the drink, so it peeks up above the rim just a touch.

- **GARNISH.** Add a straw and garnish with a bouquet of mint. This final minty accoutrement should look big and beautiful sticking out of the glass, the pièce de résistance! Don't be stingy with it.

There aren't many substitutions or changes that keep the focus of this cocktail on the mint, and that is what makes this drink such a superstar. Improvisations should stay simple, like a small dose of secondary rum and a tiny dash of bitters. Sometimes I split-base Mojitos with Planteray 3-Star and Batavia Arrack—a spirit distilled from sugar cane and fermented rice from Indonesia. This adds a subtle vegetal personality that works as a foil to the freshness of the mint. If you have cachaça or rhum agricole or Mexican aguardiente like Paranubes on hand, you could totally use one of those as the second-string rum instead—the point is just to bring a little note of difference to the cocktail. Finally, Angostura could be used to inject a dash of flavor that contrasts with the mint medley without imposing too much flavor.

MOSCOW MULE

A scintillating glass of ginger spice

My first thought when I see an iconic Moscow Mule mug in a bar is, "Wow, I wonder how many of those have been stolen? I hope they get them for free from a vodka company." Then I usually think I should order one, because the beads of sweat forming on the copper crust of the vessel look so frosty and refreshing. It's a great marketing gambit. But seriously, even though this lowbrow highball has come in and out of fashion since it was first invented in the 1940s—the first major wave of popularity happened in the 1950s to 1960s, the second in the 2010s—it's worth having in your arsenal because it is a perfectly good cocktail when made in a way that prioritizes balance. Ginger and lime work so well together, and the vodka is a neutral canvas for those other flavors to shine. Simple, uncomplicated refreshment at its finest. Mix one up next time you want happy thoughts without having to think too hard about it.

Serve:
Built in the glass,
on the rocks

Tools:
Jigger, barspoon,
offset serrated
knife

Glass:
Copper mug
(or Collins glass,
or footed Pilsner)

Garnish:
Lime wheel

RIYL:
Dark and Stormy
(page 133),
Gimlet (page 145),
Mojito (page 217)

SPEC

Żubrówka vodka	. . . .	2.0 oz
Fresh lime juice	. . . .	.75 oz
Angostura bitters (optional)	. . . .	1 dash
Fever-Tree ginger beer, to top	. . . .	4 to 5 oz

OUR APPROACH

Yes, the Moscow Mule's ultimate purpose is straightforward refreshment that gets your stomach warm and your heart stout. But that doesn't mean it can't be made with some integrity. At the very least, we can pick out a good-quality vodka, put the citrus juice inside the drink instead of leaving its proportions up to the whim and whimsy of the drinker (see the Cuba Libre, page 121), and cobble those things together with ginger beer in a way that resembles good technique. The one side step I'm taking here is adding one (optional) dash of bitters: the baking spice notes really amplify the ginger personality, and this drink is ALL about that ginger.

CHOOSE YOUR INGREDIENTS

Vodka is a strange thing. It is defined as tasteless and odorless, so the usual metric of "this tastes good" doesn't apply. (Different vodkas do have different textures though, see the White Russian on page 309 for more on that notion.) If I'm standing in front of a wall of vodka and for some weird reason don't have access to Google to find reviews or more information, I go by two things: Polish or Russian in origin, and a plain but sharp-looking label. If the bottle is super fancy, with etching and shaded opaques, I know that a lot of money was spent on the glass and not on the liquid inside, so I'm eschewing those. In the same manner, if it's a vodka that I see on billboards and TV commercials I figure they must pressure folks into drinking it, so I'm not going to fall for that. A good bottle of vodka should be around 20 bucks give or take. Don't get suckered into the stupid cheap stuff or fall for the ridiculously expensive stuff. For this Mule, I personally like Żubrówka from Poland, which has a cinnamon-y note from the sweetgrass blades infused into the spirit—that baking spice note cheers on the ginger with exuberance. For ginger beer tips, check out the Dark and Stormy session on page 133.

HOW TO MIX

● **PREP THE GARNISH.** I speak ad nauseam about how a lime wheel is an optional garnish for cocktails in other sessions, but with the Mule I almost always opt in. Why? I'll break it down for you. Remember how garnishes serve two purposes? To add aroma, and to make the drink look pretty? Well, a wheel will add a bit of fresh lime aroma, but not a ton, so most of the time the decision about whether to include one or not comes down to your preference about how the drink looks, and whether or not you think the wheel will be a bother while trying to drink the drink. In the case of the Mule, the lime wheel tends to end up resting on the rocks in the glass, which is easier to navigate around than it would be on the rim of a coupe, like in a Daiquiri (page 125) or Pegu Club (page 249), where it is apt to poke you in the face or fall off the glass entirely or splash into the drink and present a choking hazard. I also opt for a lime wheel here for its visual flourish. The Mule is a kinda boring, monochrome mix of shades of yellow and gold, and when you add a bright green lime wheel to the picture, that colorful contrast makes the whole package shine. Pretty drinks taste better! Prep your garnish now: Cut a lime wheel using an offset serrated knife, with a notch cut into the bottom so you can perch the wheel on the rim of the glass. Set aside.

● **MEASURE.** We're going to build this in the cold mug, or cool-looking glass, if that's what you've got handy. Ice first: Fill it up about three-quarters of the way with nice cubes. Then bitters go into the mix (these are optional, so if you aren't using them, skip straight to the next step). Add the lime juice, then measure the vodka. Your ginger beer is in the fridge and properly cold, right? Please tell me it's super cold, because super-cold carbonated beverages hold a tight fizz better than warm ones. Pour that super-cold ginger beer over the vodka, gently, because if you slosh it in there all the bubbles will break, and the texture of the drink will fizz out into oblivion. A tired, flaccid, bubble-less Mule is a crime worse than a stolen copper mug. (You could use the barspoon technique employed in the Ramos Gin Fizz session on page 275 to add the soda to the cocktail in a way that keeps the bubbles nice and crisp, if you fancy.) Give this a quick stir to incorporate all of the components.

● **TASTE AND ADJUST.** The drink should taste pretty good! I rarely adjust anything at this stage, but admittedly, this spec makes for a DRY Moscow Mule, so if it's too dry for you on the straw taste, you should welcome a barspoon of simple syrup (or Demerara for more heft) to the mix. If you use a super-sweet ginger beer, an extra small squeeze of perky lime juice will brighten up the drink nicely. If you add anything, give the drink another brief stir to incorporate the ingredient.

● **GARNISH.** Add your big, freshly cut lime wheel to the rim. You should be able to smell the bright acidity of the flesh and just a hint of lime oil. That combo—versus just the oils of a lime peel alone, for example—is a nice handwritten telegram peppered with good tidings. Stick a straw in that and it's done. Nostrovia! Get after it.

You know by now I'm a staunch believer that every good cocktail has at least 2 ounces of booze in it. There are exceptions, like the Pimm's Cup (page 253), Sherry Cobbler (page 285), and a handful of others; but to me, cocktails need the booze to elevate the flavors around it and 1½ ounces seems persnickety, stingy, and lacks gumption. In the Mule, because the vodka is so overpowered by the ginger and the lime, you could get away with making it a sessionable cocktail. If you want to drop the vodka a bit, I'll never tell a soul. Another thing you could do to make this drink unique: Ditch the commercial ginger beer and make a ginger syrup to pair with sparkling water instead—this gives you more control over the amount of spice and sweetness that lands in the drink. If you happen to have a copy of our other book, The Bartender's Manifesto, we have a great ginger syrup recipe on page 313 that you can use.

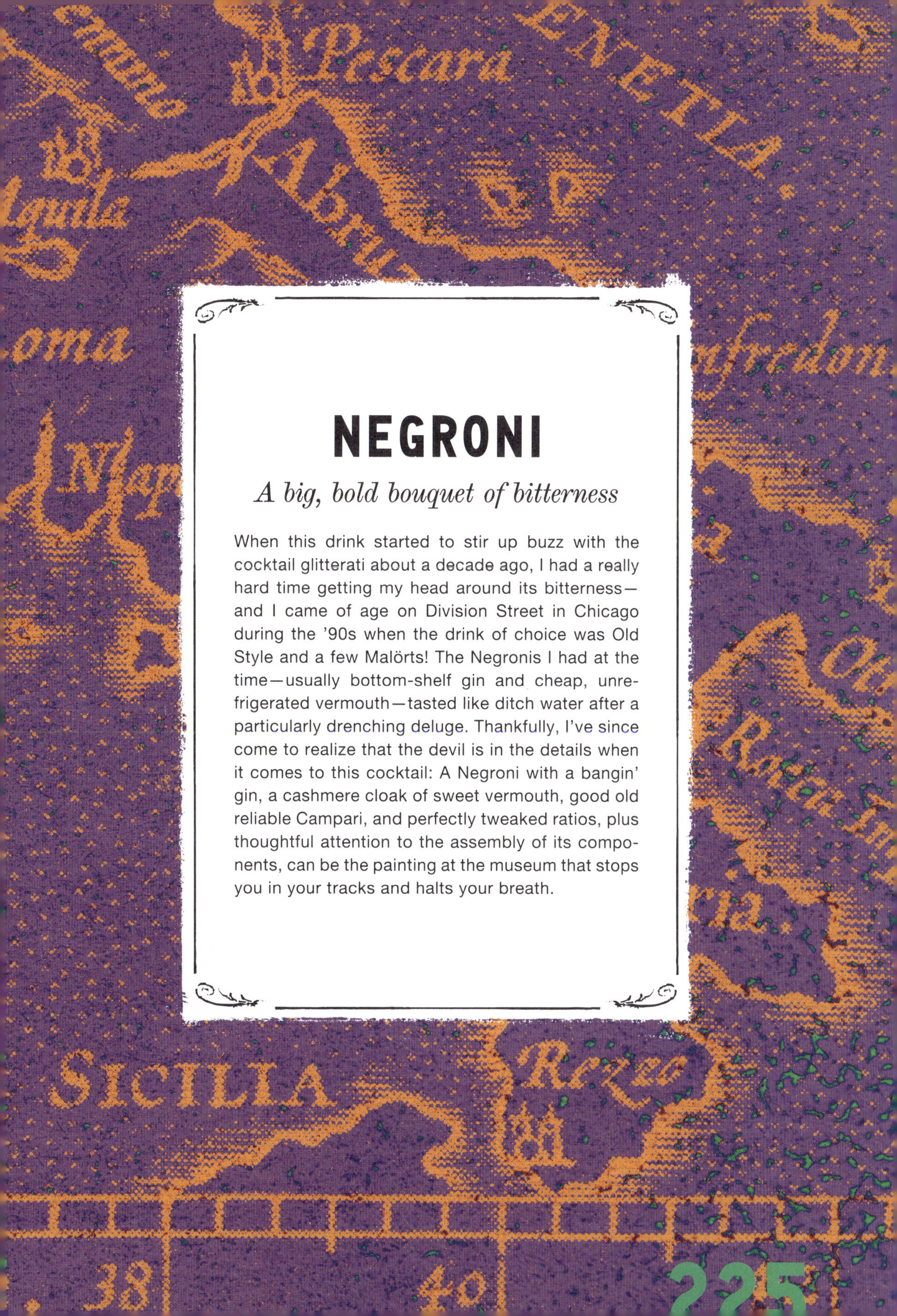

NEGRONI

A big, bold bouquet of bitterness

When this drink started to stir up buzz with the cocktail glitterati about a decade ago, I had a really hard time getting my head around its bitterness— and I came of age on Division Street in Chicago during the '90s when the drink of choice was Old Style and a few Malörts! The Negronis I had at the time—usually bottom-shelf gin and cheap, unrefrigerated vermouth—tasted like ditch water after a particularly drenching deluge. Thankfully, I've since come to realize that the devil is in the details when it comes to this cocktail: A Negroni with a bangin' gin, a cashmere cloak of sweet vermouth, good old reliable Campari, and perfectly tweaked ratios, plus thoughtful attention to the assembly of its components, can be the painting at the museum that stops you in your tracks and halts your breath.

Serve:
Stirred, large cube
or sphere

Tools:
Jigger, mixing
glass, barspoon,
Julep strainer,
Y-peeler, paring
knife

Glass:
Double Old
Fashioned, chilled

Garnish:
Orange peel

RIYL:
Hurricane
(page 165),
Jungle Bird
(page 181),
New York Sour
(page 233)

Navy Strength gin	1.5 oz
Sweet vermouth	1.0 oz
Campari	.75 oz
Orange bitters	3 dashes

OUR APPROACH

A vast majority of drinkers default to the historic approach of equal parts for the Negroni recipe—literally just 1 ounce of each ingredient—but I find that version mushy, without any of the components staking their own claim. I prefer skewing the ratios in favor of the gin and using a high-proof London dry to stand up to the ice melt needed to calm down the sugar in the Campari. For me, the big, brash Carpano Antica, or another sweet vermouth with formidable strength, stands up to the brutish gin and bully Campari. I also add orange bitters, which bring a skosh of bitterness and a big lightning bolt of complexity to the medley. For these reasons, my version of the Negroni is NOT a cute preprandial sipper. It's better served as an after-dinner Martini or Manhattan substitute.

CHOOSE YOUR INGREDIENTS

The Negroni is like the other world-famous trio: the Father, the Son, and the Holy Ghost. Campari is a vengeful deity, the vermouth the ghost, and gin the prodigal son. You are trying to make them all play nice. You don't want a gin or vermouth that is so soft it gets eclipsed by bold red bitters. Try pairing a relaxed but juniper-forward London dry like Beefeater or Fords with Cinzano vermouth, which is as complex and deep as a vermouth can be without being overpowering. To pair with over-the-top gins with bombastic flavor profiles like St. George Dry Rye, or Navy Strength stuff like Perry's Tot, I like Carpano Antica, because its texture is thick and rich, which stands up to the volume of the gin. To pair with citrus-forward gins like Bombay or Tanqueray, maybe try Cocchi Torino sweet vermouth, which leans relatively lean and somewhat jam-forward.

- **PREP THE GARNISH.** Prep your garnish by cutting a beautiful peel from the orange. Make sure there's no ugly blemishes to scar its smooth appearance, because the peel will be visible to the drinker. Trim those edges with a paring knife. Optional: Make like an Italian and grab some potato chips and olives to snack on—the saltiness balances out the sweet and bitter of the drink.

- **MEASURE.** Fill the mixing glass three-quarters of the way full of ice. Dash your bitters down the sides of the mixing glass, so they aren't resting on top of the cubes. Jigger out your red bitter liqueur and then your sweet vermouth. Pour the gin in your jigger and toss that in your mixing glass. There are only four ingredients in this drink, but each one is so wily, so distinct, so complex, that you should measure each with as much precision as you can muster.

- **STRAW TASTE.** To make sure everything is in the glass.

- **STIR.** Give the cocktail a short Chunk Stir (page 47). You don't need to wait until you think the drink is done to straw taste—taste, then stir and straw taste some more as you go, so you get a sense for how the gin's proof is tempered by water and chill as you stir—the sweetness of the aperitif will continue to even out as you go. Stir with the confidence of an Italian bartender who has learned the trade from the generations of great bartenders who came before them. Set aside for a minute and add one large cube or sphere to the Double Old Fashioned glass.

- **TASTE, ADJUST, AND STRAIN.** This drink is going to be served on ice, so you want to stop stirring it before it has achieved 100 percent water content. How do you know? The drink will taste as if it's just teetering on the edge of "too boozy." This is also a moment to consider texture and, yes, flavor: If it's too bold and bitter, you can add a bit more vermouth to polish the edges into something softer and sweeter. If it's too sweet, dose it with a bit more gin. Campari has both sweetness and bitterness, so I don't often end up adding any more during straw tastes, but you can certainly experiment with this as you're getting the hang of it. Once it tastes right to you, grab your Julep strainer (a Hawthorne will make the drink dribble down the side like it has a lip full of Novocain) to strain into your prepped glass.

- **GARNISH.** The one major thing you don't want to skip with this drink is the garnish—a spray of orange oils from a pretty peel brightens up the nose in a magical way. The orange also echoes the orange notes that you can find in Campari. Close your eyes and picture the sunny coasts of Italy when you taste it.

Emma's favorite gin Negroni features two vermouths stacked in the jigger at the same time—usually Cocchi di Torino for its jammy cherry notes, plus Dolin to welcome some dusty herbaceous undercurrents to the mix. On occasion when she's feeling the urge to splurge, she'll reach for Carpano and add that to the medley in equal parts. She rotates her gins based on whatever is on hand (sometimes using the terroir method she uses in a Gimlet on page 145) and sometimes splits the Campari measure with a rabarbaro amaro like Zucca or Nardini, or with a little Cynar (see the Jungle Bird in the Make It Personal section, page 183, for another example of how these two play well together). She'll often tip the ratios in favor of the sweet vermouths, because she likes the drink to have a lush texture.

NEGRONI FRIENDS & FAMILY

From the two cocktails that laid the foundation for the Negroni to follow—the Milano-Torino and the Americano—to a few "modern classics" that show how fantastically bartenders have riffed on the original, here is a collection of Negroni variations we've jiggered to ratios that are pleasing to our palates. Yes, some of these were invented after 2002; we make the rules, we break the rules. As with the Martini and Manhattan Friends & Family sections, use the mixing instructions in the main Negroni session as guardrails for how to mix these cocktails. As you do, note how some of these specs skew close to the original recipes the way they were created in the beginning, and in others we take liberties with adding something new to the conversation. In many, we lean into the bitterness, because it's a bitter cocktail! Forgive us, fathers everywhere, but these sins were committed in the name of deliciousness, which is no sin at all in our eyes.

AMERICANO

For the hottest days of the year, when gin cocktails bring your buzz to a head too quickly, the Americano steps in with its effortlessly cool dose of sparkling water (FRIZZANTE!) to take the edge off.

Sweet vermouth	1.5 oz
Campari	1.5 oz
Sparkling water	4 to 5 oz

Serve: Stirred, on the rocks
Glass: Collins, chilled
Garnish: Orange peel

BOULEVARDIER

Dog-ear this recipe for when it's a nice day for a cardigan. When the leaves are falling from the trees and there's a harbinger of a chill in the air. In this newfangled interpretation of the drink, rye whiskey holds its own against the walloping lush bitterness of Punt e Mes, which is a kind of hybrid vermouth-amaro. With all that bitterness in play, the amount of Campari is reduced to just a background note.

Bottled-in-Bond rye whiskey	2.0 oz
Punt e Mes	1.0 oz
Campari	.75 oz
Orange bitters	1 dash

Serve: Stirred, large cube
Glass: DOF, chilled
Garnish: Orange peel

CHOCOLATE NEGRONI

Naren Young invented this beauty at Dante in New York City and as far as we're concerned, it is un-fuckwith-able. Chocolate and Campari? Why not?! Sometimes a bit of whimsy in your bitter hipsterness is a good thing.

Fords gin	1.0 oz
Punt e Mes	.75 oz
Campari	.75 oz
Dark crème de cacao	.25 oz
Angostura cocoa bitters	3 dashes

Serve: Stirred, large cube
Glass: DOF, chilled
Garnish: Orange peel

EEYORE'S REQUIEM

As a modern Negroni I created for The Violet Hour menu, this recipe was born as a thought experiment on how to layer as much bitterness and complexity into a cocktail before it all just fell apart like a flavor Jenga, becoming the liquid equivalent of a Jackson Pollock painting.

Campari	1.5 oz
Dolin blanc vermouth	1.0 oz
Navy Strength gin	.50 oz
Cynar	.25 oz
Fernet-Branca	.25 oz
Angostura orange bitters	1 dash
Regans' orange bitters	1 dash

Serve: Stirred, up
Glass: Coupe, chilled
Garnish: Orange pigtail

KINGSTON NEGRONI

My buddy Joaquín Simó invented this tropically inclined riff on the Negroni. I up the amount of booze (of course) and then lean into the dark, brooding, funky flavors of the Jamaican rum by plumping up the Campari with some of the artichoke-based amaro Cynar. Hey! Ho! Ho-GO!

Planteray Stiggins' Fancy pineapple rum	1.75 oz
Smith & Cross Jamaica rum	.25 oz
Carpano Antica sweet vermouth	1.0 oz
Campari	.50 oz
Cynar	.50 oz

Serve: Stirred, large cube
Glass: DOF, chilled
Garnish: Orange peel, lemon peel

MEZCAL NEGRONI

I have changed more minds about the Negroni by using agave spirits as the base than I have tweaking the specs on the classic gin version. This is the perfect Negroni cousin to start messing about with, if you hate the very idea of bitter aperitifs, because the Cynar carries some of the burden the Campari normally bears on its own.

Mezcal	1.0 oz
Cocchi Torino sweet vermouth	1.0 oz
Campari	.50 oz
Cynar	.50 oz
Bittermens Mole bitters 3 drops	

Serve: Stirred, large cube
Glass: DOF, chilled
Garnish: Orange peel

MILANO-TORINO

The O.G. inspiration for the Negroni, now cheekily called a "Mi-To" by some cliques of international cocktail nerds. So effortless. So sessionable. I add orange bitters for a touch of complexity, without adding proof.

Cocchi Torino sweet vermouth	2.0 oz
Campari	1.0 oz
Regans' orange bitters	3 dashes

Serve: Stirred, rocks
Glass: DOF, chilled
Garnish: Orange peel

NEGRONI SBAGLIATO

This feels like it should be an easy intro to the Negroni, but it isn't: It is dry and long and as bitter as Tyrion Lannister from *Game of Thrones*. Delightful, but treacherous as hell under the wrong circumstances. The typical Sbag is equal parts Campari and sweet vermouth plus Prosecco, but the version from Longman & Eagle in Chicago is one of Emma's top cocktails of all time (full stop), so we're rolling with that bad boy.

Aperol	1.0 oz
Punt e Mes	1.0 oz
Prosecco	6.0 oz

Serve: Built in the glass, on the rocks
Glass: Goblet or red wine glass, chilled
Garnish: Orange peel

WHITE NEGRONI (POLKA DOT)

I'm going to cheat on this one and give you the recipe for a drink called the Polka Dot Negroni. I came up with this little ditty—a summertime version of the original—in 2016 at The Violet Hour. When you look at the drink in the glass it seems innocuous and welcoming, pale yellow as a daffodil; but when you drink it, the palate gets pelted with bitterness of summertime botanicals.

Salers	1.5 oz
Navy Strength gin	1.0 oz
Blanc vermouth	1.0 oz

Serve: Stirred, up
Glass: Nick & Nora, chilled
Garnish: Lemon pigtail, Luxardo maraschino cherry

NEW YORK SOUR

Sunday afternoon
laughter and mischief

The New York Sour is such a hidden gem! And an unexpected one at that, because what maniac would think to float a bobbling buoy of red wine on top of a Whiskey Sour?! If you look at it through a cocktail theory lens, it's kind of bonkers. Like, I don't think I would ever order a boilermaker with a chewy Cab Sauv and a chaser of Highland Malt— the finish would be too grippy, too burny—but when whiskey and wine come together with lemon and egg white, a superstar is born. The jewel-toned float of red wine shouldn't work, but it does—the flavor blossoms as it hits your taste buds first, quickly followed by the body of the Whiskey Sour. Then they combine and collapse into one integrated flavor. It's an intense narrative arc—as wild as a bronc ride and over in the bat of an eyelash. Memorable AF, and I think one of the many reasons why this drink has stood the test of time.

Serve:
Shaken,
on the rocks

Tools:
Jigger, shaker,
Hawthorne
strainer, fine
strainer, barspoon,
paring knife

Glass:
Double Old
Fashioned, chilled

Garnish:
Lemon disk,
Peychaud's
bitters

RIYL:
Bramble
(page 93),
Hotel Nacional
(page 157),
Vieux Carré
(page 301)

SPEC

Rye whiskey	1.0 oz
Second whiskey	1.0 oz
Fresh lemon juice	.75 oz
Demerara syrup (page 29)	+.75 oz
Angostura bitters	2 dashes
Orange bitters	3 dashes
Egg white	1
Red Zinfandel, to float	.75 to 1.0 oz

OUR APPROACH

This is a really solid drink already, so to maintain reason and order, while also pumping up the volume, we are going to split-base the whiskey, because I really like the complexity you get from two very different expressions of the same spirit. You can use just one solid whiskey if you prefer. We are also going to use Demerara instead of simple syrup because it bulks up the texture in a way that stands up to two whiskeys. Then we donate a few dashes of bitters to firm up the drink's tenacity. Finally, I also like to Gogh all Earless Dutchman on the garnish with a few slashes of Peychaud's on top, because it adds a floral aroma where it didn't previously exist.

CHOOSE YOUR INGREDIENTS

A New York Sour needs to be made with rye whiskey, because its assertive grain qualities stand up well to the egg white and red wine. In this recipe, we split-base the rye with a second whiskey (like a Bourbon or Irish) to soften those harsh edges just slightly. The goal is to first figure out which whiskeys work well together, and then navigate toward a red wine pick from there. You want harmony in the glass, not a cat fight. If you are using a super-soft rye like Old Overholt 80-proof, I'd go with a Pinot Noir for its light body and demure qualities. If you have the "Kickin' Chicken," aka Wild Turkey 101 Rye, go big instead—like a Cab with lots of tannins, red fruit, and forest floor notes. Mmm. For this spec, I reaaalllly like using a mix of Wild Turkey 101 and Sazerac Straight Rye paired with a Red Zinfandel. Those big Cali Zins are chock-full of juicy berry notes, oak, and vanilla, which stand up to the brawn of the whiskey.

HOW TO MIX

● **PREP YOUR GARNISH.** Make sure the bottle of Peychaud's is within reach, then cut a disk from the lemon. It will not go into the drink, so it doesn't have to be blemish-free.

● **REMEMBER GOOD EGGTIQUETTE.** Open the egg and excavate its white to use in the drink. When trying to get an egg white out of an egg, crack it on something thin and sharp (like the edge of your shaker tin) and only let the white eek out through a slit in the shell into the shaker tin. Cut off the drizzle using that sharp edge before the yolk shows up. Do whatever you want with the yolk. (For more good egg tips, see the Amaretto Sour, page 65.)

- **MEASURE.** Add the bitters, Demerara syrup, and lemon to the side of the shaker tin that does not have the egg white. You do this so you can straw taste the "body" of the drink without sucking up gooey whites. Yuck. Then add the whiskeys.

- **STRAW TASTE.** To see how big, boozy, and sweet the center of the drink tastes. Egg whites will dry out cocktails quickly, so if you have a bone-dry rye in play, consider adding a barspoon of syrup at this point. If you're nervous about this, you can always add it on the second straw taste, so just think about it for now and make a call when you wish.

- **SHAKE.** This drink is going into a DOF glass with ice, so the goal is to get the drink decently cold and slightly frothy. Cap the tins and Mime Shake (page 45) to emulsify, without ice first, just to get the ingredients mixing and mingling. Then add 5 ice cubes and Coupe Shake (page 45), like an easy canter or like a leisurely Sunday afternoon ride. Remember how using a consistent number of cubes to shake every drink will help create consistency in *all* of the cocktails you make. Shake until you hear slush in the tin.

- **TASTE, ADJUST, AND STRAIN.** Straw taste. If it's a little too sandpapery for your taste, add a little more Demerara syrup and shake again. Double-strain into your DOF glass over ice cubes.

- **FLOAT THE WINE.** It's time we all float on, alright? The act of the float might be intimidating for some, but fear not, it's actually pretty easy to do, because the wine has such a higher specific gravity that it practically *wants* to float. Measure the wine into your jigger, then hold a spoon over the ice cubes, upside down, and pour the wine over the brow of the spoon so it dribbles softly onto the tops of the cubes. Keep the edge of the jigger as close to the lip of the glass as possible so it's not flogging out in generous gushes. When done slowly and methodically, this will make your float the most intense stratum, and not fuck up the canvas of the top of the spuma that you are going to add bitters to . . . now!

- **GARNISH.** You don't want to dash the Peychaud's directly into the drink with great force because they will end up sinking to the bottom, which does nothing for the aroma of the drink. Instead, hold a napkin near the lip of the glass, then dash in one long line over the top of the drink. The napkin will catch the debris as you drag the bottle back toward you over the surface. Use a barspoon to make a dainty swirling pattern, if you please. Express the oils of the lemon disk over the top of the drink for one final chef's kiss moment of aroma, then discard the disk.

You can sneak a bit of amaro into the wine ratio to create a cool new flavor that allllmost pushes this into riffs territory. I would personally reach for something like Angostura Amaro or Ciociaro, because they have a nice, even balance and not an aggressive bitterness. Or maybe something like Nardini Rabarbaro or Sfumato if I wanted to get weird—Rabarbaro amari have a smoky note from the inclusion of rhubarb root, which gets my taste buds whirring with wonder every time. This route fits like a glove for fans of earthy, soulful spirits like mezcal and Japanese whisky.

OLD CUBAN

*If Gatsby hosted a dance
party in the Caribbean*

If the Mojito (page 217) is a beach bum, and the
Queen's Park Swizzle (page 269) is a breezy hotel
bar regular, the Old Cuban is their dapper cousin,
rocking a smoking jacket with wide velvet lapels
and a crisp panama hat. All three classics play with
similar ingredients, just in different ways. In the
case of the Old Cuban, it's the additional sparkle of
sparkling wine that sends the drink into the stratosphere of deliciousness—the way the bubbles lift
the aged rum and play with the lime juice is sublime. It is one of Audrey Saunders's finest creations.
I must have made 10 million of them when I worked
at Pegu Club, where she invented the recipe. There
were times that it was the only drink being made
in the whole place; we razed entire forests of mint
to keep up with demand. While the bar has since
been relegated to but a glorious memory, a hundred
years from now, orders for this drink will be called
around the world. It's stupid good.

Serve:
Shaken, up

Tools:
Jigger, shaker,
Hawthorne
strainer,
fine strainer

Glass:
Coupe + sidecar,
chilled

Garnish:
Mint leaf

RIYL:
Jungle Bird
(page 181),
Queen's Park
Swizzle
(page 269),
Sherry Cobbler
(page 285)

SPEC

Brugal añejo rum	1.5 oz
Banks 7 Island rum	.50 oz
Fresh lime juice	.75 oz
Demerara syrup (page 29)	.75 oz
Mint	1 sprig
Angostura bitters	2 dashes
Brut Champagne, to bottom	3 to 4 oz

OUR APPROACH

Just like Audrey does, we're following a traditional sour build for the core of the cocktail (two ounces liquor, three-quarters citrus, three-quarters sweetener) before throwing in the requisite sparkling wine. I'm going to diverge from her routine in my rum choice, though. Audrey always used Bacardi 8 rum for the Old Cuban at Pegu, which is a great place to start if you've never made one. For my version, I want to create a Havana Club 7 experience in the flavor profile. I happen to know this drink was created in homage to Havana, and in the movie *The Firm*, both Gene Hackman and Tom Cruise describe Havana Club as "more like a Cognac than a rum," which I love. Unfortunately, Havana Club is hard to get in the States (shakes fist at John F. Kennedy), so my goal here is to try and re-create that personality using two rums—the Brugal añejo and the Banks 7 Island—because together they bring similar flavors to the table. Brugal is dry like Ferrand 1840 Cognac and the Banks 7 adds just enough funk to give it a curious quality. Could you use an unaged rum in this drink and still have it taste delicious? Some purists might point fingers and accuse you of treason, but if it tastes good to YOU, then haters be damned.

CHOOSE YOUR INGREDIENTS

I mentioned my rums of choice before, so let's talk about the bubbles. Audrey uses brut Champagne in her Old Cuban, which is a prestige pick. It elevates and dries out the cocktail at the same time. That said, you can make the cocktail with another style of sparkling wine if you choose to do so—just taste your choice before you start mixing so you know how much sugar you might need to adjust the recipe with on the straw tastes. A tinny Prosecco has a very different amount of sweetness compared to a lush Grower Champagne or a chill cava, for example.

- **PREP YOUR GARNISH.** Pluck out one of the biggest and most beautiful leaves from your mint sprig. Set aside.

- **MINT AND MEASURE.** Grab your big tin and place it right in front of you. We're going to use Sasha Petraske's mint technique to make the most of our herb. (More painstaking detail on this approach can be found in the Mint and Measure section on page 271.) Dash your bitters in there, then put the mint sprig in and push it to the bottom of the tin. Add the Demerara syrup, followed by the lime. Put both rums in next. I will then push the mint down one more time at this point, so it's as submerged in the liquids as possible. Put on some music to give the rum some time to marry with the mint. You don't want to muddle the mint, because the drink is not a MINT cocktail (like the Mojito, page 217, or Mint Julep, page 213), but rather a RUM cocktail with a hint of mint. Muddling would amplify those herbaceous notes into the forefront, which is not what we're going for here. Make sense? Regarding your music of choice, here's a hot tip: There is a lot of great Latin American stuff out there that isn't the Buena Vista Social Club, so dig deeper.

- **STRAW TASTE.** To make sure everything is in the tin. Remember what I said about aiming for a lot of sweetness at this stage. It's gonna taste intense, y'all. That's a good thing.

- **BOTTOM THE WINE.** This is a good time to add the Champagne to your chilled glass.

- **SHAKE.** Add 5 cubes to the shaker tin and Coupe Shake (page 45). You have a decent amount of mint in this drink, which will get in the way of the ice breaking down like it normally does, so give it a little extra time and a little more force than you would if you were shaking a normal Daiquiri (page 125). Nothing crazy, though, because the cocktail will meet sparkling wine in the glass (aka it will gain some more dilution) and you don't want everything to come out watery. Aim for, like, 30 percent more effort than usual. I know, it's hard to read this and know what to do on the first try, but with practice, you'll find the sweet spot for this timing.

- **TASTE, ADJUST, AND STRAIN.** This should taste like a Mojito (page 217) that has been put on a stove and reduced like a demi-glace. The rumminess is super rich and intense. I know I've said this a few times already, but this exact moment is when you really need to recall how it should be like this (too sweet) on this straw taste, as the Champagne will dry out the cocktail fast. If it's not, add a touch of extra syrup now—worst-case scenario you could add more after it's all assembled and give it a quick stir. Double-strain to keep the little flecks of mint out of the glass.

- **GARNISH.** Float the reserved mint leaf on the surface of the drink.

There are times when I really want to have this be a mint bomb, so I'll treat it like a Whiskey Smash and put it on the rocks in a metal Julep tin with an obscene amount of mint in my bouquet garnish. A little spray of Angostura on the mint leaves is lovely as well, bringing a nutmeg and clove spice quality to the aroma, which extends into the drink via the flavor of the rums.

OLD FASHIONED

*The All-State cheerleader
of whiskey cocktails*

Of all the moments in history to behold a huge intuitive leap for the benefit of mankind, I'll pass on the discovery of fire or the invention of the fulcrum or the first time a wheel rolled into motion in favor of watching the first barkeep stir bitters into whiskey with sugar and a little lump of ice. The glory of that moment still reverberates a million times a night at bars all around the world. It was a moment as momentous as the introduction of the polio vaccine, or rock and roll. That's one hell of a legacy. It's one of the most quintessential and longstanding classics because its wonderfully vague definition, "spirit of any kind, sugar, water and bitters," gives the imbiber the option of tinkering with every element to their heart's desire. I realize this irks some folks, but others know it's worth the time and effort to dial in to your own preferences. Like a diamond whose existence comes from pressure, time, and heat, an Old Fashioned's beauty is just quality ingredients, technique, and water.

Serve:
Stirred, large cube or sphere

Tools:
Jigger, mixing glass, barspoon, Julep strainer, Y-peeler

Glass:
Double Old Fashioned, chilled

Garnish:
Citrus peel

RIYL:
Irish Coffee (page 169), New York Sour (page 233), Moscow Mule (page 221)

SPEC

Whiskey, usually bourbon . . . . 2.0 oz
Syrup, usually Demerara (page 29) . . . . .25 oz
Bitters, usually Angostura . . . . 1 to 3 dashes

OUR APPROACH

When I teach cocktail classes, I always get asked what my favorite Old Fashioned is. I think most of the time people expect me to call out an expensive rye or bourbon and fancy sugar plus three kinds of bitters made by left-handed albino monks who live above the tree line in Tibet. While that might be good—I'll give it a try and get back to you—my approach is quite simple. I just want to stay in step with the original spirit of the drink: whiskey, Dem, Ango, and citrus for garnish. It's one of the world's greatest examples of how "less is always more" when it comes to assembling cocktails.

CHOOSE YOUR INGREDIENTS

The most important thing to decide about an Old Fashioned is your base spirit, because the distillate stands front and center in the cocktail. Consider the mood, weather, and context in which you're drinking. An example: I like high-proof whiskey in my Old Fashioneds and when living in Louisville, I always came back to Old Grand Dad Bottled-in-Bond. Like a member of the Greatest Generation, this whiskey gets shit done without crowing about it or craving fanfare. Another example: If I'm having a round in the fall when leaves are burning far away, or in the summer by a campfire, I will slip a barspoon to ¼ ounce of Ardbeg or Laphroaig (both smoke-bomb Scotches) into my glass. If you want to stray from whiskey, which is your prerogative, Cognac makes a great Old Fashioned (Ferrand 1840 is my go-to), as we know from its close cousin the Sazerac (page 281), and an old rich rum Old Fashioned makes a perfect after-dinner drink. Or you could boldly go where many intrepid rum drinkers have gone before and try a hogo-forward Jamaican rum, like Smith & Cross, if you dare.

HOW TO MIX

● **PREP THE GARNISH.** No matter what base spirit you choose, a proper Old Fashioned always calls for an expression of oils from a citrus peel, because it's the kind of drink that needs a bullet of brightness to lift and balance out the stew of deep and dark flavors. Orange peel on a whiskey-based version pulls out the warm cinnamon spice of the spirit and sits comfortably alongside the bitters for the same reason.

A tequila-based Old Fashioned might warrant a grapefruit peel because musky notes pull out the herbaceousness of the agave spirit. A Cognac version might benefit from the bouquet of both lemon and orange peels (as a little nod to its relative the Sidecar, page 289, and tough-guy uncle the Vieux Carré, page 301). And a dark rum Old Fashioned usually needs a *couple* of lemon peels to bring extra dryness to all the molasses notes in the drink. Look at how the spirit, bitters, and syrup meld together in your version, and then think about how you can balance out the sweetness or dryness with that hit of oil. Worst-case scenario, try a few options until you find the best fit.

● **MEASURE.** Fill the mixing glass three-quarters of the way with ice. Dash the bitters in first, taking care to make sure they dribble down to the bottom of the glass instead of sitting on top of the cubes, where they won't help you make judgment calls during the first straw taste. The sweetener (in this case, Dem) follows, with the whiskey close on its heels. Like with the Martini, you want precision in these measurements, because there's nowhere to hide with only three ingredients in play. Stir for one or two rotations to get all of the ingredients swirling together.

● **STRAW TASTE.** To make sure you didn't forget anything, and to determine whether you like the balance of sweet:booze:bitter. Adjust now, to taste: maybe a barspoon more syrup, or another dash of bitters. Start minimal, then add more on the second straw taste if needed.

● **STIR.** Give it a good Chunk Stir—this is a slow and leisurely stir that'll last for less time than if you were making a drink served up; see our breakdown of different types of stir on page 47 for how to gauge this. Think about the proof and character of your stimulating liquor as you swirl that spoon around in the mixing glass—is it cask-strength whiskey or a demure, rested tequila clocking in at 40% ABV? If it's high-proof, you will have to stir it longer than you would a softer spirit to get the proper dilution. Extrapolate how this drink will taste halfway through its time sitting on a large ice cube, and what will the last sip taste like as well.

● **TASTE, ADJUST, AND STRAIN.** To get a sense for how the proof of your spirit is softening with the dilution, straw taste now. Stir some more, this time thinking about the ice in the glass and how it will further mellow things out over time. Straw taste again, focusing on the bitters in the drink and how they are affecting the booze. Do you need another dash? Or are they prominent enough in flavor to last until the last sips? Now is the time to tighten up the structure and add some complexity to the drink if needed. Strain into the glass over your one large cube of ice.

● **GARNISH.** Express the oils of the citrus peel over the top of the drink. Insert the garnish into the glass.

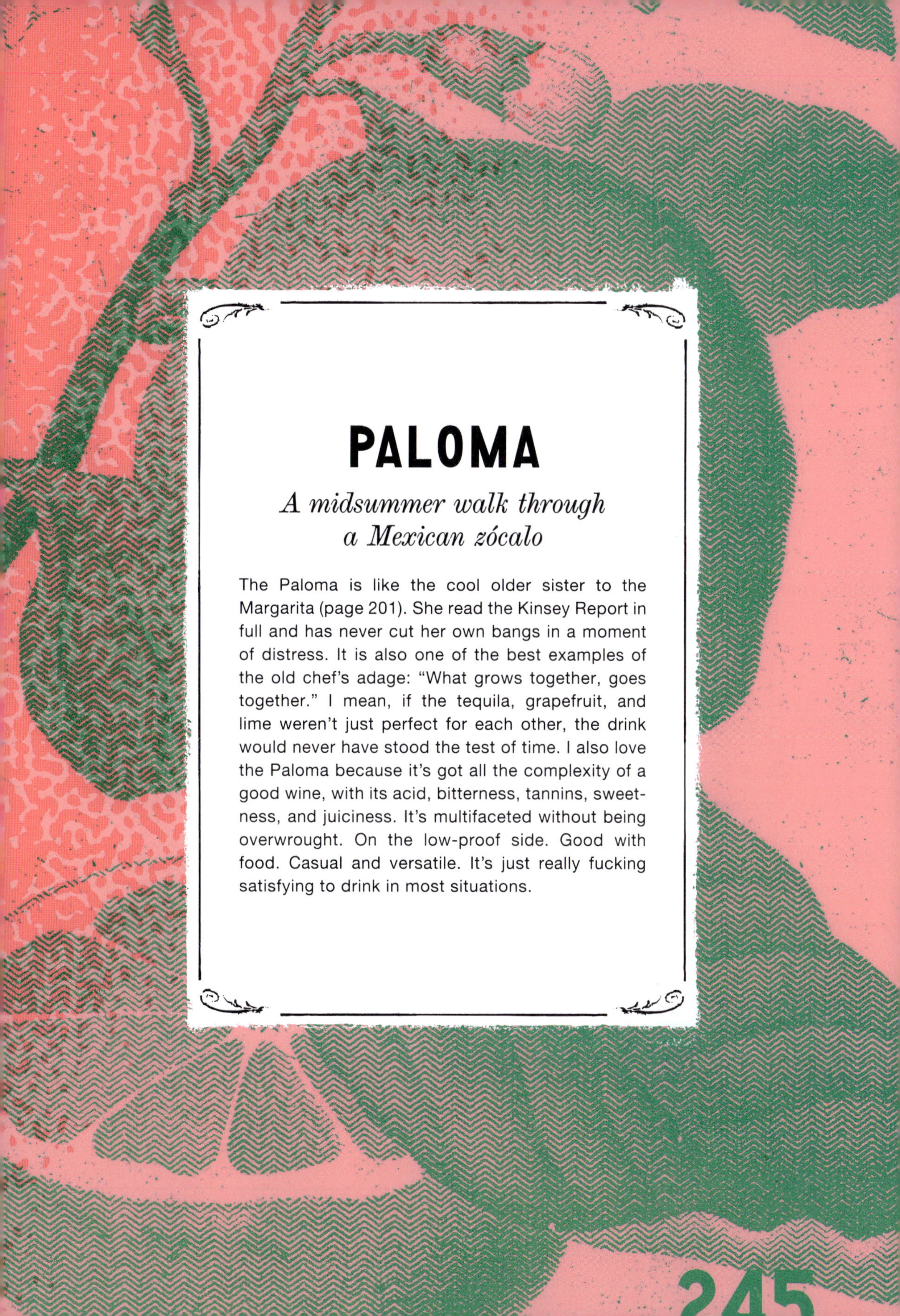

PALOMA

*A midsummer walk through
a Mexican zócalo*

The Paloma is like the cool older sister to the Margarita (page 201). She read the Kinsey Report in full and has never cut her own bangs in a moment of distress. It is also one of the best examples of the old chef's adage: "What grows together, goes together." I mean, if the tequila, grapefruit, and lime weren't just perfect for each other, the drink would never have stood the test of time. I also love the Paloma because it's got all the complexity of a good wine, with its acid, bitterness, tannins, sweetness, and juiciness. It's multifaceted without being overwrought. On the low-proof side. Good with food. Casual and versatile. It's just really fucking satisfying to drink in most situations.

Serve:
Shaken,
on the rocks

Tools:
Jigger, shaker,
Hawthorne
strainer,
fine strainer,
paring knife

Glass:
Collins, chilled

Garnish:
Lime wedge,
half salt rim

RIYL:
Hemingway
Daiquiri
(page 153),
Jack Rose
(page 173),
Negroni Sbagliato
(page 231)

SPEC

High-proof tequila blanco	2.0 oz
Grapefruit juice	1.5 oz
Fresh lime juice	.75 oz
Grapefruit bitters	2 dashes
Grapefruit soda, to bottom	4 to 5 oz

OUR APPROACH

I've seen this cocktail go two ways out in the wild: The first is just tequila and grapefruit soda free-poured with abandon. Lime wedge on the rim. The second is mixologized within an inch of its life, dressed with clarified juice and bespoke soda and small-batch spirits you can only get by traveling straight to the source and lugging the mystical "juice" home in a plastic water bottle. I'd happily drink either version, depending on the location and the weather and the company and my mood at the time, but for the purposes of this book we aim to strike a happy medium between the two routes. To treat it like a proper cocktail, albeit an easygoing one, we're putting an eye on balance and texture and temperature to give the highball a little more elegance without going nuts. In this recipe, high-proof tequila holds its ground against the waves of citrus that want to yank the drink into tart territory, while bitters bring a low earthquake rumble of complexity to the mix. We use a laid-back, commercial grapefruit soda because that's how it's usually done in Mexico—think rum and Coke vibes—but we're taking the liberty of also including grapefruit juice, which is a modern addition that we like for the way it brings extra balance to the mix.

CHOOSE YOUR INGREDIENTS

I've had Palomas made with Jarritos or Squirt and others made with Ting or Fever-Tree. All delicious. I've also had them made with freshly squeezed grapefruit juice or the grapefruit juice that comes in a carton. Still good. (This recipe was tested with the Simply Grapefruit juice brand, which has no added sugar—that's the ticket for using grapefruit juice in all recipes! It can be store-bought, just not with a bunch of bullshit in the ingredient list that you don't need.) At bars like El Gallo Altanero in Guadalajara, they dial up the intrigue by subbing in a sherbet (oleo-saccharum with juice) and sparkling water. These are all great options. The Paloma is also pretty much bulletproof with any agave spirit. I especially like them with Ocho and Siete Leguas, but if you reached for Fortaleza tequila or Banhez mezcal, it'll make you want to climb the pyramids at Teotihuacán (the pyramids of the sun and the moon, because this drink is good 24 hours a day) and praise the old gods and thank them for all the liquid joys Mexican has gifted to the world.

- **PREP THE GARNISH.** Decide if you want to rim half of the glass with salt or not. Just like with the Margarita (page 201), this is a nice accompaniment that makes the drinking experience more fun and delicious—there's a reason the Salty Dog is also a popular cocktail—but it's not 100 percent necessary. Grab the salt now, if that's the route you wanna take. Your glass is already chilled, right? Prep that rim by running a lime wedge along one half of the lip and dipping it in salt. The salt should stick. Also: Now is a good time to cut your lime wedge. Set aside for garnishing.

- **MEASURE.** First, measure out the bitters into the tin. Then add the lime and grapefruit juices, followed by the tequila.

- **STRAW TASTE.** To make sure everything is in the tin. The acid levels are going to taste sharp, and the tequila will be trying to scream its way out of the mix. These are normal things at this stage.

- **BOTTOM THE SODA.** Fill the chilled (and maybe salted) glass three-quarters of the way full of ice cubes. Then add the grapefruit soda. Set the glass aside.

- **SHAKE.** Add 5 cubes to the tin. If you are using 80-proof tequila, you are barely going to need to Collins Shake (page 46) this, because it's going to water down a bit with cold grapefruit soda. Just a quick trot of a shake will chill the ingredients and that's it. If you are using a 100-proof agave distillate, you will need to shake a bit more, because that extra proof needs a little wrangling to settle down. If you really love Palomas, make two side by side, one with 80-proof and one with high-proof. See how it takes a few extra shakes of the higher-proof one to get both to taste the same.

- **TASTE, ADJUST, AND STRAIN.** Straw taste—because this is going over grapefruit soda, you want the cocktail to taste boozy and tart at this moment, because its heaviness will mellow out when it hits the soda. Remember what your grapefruit soda tastes like? If it's suuuuper dry, and you anticipate this drink tasting too brittle once the cocktail combines with the soda, you can add a barspoon of simple syrup at this point. You could also do this after you've mixed the cocktail with the soda and ice in the glass, while you're getting used to learning how to anticipate balance. Give the shaker one more quick shake and then double-strain its contents into the Collins.

- **GARNISH.** Put a fat lime wedge on the edge and straw it. If you're drinking at a snail's pace, that wedge will come in handy about halfway through—give it a squeeze for extra brightness at will.

To take the basic Paloma into "craft" cocktail bar territory, you could swap out the sugar-filled soda and use sparkling water and simple syrup instead—start with 1/2 ounce of simple and adjust the sweetness to taste. Yes, you lose some of the grapefruit flavor with this route, so if you want to keep that in play, you could also make a grapefruit oleo-saccharum and use that instead of simple.

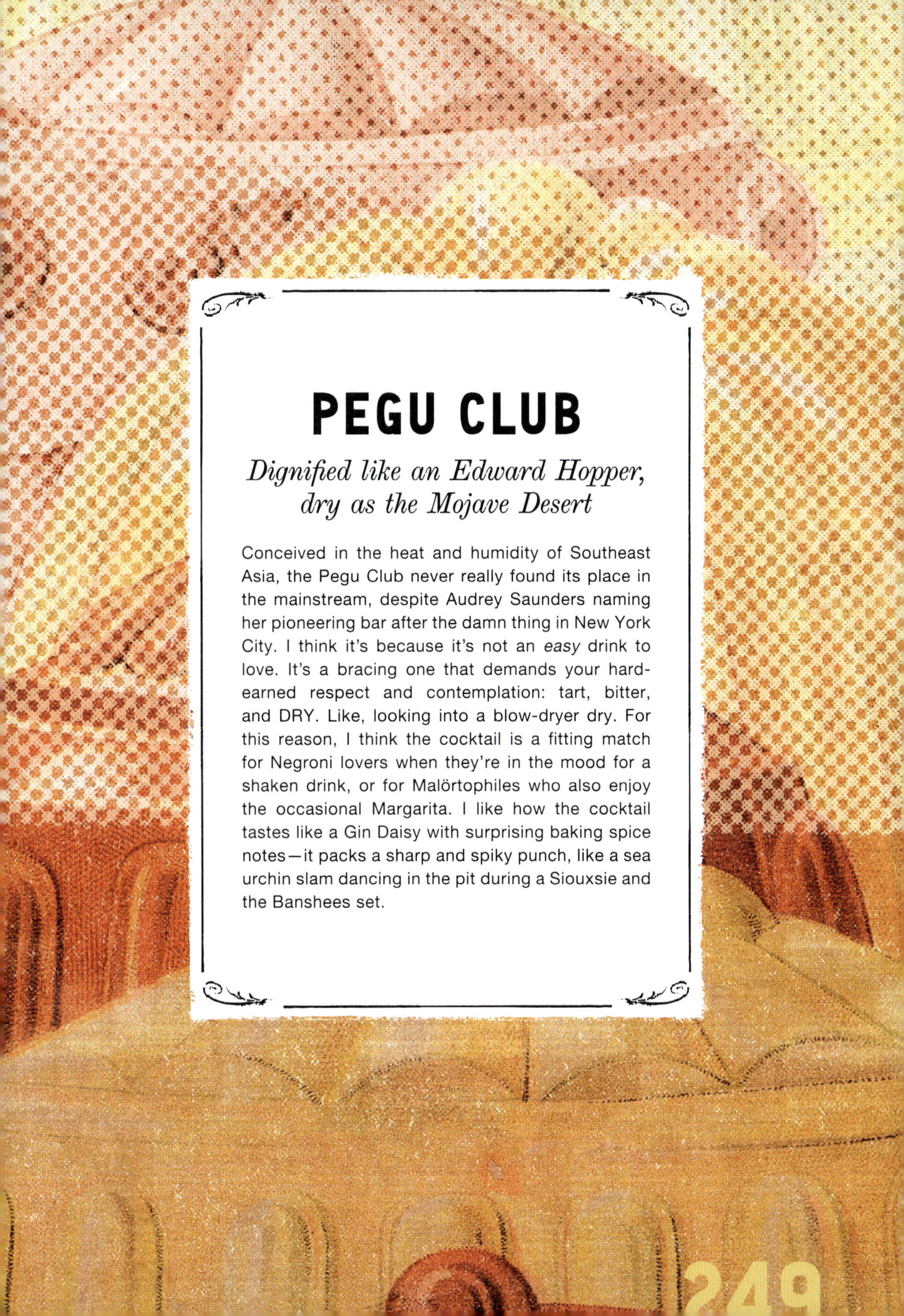

PEGU CLUB

*Dignified like an Edward Hopper,
dry as the Mojave Desert*

Conceived in the heat and humidity of Southeast Asia, the Pegu Club never really found its place in the mainstream, despite Audrey Saunders naming her pioneering bar after the damn thing in New York City. I think it's because it's not an *easy* drink to love. It's a bracing one that demands your hard-earned respect and contemplation: tart, bitter, and DRY. Like, looking into a blow-dryer dry. For this reason, I think the cocktail is a fitting match for Negroni lovers when they're in the mood for a shaken drink, or for Malörtophiles who also enjoy the occasional Margarita. I like how the cocktail tastes like a Gin Daisy with surprising baking spice notes—it packs a sharp and spiky punch, like a sea urchin slam dancing in the pit during a Siouxsie and the Banshees set.

Serve:
Shaken, up

Tools:
Jigger, shaker, Hawthorne strainer, fine strainer, offset serrated knife

Glass:
Coupe, chilled

Garnish:
Lime wheel

RIYL:
Cosmopolitan (page 117), Martini (page 205), Sidecar (page 289)

SPEC

London dry gin	....	2.0 oz
Ferrand dry curaçao	....	.75 oz
Simple syrup (page 29)	....	.25 oz
Fresh lime juice	....	.75 oz
Angostura bitters	....	1 dash
Orange bitters	....	2 dashes

OUR APPROACH

It seems to this old-timer that these days in the world of mixology, many bartenders put a premium on making giant changes to classic cocktails, like clarifying them or turning part of them into a fancy foam. I come from a time when you could add a couple of dashes of Cynar to a Manhattan and blow people's minds, so for me making small adjustments is still a cool, restrained way of approaching so many of these storied recipes. Most of these little things have been done before, I get that, but just tweaking a spec a skosh to recenter balance or bitterness or aroma can bring about a satisfying outcome in ways that adding fireworks to it just can't. So, that said, this recipe for the Pegu Club is almost exactly how Audrey Saunders makes hers. I just make a tiny adjustment. I feel like Brutus (et tu, Toby?) right now, adjusting Audrey's recipe, but my palate just needs a bit more luxury. Her palate is like a Formula One race car, all precision and speed. Mine's like a Cadillac Limo, all comfort and ease. In truth, I haven't actually changed much here—I just added a bit of sweetness via simple syrup to change the cadence of the cocktail. I also added some orange bitters to nuzzle up to the orange curaçao.

CHOOSE YOUR INGREDIENTS

I'm going to call for Tanqueray because that's what Audrey uses. Let's talk about curaçao for one quick second: You could use another orange liqueur here, but the cocktail won't have the same elegance as it will if you reach for the dry curaçao from Ferrand, as recommended. The liqueur is made with a blend of aged and unaged grape distillates, some infused with Lahara bitter orange peels from the Curaçao islands, others infused with walnut shells and prunes. Sweetened with cane sugar then aged again, it bears a distinctive, soulful personality that elevates every cocktail it touches. It's one of my favorite ways to upgrade almost any drink in a jiffy, and it tastes killer drizzled on a bit of vanilla ice cream for a grown-up orange creamsicle vibe. Bitters-wise, there weren't a lot of options on the market in 2005 when Pegu Club opened, as hard as that is to believe now. We had Angostura, and Peychaud's existed, but you couldn't just walk into any liquor store and pick up a few bottles. For orange bitters, we had Fee Brothers and Regans', the latter of which was brand new. In a real maverick move at the time, Audrey combined the two in equal parts to create a very cool "house" blend dubbed Feegan's, which went on to become the standard for many other bars around the country. The complex cardamom bomb of Regans' and the straightforward candied orange of Fee's complemented each other beautifully. Try this out or stick to your favorite brand of orange bitters (one of mine is Bittercube).

- **PREP THE GARNISH.** At the bar, we'd garnish the drink with lime wedges decorated with patterns cut into the skin side using a zester. Cute, right? But so many people immediately squeezed the lime into the drink before tasting it, which ruined all the hard work we put into creating optimal balance. Sometimes you want the option to add a little more lime juice halfway through a drink (see the Paloma, page 245) to brighten it up as it waters down, but in this case, it'll just fuck with things, so I'd suggest garnishing with a lime *wheel* instead, to avoid this unfortunate outcome. Cut the lime wheel for garnish now—cut a little notch into one side so it'll rest on the lip of the glass—and set aside until you need it.

- **MEASURE.** Into your tin, dash your bitters. Then we'd normally add the simple syrup next because we build cocktails from the least expensive ingredient to the most expensive, in case of errors that might occur while mixing. But in this case, we're going to add the lime juice next because we want to stack the simple syrup and curaçao in the jigger at the same time—see the Measure instructions for the Amaretto Sour (page 65) for the long story on stacking—because this ensures you're only adding 1 ounce of sweetener to the drink. Any more and it might come out too sweet for a bone-dry drink. Now, measure the gin and add that to the party.

- **STRAW TASTE.** To make sure everything is in the tin. Also clock how boozy and bitter this drink tastes at this stage; we will focus on the bitterness again with the second straw taste.

- **SHAKE.** Add 5 cubes and Coupe Shake (page 45) until the ice starts to turn into slush. This should sound like you have manifested a cobra in the shaker and it is hissing at you quietly. Pacing-wise, start the shake at a medium pace, gradually ramping up to a fever pitch, like when a Nirvana or Pixies track changes tempo, propelling you to fly into the pit, arms flailing, head down, center of gravity low. If it doesn't smell like teen spirit, you're not doing it right.

- **TASTE, ADJUST, AND STRAIN.** Straw taste. How is the drink's complexity? Is it a bit one-dimensional or is it splendiferous? If it's the former, would a few drops of orange bitters be beneficial? I often add a cheeky dash at this point, just to tighten up the drink. How is the texture? If it's a bit thin, you can add some simple syrup, which will thicken up the viscosity without messing with the flavor or booze content. If you want more orange spice notes, and don't mind a touch more proof, you could barspoon some more curaçao into the mix, but this drink is so dry and weird already, I'd suggest resisting the urge. In the end: You do you, because you'll learn something about your palate either way. Double-strain.

- **GARNISH.** Grab the lime wheel and place it on the rim of the drink. Revel in how the slight aroma of fresh lime juice and hint of lime peel oil stimulate the senses as you take that first sip.

There's a thrilling thing that happens to cocktails when you add citrus peel oils to the body of the cocktail. You don't always wanna do this, but I think in this case a bit of grapefruit essence goes a long way. To bring a little more complexity to this build, express the oils from a grapefruit peel into the shaker tin, then toss the peel into the mix for a royal shake (see Our Approach for the Cosmopolitan on page 117 for more), then garnish the cocktail with the oils from a little disk of grapefruit peel.

PIMM'S CUP

For a leisurely late-afternoon
lunch at the country club

When assembled extravagantly with freshly muddled fruit, gently spanked mint, bright lime juice, and
topped with a cornucopia of meticulously selected
garnishes, the Pimm's Cup is the kind of cocktail to
enjoy courtside at Wimbledon, or alongside a lavish
order of six dozen oysters. In fact, the cocktail was
conceived as a fruity digestif in an oyster house,
so it pairs wonderfully with briny bivalves. It can
also be effortlessly tossed together for a bangin'
Brooklyn block party with the neighbors or sipped
leisurely alongside a half muffaletta in the famous
Vieux Carré (the neighborhood in New Orleans, not
the drink on page 301) while a summer storm rumbles through the Quarter. I love how it can go high
or low. Either way it won't fail to delight.

Serve:
Shaken,
on the rocks

Tools:
Jigger, muddler,
shaker, Hawthorne
strainer, fine
strainer, Y-peeler,
offset serrated
knife

Glass:
Collins, chilled

Garnish:
Mint bouquet,
strawberry half,
orange peel,
cucumber wheel

RIYL:
Hurricane
(page 165),
Jack Rose
(page 173),
Sherry Cobbler
(page 285)

SPEC

Pimm's #1	1.5 oz
Fords gin	.50 oz
Fresh lemon juice	.75 oz
Simple syrup (page 29)	.75 oz
Mint sprigs	3
Strawberry	1
Cucumber slice	3
Orange wheel	1
Sparkling water, to bottom	4 to 5 oz

OUR APPROACH

The Pimm's Cup is an ensemble drink. Like a roaring Second City comedy sketch, its strength comes from how all the elements meld together to create an entire world. In my cover version, we look back to sentiments of the early days of The Violet Hour (like 2007), when we added high-proof gin for extra flavor fireworks. Our theory was that "where there is more proof there is more flavor." This is why penne alla vodka exists—the vodka makes everything around it taste more like itself. (This method is utilized in the very different Amaretto Sour as well, on page 65.) So, we're doing that here for structure and shine, and then welcoming more fruit to the shindig—the way the strawberry pumps up the fruity notes of the Pimm's and the orange adds a splash of sunshine is quite divine.

CHOOSE YOUR INGREDIENTS

I'd argue to make a proper Pimm's Cup you must use Pimm's #1, because that's the gold standard. The company has made different iterations of the liqueur over the years, though, many of which are no longer in production, but if you can find a bottle of the Winter Cup—a seasonal version made with brandy—that could be a fun rabbit hole to fall into during the colder months of the year. Gin-wise, any good London dry will do, but Fords brings a soft-handed boost of proof to the mix without impacting the flavor too much. Sipsmith, The Botanist, or another genteel gin would also slide its way into the mix without pushing any of the complexity of the Pimm's out of the picture. The gin should boost the botanicals of the liqueur, not pummel them into submission.

- **PREP THE GARNISH.** In the mize list for this cocktail, we've identified a collection of garnishes that work swimmingly with this spec (mint, strawberry, orange, and cucumber), but because this version of the Pimm's Cup is more like a lady's derby day hat versus a baseball cap, the garnishing can be decadent to the point of absurdity. Seriously. Make it a "Roman orgy," because the more lavishly decorated the drink, the more fun it is to drink.

- **MUDDLE AND MEASURE.** Toss the orange wheel and cucumber slices into the shaker tin and muddle with a vengeance. Next, add the strawberry and mint, but do not muddle in the same manner; just press them into the pulp. Measure out the simple syrup and lemon juice, then stack the gin and Pimm's to be sure that only a strict 2 ounces of booze will land in this drink.

- **STRAW TASTE.** To make sure everything is in the tin. This won't be the easiest straw taste thanks to all of the stuff in there, so you might have to swirl things around for a second to get into the liquid.

- **BOTTOM THE SPARKLING WATER.** Grab your Collins glass and fill it up three-quarters of the way with ice cubes and add the sparkling water.

- **SHAKE.** Add 3 ice cubes to the shaker tin—not 5, because this is a lower-proof drink served on rocks and sparkling water, meaning you won't need as much dilution as you would with a Pegu Club (page 249) or Jack Rose (page 173), which don't have ice or soda in the final build. Shake for a length of time that lands somewhere in-between a Collins Shake (page 46) and a Rocks Shake (page 46) because the organic flotsam in the tin will interfere with getting the water content you need out of your cubes. All of this junk in play means you'll need to give the shake a little more oomph, too—put your back into it! Stop shaking when the tins feel good and cold.

- **TASTE, ADJUST, AND STRAIN.** The drink should taste kind of like a well-composed gin sour: The citrus juice, sweetener, and spirit should taste relatively balanced, if not a bit sweet and "hot" or boozy, because you're about to thin it all out with the sparkling water in the glass. If it's tasting a bit wimpy, or thin, bump a barspoon of simple syrup into the mix to fortify its texture. Double-strain into your prepped Collins glass.

- **GARNISH.** Grab a straw and hold it about 1 inch above the drink, oriented horizontally. Spank the mint over the top of the straw to add aroma, then insert the bouquet into the drink. Then dress with the citrus peels, berries, and what other extravagances you previously prepared for garnish. Make this as pretty as a Picasso painting: First add the mint bouquet, then nestle in the peels and berries in a way that's visually appealing.

The fruit salad that gets muddled into this drink is just a combination that I personally like, because there is a sweet component (strawberry), a slightly acidic component (orange), a savory component (the cuke), and an herbal component (the mint). You can switch out the strawberries for raspberries or blackberries, the orange for white grapefruit or pomelo, the cucumber for honeydew melon or guava, and the mint for rosemary or tarragon. Think about what you really enjoy the most, and experiment with it. Have those choices reflected in the garnish!

PIÑA COLADA

Private cabana, open tab vibes

This cocktail is a vacation in a glass. Literally, the song it's most associated with—you know the one about getting caught in the rain—is called "Escape." While drinking a Piña in the rain is a bad idea—the rain will fuck up the water content in your drink mas pronto—when made right, it's a fruity, freezing intoxicant perfect for when you have nothing to do and nothing to prove. Or in the middle of a Chicago winter when it's –17°F before the wind chill and the snow is piling up. You don't even need a fire, a bearskin rug, and Sade on the hi-fi to make it a vacation. One sip and you're there.

Serve:
Blended,
on crushed ice

Tools:
Blender,
Hawthorne strainer

Glass:
Hurricane, vintage
tiki mug (or a pint
glass if that's what
you've got), chilled

Garnish:
Pineapple
wedge, Luxardo
maraschino cherry

RIYL:
Espresso Martini
(page 137),
Porn Star Martini
(page 265),
White Russian
(page 309)

SPEC

White rum	1.5 oz
Aged rum	.50 oz
Fresh lime juice	.75 oz
Pineapple juice	2.0 oz
Cream of coconut (Coco López)	3.0 oz
Demerara syrup (page 29)	.50 oz
Angostura bitters	3 dashes
Coffee bean	1
Frozen pineapple chunks	8.0 oz

OUR APPROACH

I love the Piña Colada they serve at Sweet Liberty in Miami, so I am taking a page from the book of the late great John Lermayer, who transformed this mediocre mix into a real banger with the simple addition of a few coffee beans. It's madness the way they cut down on the perceived sweetness of the drink, without adding a "coffee flavor" to the cocktail. Madness! I'm also adding bitters with the utmost restraint, because Angostura's cinnamon, allspice, and clove notes go so well with coffee and coconut but can push this into riffs territory if employed with too much zeal. Finally, the biggest threat to blender drinks is too much ice—you want a thick, lush texture, but the more ice you add, the more the cocktail waters down, so I'm using frozen pineapple chunks instead of ice to get the drink cold and flavorful, with a wicked good texture. Damn the torpedoes and batten the hatches, you could use this trick to get more pineapple flavor (without dilution) into a frozen Jungle Bird (page 181) or a blended Hotel Nacional (page 157) as well!

CHOOSE YOUR INGREDIENTS

I like using a large measure of white rum in my Piña Colada, because it's something of a neutral canvas, and easy to balance with the other ingredients. Then I add a little hardiness with a splash of aged rum, which toughens up the spine of the drink with woody molasses notes. For both rums, you could use something aged or funky or dry as a bone. You could use three or four rums if you wanna go really wild, just keep the total measurement at a nice and tidy 2 ounces. It's up to what you prefer. We tested this spec with tried-and-true Planteray 3 Star, plus Planteray 5-Year, and it tasted great. Like applying sunscreen on a sandy beach, no sunburns! For the pineapple juice, this drink will taste better if you use the fresh stuff instead of the canned stuff. See the Hotel Nacional session on page 158 for more on this.

● **PREP THE GARNISH.** This cocktail screams unbridled maximalist, so there is no garnish that is out of bounds. Floats of bitters, vintage stir sticks, and parasols for sure! Banana dolphins? FUCK yeah! Who cares that there's no banana in the build? At its most basic, the Colada is a drab shade of white, so think of that as a blank slate and go crazy with your colorful garnishes. For the purposes of this session, let's start with a pineapple wedge and a cherry to bring poolside vibes to the party. Cut a notch into the tip of the pineapple wedge so it'll perch up on the rim of the glass with ease.

● **MEASURE.** We're blending this cocktail, so no need to grab a shaker tin. Start by adding the cheapest ingredients—the coffee bean, bitters, and Dem—to the jar of the blender, then the coconut cream. This is a messy business. There will be spills and cursing. Now add the pineapple juice, then lime juice, then both rums. Toss in the frozen pineapple chunks.

● **BLEND.** If you've got a Vitamix, you have some control over how this plays out—start the speed on low, blending slowly to get everything banging together, then increase the speed in increments so the contents really get whirring. If you don't have a Vitamix, just hit the "on" switch and let 'er rip. It'll sound very loud and crunchy, but it'll get the job done. Just don't forget to securely fasten that lid in place so your work station doesn't end up covered in Colada. Once the texture becomes nice and smooth, and you think there's no pineapple chunks left, stop blending.

● **TASTE, ADJUST, AND STRAIN.** Straw taste. Right now, you have the over-the-top sweet and rich qualities of the coconut cream on one side and the puckering lime on the other, with the pineapple right in the middle displaying both sweet and acidic personalities. Is it too sweet? Add a bit of lime juice for balance. If it's weak and ghostly, add Dem. Remember this will be served on crushed ice, so if it's a bit too sweet in this moment, that'll smooth out in the glass. Once you're happy with the balance, take a barspoon and run it around in the cocktail and see if you can feel any little "clinks" against frozen pineapple nubbins. Blend again if needed, to kill these stragglers. You could pour this right from the blender into the glass over crushed ice, but it's easier to pour first into a big shaker tin and then strain from the tin into the glass.

● **GARNISH.** Add the topper of your choice and garnish. Straw it.

Let's talk about floats. The Piña Colada is a great canvas for drizzling a liqueur or spirit on top of the drink for a new aromatic experience, because the specific gravity of the Piña is so dense, anything lighter than an anvil will float. Obviously, a bit of spiced rum or funky rhum agricole or Jamaican rum will take you down a logical tropical path. But you could also float a 1/4 ounce of lime juice and barspoon of Bénédictine. Or give a bit of Cynar or Ramazzotti a go. Consider what you want to smell and then taste as it slowly melts into the body of the drink. Also think about if you want your last sips boozier, drier, or more bitter than the first. This is an interesting example of changing the narrative arc of a cocktail through technique (see Narrative Arc on page 44). Extra Credit: Google the Champagne Piña Colada from the London bar Coupette, which takes the poolside vibes out of the equation in favor of private club ones.

PISCO SOUR

The heady high from a window-seat view of the Andes

Pisco—the unaged South American brandy made from grapes—is one of the coolest, most underrated spirits in a bartender's arsenal. It tastes like liquid sunshine. So bright and floral, it's reminiscent of wandering through a field of wildflowers with a warm breeze on your cheeks. Or the high-altitude high one gets from climbing to the top of Machu Picchu. When shaken together with citrus and egg whites, it becomes a cocktail made for summer day-drinking. Even better when paired with grilled meats or fresh ceviche, as is often the case in countries like Peru and Chile. People from both locales have long argued over whether the cocktail should be made with lemon or lime, but to me they are equally radiant.

Serve:
Shaken, up

Tools:
Jigger, shaker,
Hawthorne
strainer,
fine strainer,
paring knife,
toothpick
(optional)

Glass:
Coupe, chilled

Garnish:
Bittercube
Grapefruit
Hibiscus bitters,
lemon disk

RIYL:
Corpse Reviver #2
(page 113),
French 75
(page 141),
Mai Tai
(page 189)

SPEC

Pisco	2.0 oz
Fresh lemon juice	.75 oz
Simple syrup (page 29)	1.0 oz
Egg white	1

OUR APPROACH

It's difficult to dramatically improve on this simple sour because the original build is pretty ideal just the way it is. In some bars in Lima, the typical ratio is 3 or 4 ounces of pisco to 1 ounce of citrus and 1 ounce of simple syrup, but for some drinkers that large amount of booze in one glass will render them legless in a jiffy, so we're keeping a standard 2 ounces in this spec. If you must tinker with things, you could split-base the spirits if you have access to a bunch of cool piscos, just like we do with rum in the Daiquiri (page 125). I don't have a ton of pisco on hand, and finding the good stuff in the US can be such a tiresome expedition, so in my version I just tinker with the garnishes. First, I express lemon oils over the top of the drink to spike it with extra sunshine. Then I switch up the bitters by using Bittercube Grapefruit Hibiscus bitters (formerly called Jamaican No. 2 bitters) instead of Ango, because the hibiscus notes of the bitters totally jam with the floral notes of the pisco.

CHOOSE YOUR INGREDIENTS

Pisco is a spellbinding spirit, especially when you can get your hands on one that's made with craft and tradition in mind, with a rainbow of options for styles and countries of origin (namely, Chile or Peru). For example, Acholado piscos are blends of multiple grape varieties, so their personalities can vary, whereas single varietals like Quebranta (earthy) and Italia (floral) bring singular flavors to the forefront. Look for the brands Piscologia or La Botija for best results. Also, as I mentioned, I put a modern spin on this Pisco Sour by using Bittercube Grapefruit Hibiscus bitters, but since you probably already have Angostura on hand, that works just fine, too. Another option: Amargo Chuncho bitters are formulated more like the original bitters used to make the drink in the 1920s in Lima, so that's a fun route to go if you are a history nerd.

HOW TO MIX

● **PREP THE GARNISH.** Cut a disk of lemon skin from the fruit. Set aside for garnishing. Make sure your bitters are ready to grab and dash on the fly. If you want to swirl the bitters on the surface into a cool pattern, grab a toothpick or knife or other pointy device to assist in this quest.

● **MEASURE.** Crack the egg on the edge of the tin, not on a flat surface like if you were making scrambled eggs, so that you're making as small an opening as possible, for the most control over what comes out. Plop the egg white into the smaller side of the tin, trying to make sure no yolk gets in there—you can use that for something fun later, like an omelet. Cap the tin and shake for a few seconds to aerate the egg whites. Open up the tin again and add the simple syrup and the lemon juice. Precision with both of these measurements will serve you well in the long run. Now, flip your jigger and pour out a nice flat 2 ounces of pisco. We're not going to straw taste this one, because the egg whites have not yet integrated with the rest of the ingredients, so you won't get a full snapshot of the balance and flavor of the cocktail at this point.

● **SHAKE.** Mime Shake (page 45) first—that is, shake without ice to allow the ingredients to properly gel together. Set the tin aside for a minute, because the acid in the lemon juice will work quietly on the proteins of the egg white, making them fluffier. Now, add 3 ice cubes and Coupe Shake (page 45), shake, shake. Pay attention to the way the cocktail feels inside the tin as you do this; I know an egg white drink is done when I feel the liquid inside the tin tighten up and "drop" down, like a good EDM beat drop or a tire bumping up and down as it rolls down a driveway into oncoming traffic. This is hard to explain in writing, but it's almost like you can feel the cocktail become a cohesive thing inside the tins.

● **TASTE, ADJUST, AND STRAIN.** Straw taste. Egg whites tend to make drinks taste dry, so if you need to add a barspoon of simple syrup to realign the balance, go forth and do it. In the event you shook the drink for a little too long, this addition of syrup will also buff up the texture into something less wimpy. Tap the tin on the bar top or counter a few times to compact the bubbles. You've seen baristas do this after steaming milk to get nice, even, tight foam, right? Right. Crack open the tins and double-strain the liquid from one side of the shaker to the other side of the shaker. Rinse your fine strainer and pour the iceless drink through the strainer again into the glass. This back-and-forth should result in a lovely smooth egg white top. (Use this technique in other egg white drinks, like the Amaretto Sour, page 65, or the Clover Club, page 109.)

● **GARNISH.** Aromatic bitters really gussy up the entryway into the drink. I just love the way you get that dark spicy smell as your nose nears the glass, but then the cocktail itself bears no trace of that ingredient—it makes for a surprising and delightful narrative arc. Revisit the Clover Club (page 109) if you need some guidance on how to best slash and swirl bitters on top of an egg white drink. Squeeze the lemon disk about 6 inches above the cocktail, sending its oils over the drink in aromatic glory. Discard the disk.

Truth or dare? Dare? Get out your blender! Add all of the ingredients, except the egg white, to the blender jar, plus 1/4 cup of crushed ice. Blend until smooth. Add your egg white and blend again for 3 to 5 seconds. NO MORE! Otherwise, it'll get too frothy. Pour into your tropical glass and drink up, mateys. As an aside, we know that the close cousin of this drink, the Pisco Punch, is a thing that's delicious, right? To me, that proves that pineapple and pisco are good bedfellows, so you could take inspiration from that combo and make a frozen Piña Pisco Sour by using 8 ounces of frozen pineapple chunks in the blended version instead of ice.

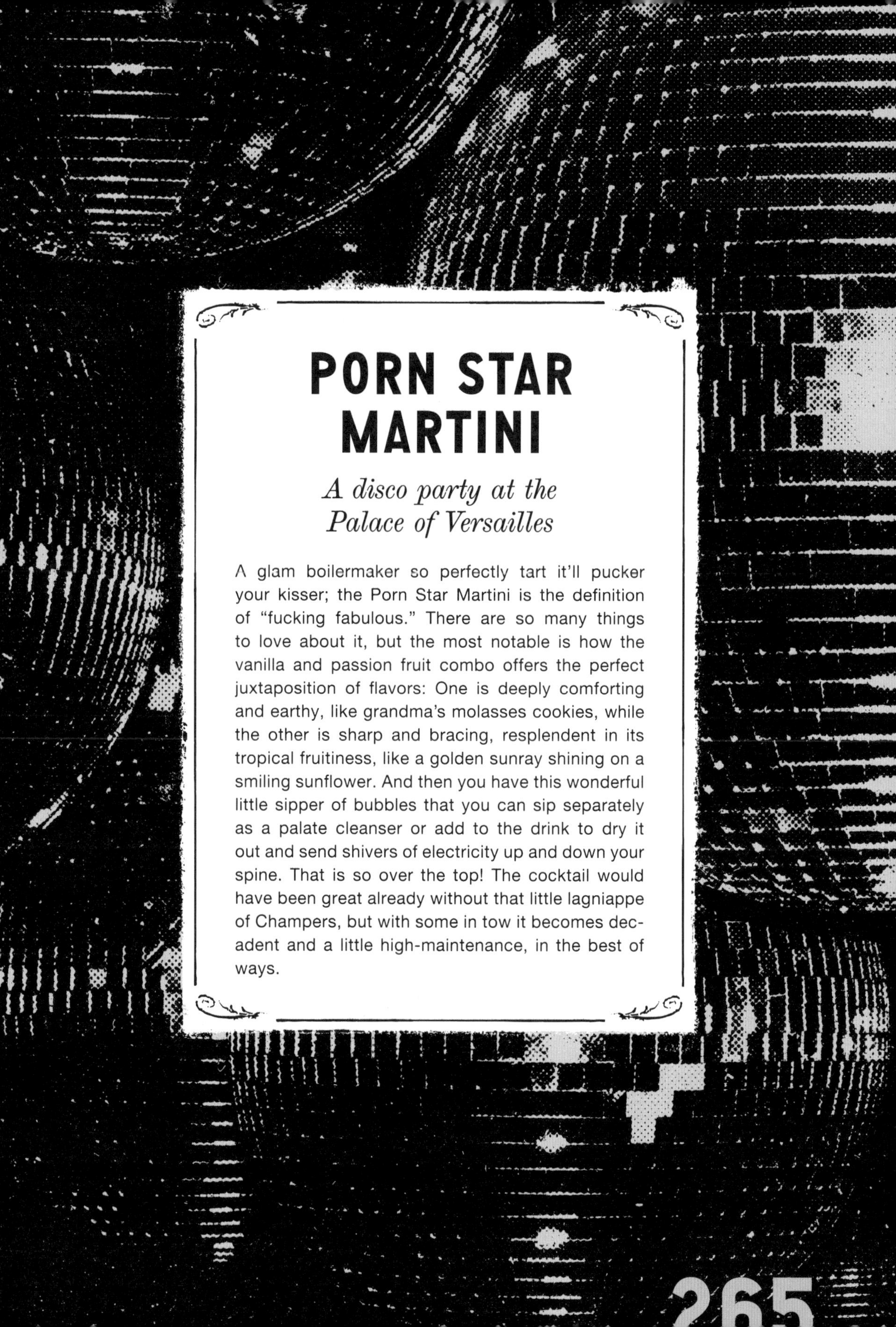

PORN STAR MARTINI

A disco party at the
Palace of Versailles

A glam boilermaker so perfectly tart it'll pucker your kisser; the Porn Star Martini is the definition of "fucking fabulous." There are so many things to love about it, but the most notable is how the vanilla and passion fruit combo offers the perfect juxtaposition of flavors: One is deeply comforting and earthy, like grandma's molasses cookies, while the other is sharp and bracing, resplendent in its tropical fruitiness, like a golden sunray shining on a smiling sunflower. And then you have this wonderful little sipper of bubbles that you can sip separately as a palate cleanser or add to the drink to dry it out and send shivers of electricity up and down your spine. That is so over the top! The cocktail would have been great already without that little lagniappe of Champers, but with some in tow it becomes decadent and a little high-maintenance, in the best of ways.

Serve:
Shaken, up

Tools:
Jigger, shaker, Hawthorne strainer, fine strainer, paring knife

Glass:
Coupe, chilled + shot glass

Garnish:
None

RIYL:
Brandy Crusta (page 101), Jet Pilot (page 177), Jungle Bird (page 181)

SPEC

Vanilla vodka	2.0 oz
Chinola passion fruit liqueur	.50 oz
Vanilla syrup (page 31)	.50 oz
Fresh lime juice	.75 oz
Peychaud's bitters	3 dashes
Sparkling wine	3 to 5 oz

OUR APPROACH

The whole concept of having the main cocktail and the sidecar of bubbles separate is more than just fun—it creates balance with seemingly disparate things. Like how the Singapore Sling at the Raffles Hotel only tastes good alongside fistfuls of salty peanuts. Or how a shot of espresso pairs well with a shot of Carpano Antica. It's all in the back and forth, and in some of those cases the cocktail simply wouldn't taste balanced without its counterpart. That said, in this session we approach the drink more like an Old Cuban (page 237), with the sparkling wine integrated into the cocktail, to make the flavor experience unfold differently. Three flexes make that work: First, some recipes include lime juice, while others do not, but I like fresh lime because without the extra acid, I find that the drink skews too sweet. Also, this recipe originally had four (four!!!) fresh passion fruit halves scooped into the tin. I'm sure the mixing process was smooth and easy because the bar made so many of them but utilizing fresh fruit and granulated sugar has too many variables for what we are trying to accomplish in this integrated version. There's something very *not* elegant about having chunks of passion fruit swimming around in a cocktail. When you use a commercial liqueur instead of fresh fruit, it brings great consistency to the ritual of cocktail making, ensuring better results every session, so we're welcoming Chinola to this build. And finally, Peychaud's bitters perform spectacularly in this drink, bolstering the vanilla notes of the vodka and syrup. A lovely trio of vanilla flavors for a lovely little tipple.

CHOOSE YOUR INGREDIENTS

Vanilla gets a bad rap. It is considered the most popular flavor in the world, and while often ubiquity is a harbinger for boredom, I totally get why this drink features vanilla in multiple applications. I think vanilla is floral and elegant, sweet, and plays well with others. I imagine Dolly Parton smells like vanilla. It's an orchid, for Pete's sake! What's not to love? Okay, so there were some truly brutal vanilla vodkas produced in the '90s, but you can get good ones now. I have an especially soft spot on my tongue for the Cîroc version. If you want to stick it to the man and make your own, get a good, expensive single origin vanilla bean from somewhere like the Amazon jungle. Split it with a paring knife and steep it in your favorite vodka for a few hours. (Strain out the bean before you put the bottle back on the shelf, otherwise the vodka flavor will get bizarre and bitter as it continues to steep.) Also: I love Chinola passion fruit liqueur for all my passion fruit liqueur needs because it's tart and bright and sweet. I literally lust after this flavor.

HOW TO MIX

- **BOTTOM THE WINE.** Add 2 to 3 ounces of the wine to the bottom of your chilled coupe. (Wanna know why? Read more about "bottoming" in the Tom Collins, on page 299.) While you're at it, pour 1 to 2 ounces of wine in the shot glass and set that aside. Bonus points if you store this sparkling sidecar in the freezer or the refrigerator, if those are close by, so the liquid doesn't warm up and lose some of its snappy bite.

- **MEASURE.** In the shaker tin, add your bitters, then the lime juice. Stack the vanilla syrup and the passion fruit liqueur up to the 1-ounce level. NO MENISCUS! Balance is the key to happiness. Donate the vanilla vodka.

- **SHAKE.** Add 5 cubes to your shaker and Coupe Shake (page 45). This doesn't need a ton of effort—you just want the drink to get nice and cold so when it hits the sparkling wine the two components gel together seamlessly.

- **TASTE, ADJUST, AND STRAIN.** Straw taste. Home in on the balance at this stage—it should be pushing the envelope of the sweet side, because the sparkling wine will dry it out. If it's not sweet enough, you have two options to fix this. If you like the flavor of the drink but want to buff up the texture, add a barspoon or so of simple syrup, which will blow up the soft round qualities of the drink without changing its flavor. Alternatively, if you think it could use a bit more vanilla character, you can use a barspoon or so of the vanilla syrup instead. Double-strain.

- **NO GARNISH.** Note how this is one of the only drinks in the book that does not call for a garnish: The cocktail smells so beautiful on its own, it's not needed! Take a nice big whiff before you indulge in that first sip. You have choices with the extra bubbly in the shot glass: Gulp it down before the cocktail, or after it's drained, or you can top up the drink in the coupe as it dwindles. Your choice.

My addition of Peychaud's bitters is a flex, I know. I love the way they have a big vanilla note that hooks onto the syrup beautifully, giving it a leg up in the drink. But if you don't want that vanilla to stand out as much, give grapefruit bitters a try—they add a dimension of slight tangy bitterness that's a touch mysterious and fun at the same time. You can also use a mindful and demure sparkling rosé instead of regular sparkling wine—ideally a fruity one with berry notes—if you want to fluff this up a bit.

QUEEN'S PARK SWIZZLE

*The more put-together cousin
of the maligned Mojito*

With its stunning three-layered assembly, the Queen's Park Swizzle (QPS for short) is like a Mojito (page 217) dressed for a carnival. More intense, because there is no sparkling water. Also more fun, because of the crushed ice. And it's more complex and edgy thanks to the Angostura bitters. I remember the first time I saw one. I was working at Milk & Honey, and it was like when Gatsby first saw Daisy. Back then, no bartender worth their salt would deign to entertain the idea of pulling out a dusty muddler and making one, but I reveled in it. It was also the first cocktail that made a whole room stop, shut up, and just watch it glide to its final resting place in front of the luckiest person in the bar. A flurry of QPS orders came in immediately after that.

Serve:
Built in the glass, on crushed ice

Tools:
Jigger, swizzle stick, Julep strainer

Glass:
Collins or footed Pilsner, chilled

Garnish:
Angostura bitters, mint bouquet

RIYL:
Airmail
(page 61),
Aviation
(page 73),
Stinger
(page 293)

SPEC

First rum	1.5 oz
Second rum	.50 oz
Fresh lime juice	.75 oz
Simple syrup (page 29)	.75 oz
Mint leaves	17

OUR APPROACH

This cocktail, much like the Mojito, is all about the mint, but now . . . WITH BITTERS! You could mix the Ango float into the drink, but I like to let it ride on top and have the last couple of sips taste wicked bitter. It reminds me of being a teenager, when my friend and I would appropriate some of his parents' Jack Daniels and put it in the bottom of our three-foot bong with ice. We would do a few monster rips, then strain out the ashes and ice and drink the whiskey. That's fucking Molecular Mixology, in the early '80s no less. So, with this spec, I'm looking at the QPS more like a Pousse Café—a famous drink with a rainbow of layers of booze—rather than an integrated cocktail. The mint should be packed in, and the swizzle technique is key to getting the whole thing ice cold.

CHOOSE YOUR INGREDIENTS

I like big, round rums in my QPS, because the thick texture tempers the sharp bite of the mint while the vanilla notes nuzzle into the baking spice of the Angostura. So stay away from those super dry expressions of the spirit for best results. Ten to One Caribbean white or dark rum works well, as does El Dorado 3-Year. If you want to stay true to the island of origin, you can use the Angostura White Oak. You could also choose a base spirit according to seasonality: Go with darker rums as the weather gets colder, stack up two unaged rums for summertime sipping, or just balance the light and dark for ultimate year-round quaffability. I've found the lighter the rum, the less time it takes to drink. Maybe that's just me though. Take a peek at the Jet Pilot session on page 177 if you want some more thoughts about how to pick and layer multiple rums in a cocktail.

HOW TO MIX

● **PREP THE GARNISH.** Pick mint for both the inside of the drink and the garnish. When you have mint in the bottom of a glass, it needs to be all leaves, no stems, because if you include the stems the herb won't sit nicely on the bottom. If there are leaves that have little holes in them from insect dinner, use those! They are the most flavorful and fragrant and won't be scrutinized by thirsty eyes. For the garnishing mint, keep aesthetics in mind: The bouquet should be bountiful and blemish-free.

● **MINT AND MEASURE.** We're going to build this in the glass as it was originally intended. It starts with the mint. With drinks like this, which are ALL about the mint, I use Sasha Petraske's mint trick. You put tender, bendy leaves in the bottom of the Collins glass, then with your spoon or your swizzle stick, trap the mint and pull it up the sides of the glass, like you're painting the inside with mint oils. Smell this. It's the most glorious version of mint. Now lower that green glory all the way down to the bottom of the glass. Add the simple, lime juice, then the rums. Resist the urge to muddle. Walk away for a minute. Fold some laundry, crush your ice, get your straw ready for the first taste. This beat or two lets the booze pull out some of the oils from the mint into the liquid. If you were to muddle the mint, it could extract too much bitterness from the herb, which can tilt the balance of the drink sideways.

● **STRAW TASTE.** To make sure everything is in the glass. It should taste like a more bombastic, boozy version of a Mojito or a warm Daiquiri with mint. Sweet. Herbaceous. Boozy! Bookmark the intensity of these qualities in your mind.

● **SWIZZLE.** This drink uses a swizzling technique: a flurry of movement that sends a lot of energy into the ice, diluting and chilling the cocktail at the same time as it integrates the components. To start, don't overfill your glass with ice because those little pebbles will end up all over kingdom come. It's best to swizzle as you burrow into a small amount of crushed ice first. So fill the glass about halfway full with crushed ice now. Get the business end of the stick about three-quarters of the way down the glass. Use your very best *Castaway* fire-starting skills to spin the stick quickly in both directions. Move the five little nubbins up and down as well, making sure all the ice has been swizzled. Do this with a LOT of energy! Do it until a frost appears on the outside of the glass—a layer so slick it takes BOTH hands to pick it up safely. That's how you know the cocktail is cold as fuck. Add a bit more crushed ice and swizzle some more.

● **GARNISH.** Top with more ice, well above the rim of the glass—I like to form a cone using my Julep strainer instead of my hand, because it's more sanitary. Take the glass in one hand and the bottle of Angostura in the other, gently dash the bitters on top of the drink while spinning the glass with the other hand. You are trying to drip the most distinct layer of dark bitters along the crest of the ice. Use your straw to make a little pathway into the ice, then use that same straw to spank the mint above the drink, expelling its oils across the surface in a symphony of aromatics. Insert the straw and then the mint garnish, and be sure to take a deep inhale of that bountiful herb before you take the first sip.

When I worked at Milk & Honey, I was enraptured by Peychaud's bitters. (I still am, as you may have noticed in the dozen or so drinks I add the bitters to in this book) Back in the day, I started making the exact same drink as the QPS but with a startlingly red Peychaud's float instead of the Angostura float. I think it made the green of the mint even greener, and I loved the vanilla and anise notes on the aroma. Sasha Petraske started calling it a Maloney Park Swizzle, and the name just stuck This is the ultimate way to personalize a drink—switching one thing for another and then having it get named after you! I also like a QPS with a bit of the Bittercube Cherry Bark bitters—I think of those bouncy cherry notes as a nice juxtaposition to the mint—or you could go with Bittercube's Blackstrap bitters to give a tip of the hat to the Dark and Stormy.

RAMOS GIN FIZZ

Saturday morning brunch
at a sidewalk café in Paris

The Ramos Gin Fizz is a damn delicious drink, with great texture from egg white, fat from the heavy cream, a premonition of effervescence from the sparkling water, the glory of gin, lemonade-adjacent acidity, and the aching beauty of orange flower water. This deft combination made the cocktail a big thing when we started the first wave of mixology back in 2000-ish. In retrospect, we all had an unhealthy fixation on this drink. In some circles it looked like borderline worship. We'd make an overwrought spectacle out of how many minutes it took to shake—and charged out the wazoo for the time and effort—creating an almost undrinkable texture. Years later, I now look at it as more of a lovely little brunch drink. When you spend less time hemming and hawing over the shaking and the tapping and the chilling, it's a lot more enjoyable to just neck it in a few minutes and move on.

Serve:
Shaken,
on the rocks

Tools:
Jigger, shaker,
Hawthorne
strainer, fine
strainer, pipette
(or tiny straw),
barspoon

Glass:
Collins, chilled

Garnish:
Orange flower
water

RIYL:
20th Century
(page 57),
Queen's Park
Swizzle
(page 269),
Tom Collins
(page 297)

SPEC

Gin	2.0 oz
Fresh lemon juice	.75 oz
Simple syrup (page 29)	1.0 oz
Heavy cream	1.0 oz
Orange bitters	1 dash
Egg white	1
Sparkling water, to top	3 oz

OUR APPROACH

The Ramos is all about texture. Together, egg white and cream create a lovely meringue, which makes the cocktail stunning to look at and fun to lick off your top lip. But you can get that fluffy structure without shaking it to the point of almost-butter, or trying to make volume rise like a liquid core sample with the soda, which makes it difficult to drink. How? We are going to shake a bit more than a coupe drink to get the right fluff in play without going overboard. In fact, I challenge you to make this cocktail start to finish in three minutes. Like the whole damn process from chilling your glass to the first sip, should be three minutes. TOPS. Set your watch to Sam Cooke's "You Send Me," and get at it. In this version, I also added some orange bitters for structure—the way they amplify the orange notes of the orange flower water is supercalifragilisticexpiali-delicious.

CHOOSE YOUR INGREDIENTS

If you are drinking this cocktail in the morning, treat yourself to an easygoing, bright, and citrusy gin. I really like the Citadelle Jardin d'Été or Hendrick's, but I'm also never mad at a London dry like Tanqueray either, because at 47.3% ABV, its extra proof gives the drink supreme spunk and stamina. For the sparkling water, try something with a cool mineral content, like Topo Chico, to see how its earthy qualities tie into the cream (or reference the Aperol Spritz on page 69 for more ideas). Finally, orange flower water is nonnegotiable, but this is a good time to put a drop on the back of your hand and give it a taste, so you can see how overwhelmingly floral it is. Keep that at the top of mind, because it's the first thing that's going into your tin—a dangerous thing, if you add too much to begin with, because you can't mask it with other flavors later.

HOW TO MIX

● **MEASURE.** Put 3 drops of orange flower water in the shaker. You can use a tiny straw if you don't have a pipette. Be judicious! Add too much accidentally, and it's going to smell like walking into the perfume department at Macy's in Herald Square. You are going to add more for aromatics later, so it's A-OK to only add a single drop here if you're nervous. Now do your egg white (see Remember Good Eggtiquette on page 234). Then add the bitters, followed by the heavy cream. Let the jigger hang over the tin for longer than usual, to drip the last droplets of cream into the tin. Wash your jigger or toss it in the sink and grab a clean one. Add the simple syrup, the lemon juice, and then the gin. Before you shake, grab the Collins glass and fill it three-quarters of the way full with ice cubes. You aren't bottoming the soda in this cocktail like you do with others, but you want the glass to start chilling now.

● **SHAKE.** This is no big deal. Cap the small tin and Mime Shake (see our guide on types of shakes on pages 45–46)—that is, shake without ice first to seamlessly integrate the heavy ingredients with the lighter ones. You want to Mime Shake for 15 seconds, at least, to get all the components shimmying together properly. Then add 2 cubes to the shaker and Coupe Shake (page 45). (Seriously, just 2 cubes, because later we're going to add 2 more and shake again.) Aim for a long, steady, sturdy shake, nothing crazy in terms of strength or pace, but keep at it until the tin starts to really bite at you with its icy cold teeth.

● **TASTE AND ADJUST.** What are you looking for with the straw taste? You have a lot of things in this build that "eat up" sugar (aka, dry out the drink): a whole egg white, 1 ounce of cream, and fresh citrus juice, so when you taste, pay attention to the balance of sweetness to dryness. The texture is going to be super lavish because of the fat in the cream, but you don't want it to taste too dry, because it will further dry out over ice and sparkling water in the glass. So don't hesitate to add a drizzle of simple syrup now and shake again for a beat just before you pour to kick things into balance.

● **SHAKE AGAIN, THEN STRAIN.** Add 2 more cubes to the tin and Rocks Shake (page 46) this time. When the cubes have mostly dissolved, making a "plink" sound, you can stop shaking and double-strain the cocktail into the Collins glass. (If there is a little bit of cocktail left over in the tin after you strain, you can toss it back into your eager maw. This is what I call the "naughty taste." I have occasionally drunk out of jiggers and tins behind the bar, and it's so verboten that it makes me feel naughty.)

Now, pick up the glass and tap it on the counter a few times. Let it sit for 30 seconds. Then take the nonspoon end of the barspoon and slide it into the center of the cocktail so that it sinks about halfway down into the glass. Pour the sparkling water down the spoon and into the glass. When you do this, the cocktail will fizz like an elementary school science fair volcano as the whipped egg white and cream meet the sparkling water. Do this slowly, so the foamy lid of the drink doesn't overflow outside the glass. A gentle trickle will do.

● **GARNISH.** Put a couple drops of orange flower water on top of the drink. Again, with the utmost caution so you don't overdo it and end up with a drink that smells like your Great Aunt June. NO STRAW. The first sip should give you a serious dairy mustache.

I love the blender version of this cocktail. It's a tipple that you want to drink in treble and takes less than a minute to make. Prep the Collins glass with sparkling water first. Set aside. In the blender, add the rest of the ingredients, plus 1 cup of crushed ice. (You could put a drop of good-quality vanilla extract, but only a drop, to make the cocktail taste warmer and more comforting. Or, at Junebug in New Orleans, they split-base the citrus measure with lemon and lime and use soft serve instead of cream! This is wild, but within the realm of possibility—it just reads more like a dessert drink vs. breezy brunch number. Omit the simple if you go this route, since soft serve already has sugar in the mix.) Now, blend slowly and carefully so that you don't overwhip the cream. Stop when it looks as though the ice has completely integrated into the drink (i.e., no big chunks left). Pour the frozen cocktail into the prepped Collins glass.

SATURN

*A beach bum dressed
in a Savile Row suit*

The Saturn is a gin drink lurking within the tsunami of rum cocktails that make up the tiki canon. Bright and sunny yellow and tart and garnished within an inch of its life, it is a killer option for when you want to wander off the beaten path of tropical drinks or spark a light of curiosity in a drinker's unsuspecting eyes. It is also a study in opposites, which I love. For every sharp, there is a round. For every bright, a shadow. On the light side, you have the juniper from the gin and the searing tartness of the passion fruit and lemon juice. Holding those close are the nuttiness of the orgeat and the deep flavors of the spices in the falernum and Angostura. This beautiful opposition is what I call juxtaposition—when unlikely things come together in harmony, it can make a drink more interesting.

Serve:
Shaken,
on crushed ice

Tools:
Jigger, shaker,
Hawthorne
strainer, Julep
strainer

Glass:
Collins, chilled

Garnish:
Peychaud's bitters,
mint bouquet

RIYL:
Bee's Knees
(page 81),
Negroni
(page 225),
Mai Tai
(page 189)

SPEC

Fords gin	1.5 oz
Hayman's Navy Strength gin	1.0 oz
Chinola passion fruit liqueur	.75 oz
Orgeat (page 31)	1.0 oz
Falernum	.25 oz
Fresh lemon juice	.75 oz
Angostura bitters	1 dash
Demerara syrup, to taste (page 29)	to taste

OUR APPROACH

In my cover version of this drink, I wanted as much gin bang for my buck as possible—drink more gin!!!—so I up the percentage of gin from 2 ounces to a sly 2½. I also want to get as much silkiness out of the orgeat as possible, so I dropped the falernum and doubled up on the nutty syrup. This creates more of a "rum" vibe in the cocktail (because rum's texture is big and round and sweet, like the orgeat) while still communicating all the botanical complexity of gin. There's no Angostura in the original recipe, but it helps sync up the disparities among the passion fruit, orgeat, and gin, which all have wildly different textures and personalities. The baking spice notes match the frequency of the ones in the falernum, too, so it's nice and matchy-matchy in that sense. Finally, a lot of people garnish this with a cherry and lemon peel skewered to look like the planet Saturn, but we like the aromatic majesty that happens with a float of Peychaud's and a mint bouquet instead, the same way they do it at Fives bar in New Orleans.

CHOOSE YOUR INGREDIENTS

I want my gin to be as aggressive as a Millwall hooligan. It should taste like falling out of a juniper tree and hitting every single fucking branch on the way down. Like getting mugged by a North Pole elf wielding a wreath of pine and mistletoe. Like rolling down a hill in backwoods Oregon, plush Douglas fir needles stabbing your eyeballs and getting lodged in your nostrils. Why? As one of the only gin cocktails in the tiki realm, the Saturn is an anomaly, right? An underdog! And with quirky underdog cocktails like this one, the best thing we can do to make them shine is capitalize on the point of interest that makes them unique in the first place. In other words, this is a weird gin cocktail that exists within a category that's otherwise just an ocean of rum drinks, so let's sound the alarms and make it the most GINNY gin cocktail we can. For this reason, bring on the London dry gins and the Navy Strength gins, and the juniper-forward American gins! Try Copper & Kings The Moons of Juniper or St. George Terroir if you need a starting point for this adventure.

- **PREP THE GARNISH.** Procure an absurdly abundant bouquet of mint—one that is soft on the eyes, without dry ragged edges or the like—and set aside. Make sure your Peychaud's are nearby.

- **MEASURE.** The Angostura will be dashed into the shaker tin first. I always do bitters first for a couple reasons. First, so I don't forget them. Also, because they are the cheapest ingredient due to the amount you throw in (literal dashes instead of ounces), so if you mess up and hit "repeat" on measuring, you won't be wasting a ton of dough. After the bitters, add the lemon, falernum, and orgeat, followed by the passion fruit liqueur. Next the gins.

- **STRAW TASTE.** See how big and rambunctious the sweetness is in this drink? How thick and gooey is its texture? That's a good thing! It's all gonna smooth out once it hits crushed ice. Speaking of which, right now is a good time to fill the Collins glass three-quarters of the way with crushed ice. Set aside.

- **SHAKE.** We would usually do a whip shake for this tiki tipple, since it is served on crushed ice (see the Daisy de Santiago on page 129 for more on this technique), but instead we're going to Rocks Shake (page 46) the Saturn with 5 uniform ice cubes. This is because there's a ton of booze and sugar in this drink—the gin, liqueur, falernum, and bitters all add proof, and two of those add sweetness in addition to the orgeat—so you need it to add a good deal of dilution from the ice to achieve balance.

- **TASTE, ADJUST, AND STRAIN.** Straw taste. If all the booze has calmed down, you can strain into your prepped Collins glass. If you're not sure, go ahead and shake for another 10 seconds or so, just to be safe. Think about the balance of sweetness to acidity in this moment also: With so many sweet elements in play, you might want to add a touch more lemon juice to lift the texture and liven up the brightness of the cocktail before you strain. Remember that you can always add more juice later if you need it, but you can't take any away if you overdo it, so start with a little squeeze of citrus, give it a quick stir and straw taste, then add more if needed. Finally, in the unexpected event that you over-diluted the drink when you shook it, you might add another dash of Ango to buffer up the backbone with a bit of spice and fortitude. Use your Julep strainer to add a dome of crushed ice.

- **GARNISH.** Add that prepped mint. Then, dash bitters around the top of the drink, softly, so they aren't shooting down into the cocktail. You want them to float so all of those gorgeous vanilla and fennel aromas greet the nose of the drinker when they raise the glass! Now add a straw and get after it.

Use Kirk's Fassionola (page 31) instead of the passion fruit liqueur for a slightly different take on the Saturn. Fassionola is more complex than straight-up passion fruit, featuring hibiscus, which has a cool grippy texture thanks to the presence of the tartaric acid (named by the same person who named allspice and the walkie-talkie), and guava, which rumbles with a low tropical note. I really like when this drink is red, too, which it is with Fassionola. I will swear, to my dying Corpse Reviver #2, that the color makes the drink taste better. (Fun fact: Swapping Fassionola for passion fruit is also what we do in the Hurricane recipe on page 165. Try it out there, too.)

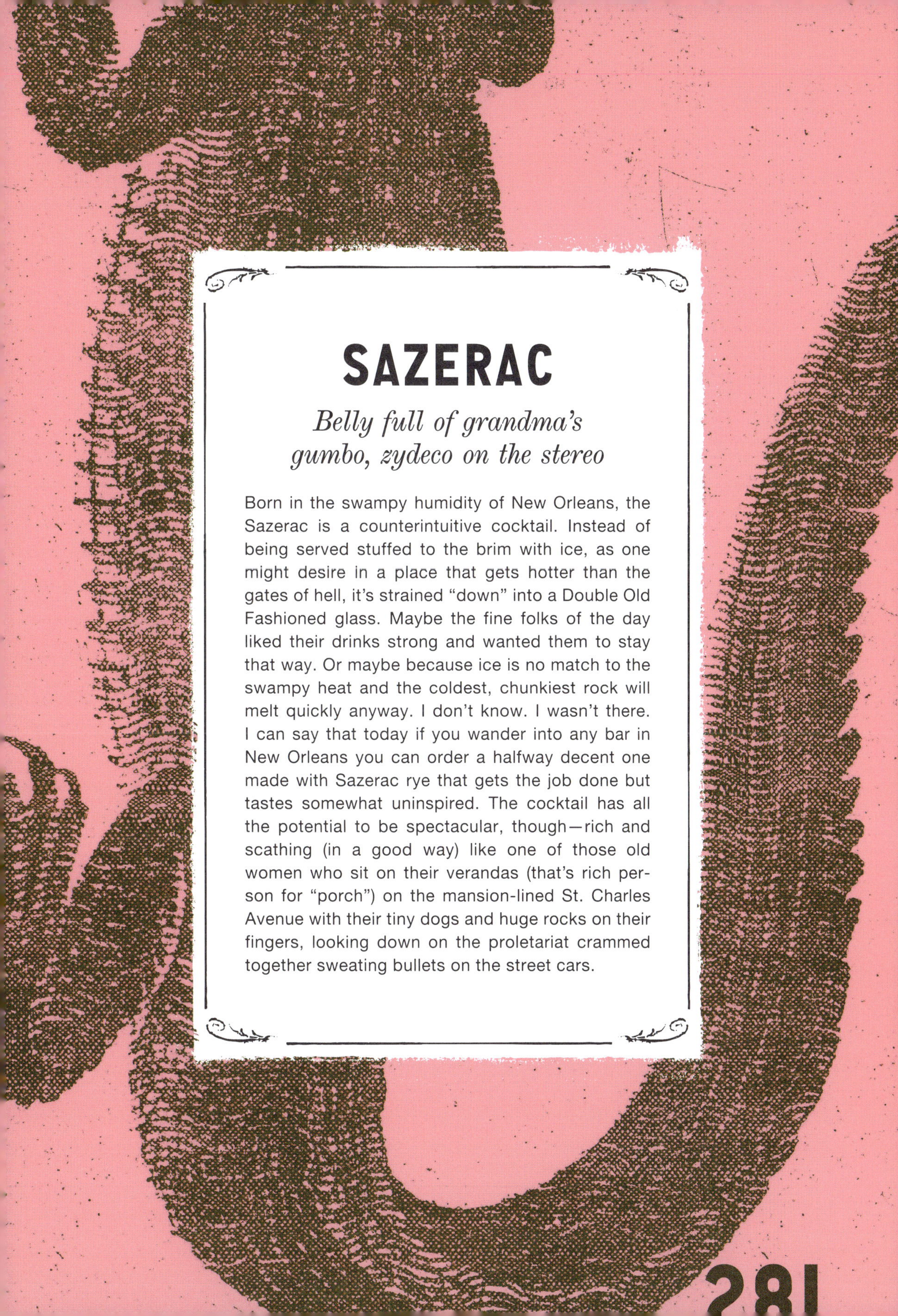

SAZERAC

*Belly full of grandma's
gumbo, zydeco on the stereo*

Born in the swampy humidity of New Orleans, the Sazerac is a counterintuitive cocktail. Instead of being served stuffed to the brim with ice, as one might desire in a place that gets hotter than the gates of hell, it's strained "down" into a Double Old Fashioned glass. Maybe the fine folks of the day liked their drinks strong and wanted them to stay that way. Or maybe because ice is no match to the swampy heat and the coldest, chunkiest rock will melt quickly anyway. I don't know. I wasn't there. I can say that today if you wander into any bar in New Orleans you can order a halfway decent one made with Sazerac rye that gets the job done but tastes somewhat uninspired. The cocktail has all the potential to be spectacular, though—rich and scathing (in a good way) like one of those old women who sit on their verandas (that's rich person for "porch") on the mansion-lined St. Charles Avenue with their tiny dogs and huge rocks on their fingers, looking down on the proletariat crammed together sweating bullets on the street cars.

Serve:
Stirred, down

Tools:
Jigger, mixing glass, barspoon, Julep strainer, Y-peeler, atomizer (optional)

Glass:
Double Old Fashioned, chilled

Garnish:
Lemon peel

RIYL:
Hemingway Daiquiri (page 153), Irish Coffee (page 169), Vieux Carré (page 301)

Rittenhouse rye whiskey	1.0 oz
Ferrand 1840 Cognac	1.0 oz
Demerara syrup (page 29)	.25 oz
Peychaud's bitters	5 to 7 dashes
Herbsaint, to rinse	

OUR APPROACH

My friend Kirk Estopinal from Cure in New Orleans makes the best Sazerac of all time. When he worked with us at The Violet Hour in Chicago, his version was almost red with Peychaud's—literally bleeding with bitters. I think the care he used in getting the right amount of lemon oil on top of the cocktail was paramount. Instead of just letting it rip, he would gently squeeze the lemon disk about a foot above the drink letting the oils drift down, feather-like, to grace the surface. Like Kirk, I'm going to also employ a ludicrous amount of Peychaud's, then fuck with the spirit base as well. I've said many times that the easiest way to make your drinks more complex is to split-base your spirits, but in most cases, I'm talking about the same spirits, like two gins in a Martini or a bourbon and rye in a Manhattan. In the case of the Saz, the rye is dry with baking spices, caramel, toffee, and vanilla notes, while brandy has stone fruit (like apricot), plus floral notes like orange blossom, and woody notes like cigar box. These things complement one another beautifully.

CHOOSE YOUR INGREDIENTS

Because this drink has all the same simplicity of an Old Fashioned, it's an opportunity to use really fucking good rye whiskey. Old Overholt 100 is one of my favorites. Or you can't go wrong with the Knob Creek rye or the Michter's Straight Rye, either. All three sit comfortably between the whiskeys that teeter on the bottom shelf and the super-fancy ones that are egregiously expensive. For the Cognac, go straight for the good stuff—Ferrand 1840 is bulletproof. Now, you might be tempted to grab an absinthe in place of the Herbsaint, but I'd suggest resisting the urge—Herbsaint is a softer version of absinthe, with less proof and a come-hither sweetness, which makes it an alluring fit for the Sazerac.

HOW TO MIX

• **PREP THE GARNISH.** Pull a lemon peel with a Y-peeler.

• **RINSE.** I like to take my time and make this cocktail in a leisurely manner because it's a New Orleans drink, sultry and dignified, so you don't want to break a sweat. Fill the DOF glass with crushed ice and add 3 dashes of Herbsaint. Swirl that around so it coats the inside of the glass and set aside. If you have an atomizer, you could use that instead of rinsing the glass: Just spray a spritz or two from above the DOF so that the molecules of Herbsaint distribute themselves evenly over the interior of the glass.

● **MEASURE.** Fill a mixing glass three-quarters full of ice and add the completely irresponsible amount of Peychaud's bitters. (You are not allowed to even THINK the word Angostura while making this drink.) Give this a quick swirl with a barspoon to make sure the bitters don't get stuck on top of the ice cubes. Then add the Dem, and stack the Cognac and whiskey in the jigger, and pour that 2-ounce measure into the glass. Don't be sloppy and pour the spirits into the jigger in a way that blooms up like a soufflé over the rim of the instrument. A sharp 2 ounces with no extra drops is the goal.

● **STRAW TASTE.** To make sure everything is in the glass. What you're looking for here is the balance of bitter to sweet to spirit. The cocktail isn't going to change a ton during the stirring process—the three will come into harmony as the sweetness reduces and the "heat" of the spirit softens—but this is a good moment to decide to add a bit more whiskey or Cognac, if you think that'll be pleasing to your palate.

● **STIR.** Coupe Stir (page 47) for about 30 rotations or so, then walk away for a moment to let the ice melt a bit more. Maybe change the music to one of the greatest hits of Dwayne Michael Carter Jr. (aka Lil Wayne) for a hot NOLA vibe. Come back, stir some more. Keep an eye on how much liquid is in the mixing glass as you stir—the goal is to almost (almost) double the volume of the drink during this process.

● **TASTE, ADJUST, AND STRAIN.** Is it cold enough? With just enough water content to make sure your eyes aren't going to water with booziness if the drink ends up near room temperature as you're drinking it? If not, stir some more. Taste it again to make sure you've hit the right balance. I seriously doubt you'll need more bitters at this stage, but if that's your jam, then jam away. Return to the Double Old Fashioned glass with the Herbsaint—tilt it at an 85-degree angle over a sink or trash can so the liquid comes almost to the lip of the glass. Swirl to coat the entire inside of the glass, then dump the ice. Smell the glass—if it doesn't smell like a huge bombastic assault of anise, add one more dash of Herbsaint plus more crushed ice and rinse again. Once the Double Old Fashioned glass is ready, strain the prepared cocktail into the cold glass.

● **GARNISH.** The most spectacular thing about the Sazerac is the careful layering of volatile aromatic components. The first sniff can be a real showstopper, as the Herbsaint rinse says hello with a smack of herbaceous fennel and anise. When the lemon oil is introduced, the combo soars. With a deft hand you have created something that is neither black licorice nor lemon oil, but both, like the early evening sunlight that bounces off pink houses in the French Quarter. Soon enough the lemon molecules will escape into the sultry air and the brawn of the Herbsaint will muscle forward to escort you to the end of the drink, which is now combined with the randy aroma of the whiskey. With the flourish of a street magician, squeeze the peel 4 to 6 inches above the glass so the oils drift gently down on the cocktail. Insert the peel. Imbibe wistfully.

Resist the urge to fuck with this one too much. Instead, I'll give you a fun tip: One nice move I've seen is where you chill the glass with crushed ice and the Herbsaint as usual, then you pour out the diluted Herbsaint into a very small glass, add a bit of simple syrup, and then add more crushed ice and a lemon twist so you get a tiny "Herbsaint frappé" on the side of your cocktail. Classy. As. All. Get. Out.

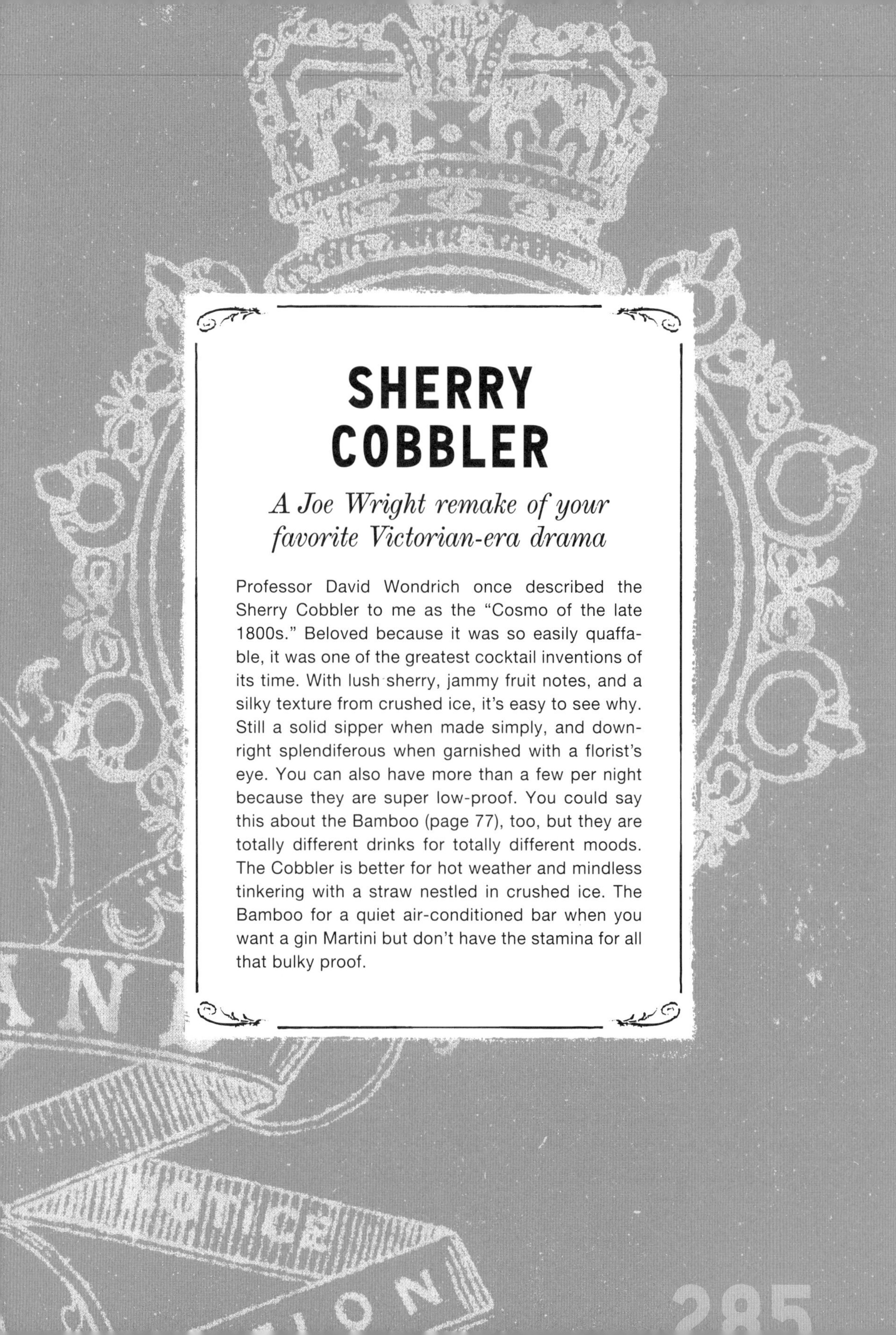

SHERRY COBBLER

A Joe Wright remake of your favorite Victorian-era drama

Professor David Wondrich once described the Sherry Cobbler to me as the "Cosmo of the late 1800s." Beloved because it was so easily quaffable, it was one of the greatest cocktail inventions of its time. With lush sherry, jammy fruit notes, and a silky texture from crushed ice, it's easy to see why. Still a solid sipper when made simply, and downright splendiferous when garnished with a florist's eye. You can also have more than a few per night because they are super low-proof. You could say this about the Bamboo (page 77), too, but they are totally different drinks for totally different moods. The Cobbler is better for hot weather and mindless tinkering with a straw nestled in crushed ice. The Bamboo for a quiet air-conditioned bar when you want a gin Martini but don't have the stamina for all that bulky proof.

Serve:
Shaken,
on crushed ice

Tools:
Jigger, shaker,
Hawthorne
strainer, fine
strainer, offset
serrated knife

Glass:
Double Old
Fashioned, chilled

Garnish:
Lemon or orange
peel, seasonal
berries, mint
bouquet

RIYL:
Bijou (page 85),
New York Sour
(page 233),
Tom Collins
(page 297)

SPEC

Amontillado sherry . . . . 4.0 oz
Demerara syrup (page 29) . . . . .75 oz
Orange bitters . . . . 2 dashes
Seasonal fruits of your choice, to muddle

OUR APPROACH

The key to a good cobbler is that it should remain wholly uncomplicated. It doesn't need mixologizing, it just needs solid construction and great ingredients. For this session, we're starting with the most basic cobbler recipe out there. The only flex is that I add orange bitters to my build, because it's mostly unobtrusive, adding just one small, intriguing facet of flavor. I think a fig or date bitters would also sing in this. Proceed with restraint as you devise your own approach! You don't need things that compete with the delicacy of the sherry; you need things that happily skip alongside—bitters, interesting seasonal berries, or flavored syrups (like cinnamon or vanilla, page 30) are great examples of how to lift up the fortified wine instead of overshadowing its compelling complexity.

CHOOSE YOUR INGREDIENTS

For the sherry component of the Sherry Cobbler, style is everything. Emma and I like amontillado for this build, because it has enough heft to carry the weight of the fruits, its nuttiness offsets the sweetness of said fruits, and its nice round texture holds its own against the crush of crushed ice. Alternatively, oloroso and PX sherries are jam-packed with jammy fruit notes and a thick texture akin to a good, heavy sweet vermouth, which is delightful in the winter; and fino sherry has crisp, dry minerality that sings during summer months. A combo of different sherries will never set you down the wrong path. Know the difference between these genres and you'll be able to improvise as effortlessly as Jon Batiste tickling the ivory keys. When choosing what fruit to muddle, think seasonally. Fresh fruit is always going to taste better when it's ripe and in-season. Unless it's IQF—which means each piece of fruit is individually frozen shortly after harvest—in which case, fine, go ahead and prove me wrong. Anyway, almost every sort of fruit goes with sherry, so if you're working with oloroso or PX because it's fall or winter, think about contrasting those jammy notes with an Angostura-soaked grapefruit wedge (like in the Jet Pilot page 177), or instead lean *into* the vibes with a couple of crushed pomegranate seeds, thinly sliced pears, or kumquats, cut in half. If it's spring or summer, keep it simple with blackberries or strawberries.

HOW TO MIX

● **PREP THE GARNISH.** Think about picking aromas that either echo, complement, or juxtapose the qualities of the sherry and the fruits you use in the drink. I like to sometimes think of the cobbler as a cheese board: The sherry plus Demerara are the candied almonds, then you need some sort of fruit paste or preserves, like quince or blueberry, to balance that out, right? Pick out seasonal berries to serve this purpose. Then there is the "vegetable" component of the board, which could be fulfilled by the herbaceous mint sprigs. To top it off is the acidic portion, being pickles on the board: We use lemon or orange wheels, which add just a whiff of citrus to the aromatic blend. As you prep, make sure your berries are fresh and your citrus wheels have notches cut into the bottom in the event you want to perch them on the rim of the glass instead of nestling into the crushed ice.

● **MUDDLE AND MEASURE.** Dash the orange bitters in the tin. Proceed by muddling your fruits in the mix. In most cases, just a few gentle presses will get the juice out and the pulp mashed up enough so that they'll shake together with the other ingredients. You don't need to murder them. Now, add your Demerara syrup. I like Dem in this drink because it has darkness that matches the richness and complexity of the amontillado (also the case with oloroso and PX; if you use fino, consider a simple syrup instead for brightness). Now measure and add your sherry.

● **STRAW TASTE.** To make sure everything is in the tin.

● **SHAKE.** Whip Shake (page 46) this real quick, without thinking too hard about it. Just enough to chill everything. That is: Add about 2 ounces of crushed ice to the tin and shake until you can't hear the rocks hitting the metal anymore. Use a pace that's akin to the one set by The Young Rascals on the track "Groovin'." Or you could get a bit fancy and roll this mixture back and forth between the two tins a few times instead—bartenders call this "throwing"—to aerate the sherry and add dilution and chill at the same time. Either way, make the timing of this act as fleeting as the memory of a summer fling.

● **TASTE, ADJUST, AND STRAIN.** You should taste a lot of lush sweetness, almost too much, because the cocktail will soften as it sits over the crushed ice in the glass. Add more Demerara syrup or simple to the mix now if you don't feel like it's quite right. If it's cold outside I might feel inclined to add a modicum of Angostura bitters to coax the baking spice notes out further. This also helps if you've perhaps overdiluted this low-proof beauty and need to bring some thunder back into the cocktail. Grab a chilled glass, fill it three-quarters of the way with crushed ice, and double-strain the drink into the glass. Top with crushed ice again, so it looks like a mountain, not a molehill.

● **GARNISH.** Now garnish this like a sumptuous cornucopia of colors and aromas. Stick a straw into the mountain of crushed ice, and suck it down with glee.

Emma was enamored by the Sherry Cobbler at the Broken Shaker when the Chicago location first opened. It had three sherries, some white rum for backbone (see the Pimm's Cup, page 253), and an oleo-saccharum of strawberries and oranges. That is a great example of how you can explode a simple cocktail into something super complex. Sometimes I go in the opposite direction, applying as much restraint as I am capable of, to show you how sometimes less can be more: Try using only orange wedges and orange bitters and falernum instead of Demerara. This combo rounds out the fruity parts of the drink's "orange" personality with some darker spindles of structure while welcoming whispers of sweet clove and nutmeg to the party. I like the way those spices amplify the darker nutty notes in the amontillado. This is a great fall cobbler, best imbibed during those weird heat waves that sometimes spring up out of nowhere.

SIDECAR

*If Escoffier riffed on the
classic Margarita*

The Sidecar is not a classic that comes to mind immediately for everyone—it's more of the B-side only your extra-hip "I knew that band before it was cool" friend calls for at the bar—but I know this drink like the back of my hand, with a stamp that says I paid to get in. With the miracle of aged brandy at its core, and ripples of warm orange chanting chorus, the drink tastes as good on the hottest day of the year as it does on the coldest and most blustery. It's approachable enough for cocktail neophytes who love Cosmos (page 117), and complex enough to get a "hell yeah" from the most jaded of mixologists. It's a skosh more refined than a Margarita (page 201), not quite as bullish as a Pegu Club (page 249), which has a stiff upper lip. And you can dress it up for fancy occasions with a simple whimsical sugar rim. Without one, the drink bears the gravitas of Sartre and Rodin arguing "art versus craft" in a Paris bistro. Simply put: It's one of my all-time favs.

Serve:
Shaken, up

Tools:
Jigger, shaker,
Hawthorne
strainer,
fine strainer,
paring knife

Glass:
Coupe, chilled

Garnish:
Orange disk,
half sugar rim

RIYL:
Brandy Crusta
(page 101),
Hotel Nacional
(page 157),
Porn Star Martini
(page 265)

SPEC

Cognac	2.0 oz
Fresh lemon juice	.75 oz
Ferrand dry curaçao	.75 oz
Demerara syrup (page 29)	.25 oz
Orange bitters	3 dashes

OUR APPROACH

This glorious three touch cocktail is a study in minimalism. It is also one of my favorite cocktails to approach through the lens of "echoing," which is where I laser in on a single ingredient or flavor in the drink and find sneaky ways to get more of that element into the recipe. In the Sidecar, I think the "orange" element is the drink's lynchpin, so I layer the orange curaçao with orange bitters *and* an orange peel garnish. Between the warm sweet notes of curaçao, the candied flavor of the bitters, and the smack of fresh citrus in the garnish, threading these many elements together creates a very intriguing and complicated orange profile.

CHOOSE YOUR INGREDIENTS

Brandy is magical. I don't know the science, but in my experience when you are making a distillate with grapes, cool shit happens. I put Cognac in this recipe because it's classy, but there are plenty of beautiful grape-based brandies from other regions that will also get the job done. Try Brandy Sainte Louise on for size! Now, a brief lesson on orange liqueur, the Margo Martindale of ingredients, because it can work with everybody and always knows the assignment. When I started out bartending, we only had access to triple sec, which was essentially garbage. Later there were the snooty orange liqueurs Cointreau and Grand Marnier, which we called "grandma" for short. They sat up on the top shelf, only pulled down to be swirled in a snifter. Marie Brizard was the go-to middle ground after that, and these days there is the Ferrand dry curaçao, which is a total banger. I like to drink it on the rocks with an orange peel expressed and inserted. If you're new to the ingredient, make the cocktail with one of the basic orange liqueurs first, then try it again with the Ferrand to see the striking difference in elegance it brings to the glass.

HOW TO MIX

● **PREP THE GARNISH.** Slice the orange disk from the fruit and set aside for garnish. The Sidecar is a pretty drink, with a deep orange hue and alluring sugar rim that beckons those plagued by thirst to come hither, but the orange disk is getting used just for its oils and not for its appearance in the glass, so you don't have to worry about maculations, marks, and moles on the skin. For the sugar rim: Place a pile of sugar on a flat surface. Take a citrus wedge and rub it in a straight line on the outside rim of half the glass. You can use a bev nap to touch up the lines if any drippage happens. Now, roll the outside of the glass through the flat sugar slowly, making sure none of it gets on the inside of the glass. Holding the glass upside down, tap the bottom of the glass over a sink to discard excess granules of sugar. Place the glass in the freezer so the sugar concentrates while you mix the cocktail.

● **MEASURE.** First add the bitters, then stack the Demerara syrup and the orange curaçao, so the total measure of both ingredients comes out to an even 1 ounce. Then add the lemon juice. Get the Cognac in there to mingle next. Measure everything as precisely as you can, because there are so few ingredients in this drink even the smallest misstep might result in bad balance.

● **STRAW TASTE.** To make sure everything is in the tin. Right now, the cocktail should taste tart and chewy and booze-forward. Like a maximalist marmalade. Or fresh-from-the-oven apricot cobbler, but room-temp instead of piping hot.

● **SHAKE.** To the tin, add 5 cubes and Coupe Shake (page 45). This drink is super boozy because proof is included in both the spirit and the liqueur, and it's extra sweet, too, because it's got both Demerara syrup and liqueur, so it's going to need a bit more shaking than a plain old sour made with only simple syrup (like, say, a Gimlet, page 145). This is a bigger drink than your typical sour also, so the shake will feel slightly different than a straight Gimlet would. You'll develop good instincts over time and with many sessions—for now, just aim for a groovy shake à la Winona Ryder's levitating dance at the end of *Beetlejuice*. Shake, shake, shake, señora! Work it all the time.

● **TASTE, ADJUST, AND STRAIN.** Straw taste. At this point the darkness of the Cognac should have lifted like a sunrise into the medley of citrus juice and liqueur. If it's still really sweet right now, shake a bit longer—the drink won't be going over ice in the glass so it's not going to change much down the road. It's just going to get warmer, and as it warms it'll taste sweeter, so you want to strain it out of the tin when it's extra cold and lightweight instead of too boozy and rich. Double-strain into your coupe.

● **GARNISH.** Express the oils of your prepped disk over the surface of the drink, liberally. Discard the disk.

To amplify the citrus notes of this cocktail in a cool way, you can royal shake with an orange peel or a lemon peel, as we did with the Cosmo (page 117). You can also change the aromatic garnish to a spray of bitters, or a combo of lemon and orange oils. If you want to add some dimension that tastes a bit like old antique books, slide a bit of Bénédictine into the orange curaçao ration. Or if it's hot out, recognize that this is just a French margarita and blend it with 2 ounces of ice!

STINGER

*The icy cool blast of
after-dinner mints*

To me, the feeling of crushing an ice-cold Stinger is the closest thing to the joy a child gets from successfully running down the ice cream truck with a pocket full of change. It is a bewildering cocktail on so many levels, because it breaks every rule I know. It's shaken when convention says it should be stirred, composed of all sweet ingredients and no citrus or bitters for balance. Plus Cognac and crème de menthe seem like water and oil: Cognac is like a refined smoking jacket of leather, fig, and oak, while crème de menthe is a big sip of ice-cold menthol, smokin' Newports back by the dumpster—they are polar opposites, but when you put them together and shake the living snot out of it, you get a delicious drink. With an intense boozyness and palate-cleansing minty-ness, somehow it just works.

Serve:
Shaken,
on crushed ice

Tools:
Jigger, shaker

Glass:
Double Old
Fashioned, chilled

Garnish:
Mint bouquet

RIYL:
Bijou (page 85),
Brandy Alexander
(page 97),
Gin Blossom
(page 210)

SPEC

Ferrand 1840 Cognac	1.5 oz
Tempus Fugit white crème de menthe	1.5 oz

OUR APPROACH

When we started working on our specs for the classics at The Violet Hour back in the day, I immediately thought there should only be ¼ ounce or so of crème de menthe in this cocktail, because it's such a flavor bully. I didn't want it stealing the mic. I also figured stirring and straining the drink over a big chunk of ice would be the way to respectfully treat the Cognac. ALL OF THESE THOUGHTS WERE WRONG. Our best build turned out to come from Dale DeGroff's recipe from the 1970s: equal parts crème de menthe and Cognac, brutally shaken and strained over crushed ice, then garnished with a big bouquet of mint. In a 2016 interview, DeGroff emphasized that serving the cocktail on crushed ice makes it clean and cold, the "wonderful icy mint was like an adult York Peppermint Patty." I should have just looked up King Cocktail's version in the first place to save myself the consternation and liquor waste. In the words of Canadian legend Alanis Morissette: You live, you learn.

CHOOSE YOUR INGREDIENTS

You'll notice we call brands out by name in the spec. This is no accident, because the combo of Ferrand and Tempus Fugit is as groovalicious as Sonny and Cher. (Giffard sorta works, but its minty qualities tend to poke at the Cognac, whereas the Tempus Fugit snuggles up to it. For us, anyway.) The reason that we keep coming back to these brands is because they were made with an eye focused on cocktail making. When I was coming up behind the stick, most of the "top shelf" spirits were made only for sipping, so they were often not great in a mixed drink scenario. The ancillary liqueurs were made as cheaply as possible, so they brought down the quality of a drink. Now we have companies making quality products intended to lock shields with bold flavors. These are two of them, so I highly recommend using them. On a related note: We call for the white version of menthe in this cocktail instead of the green version because it was made with high-quality ingredients and bears an exceptional balance. I have yet to find a green version of the liqueur that tastes as good. Most of them are thin and syrupy and lacking in complexity. That said, I love a green Grasshopper—the color makes it taste more minty—so I've been known to split-base the liqueur on occasion. Right now at The Elbow Room in Vancouver, Washington, for example, I use 1 ounce of white and ½ ounce of green against the same measure of Cognac, so the integrity of flavor remains mostly intact but you get that gorgeous screamin' green sheen.

- **PREP THE GARNISH.** Pick your mint bouquet for garnish based on which bundles look and smell the freshest. Set aside for later.

- **MEASURE.** In a shaker, start by tossing the white crème de menthe and Cognac together superciliously.

- **STRAW TASTE.** Yes, there are only two ingredients in play here, so the odds of forgetting to add one are slim, but give this a straw taste anyway, noting how big, boozy, and fucking SWEEEEET the combo is at this stage. Tucking this information away in your working memory for a few minutes will be helpful for when you start shaking and straw tasting next.

- **SHAKE.** Add 3 ice cubes instead of 5, because you are going to shake savagely to get most of the ice's water content into the drink but then serve the cocktail on crushed ice, so you don't need those extra cubes' worth of dilution. Make sense? Now Rocks Shake (page 46), viciously. Shake as if the shaker is going to come out of your grasp and fly across the room. Just remember to always point the shaker away from things that break or might need a trip to the ER. Hold onto a counter, hook your foot under something heavy, and SHAKE! Stop shaking when it sounds like the ice is gushing like a waterfall instead of rocking and rolling around inside the tin.

- **TASTE, ADJUST, AND ROLL.** The act of shaking is using the water content of the melting ice in the tin to cut the sweetness of the crème de menthe, so if it's tasting too sweet on this straw taste, cap the tins again and keep shaking. Always shake half the amount of time you initially shook at this stage, to avoid egregious overshaking. Taste again. If it needs a bump of simple syrup because you shook too long and now it's watery, that should guide the mix back into balance. Once it tastes like a cohesive cocktail, but still one that's quite robust in strength and personality (because it will dilute over the crushed ice after a while), roll it into your DOF glass over crushed ice.

- **GARNISH.** A beautiful bouquet of mint spanked above the drink before garnishing ensures a wicked echo of the white crème de menthe. To do this: Hold a straw over the top of the drink horizontally, about 1 inch from the surface of the drink. Then smack the mint on the straw. This will send its aromatic oils careening over the cocktail.

For Emma, the way to make this drink sparkle is to lean into its minty qualities, so just as we do in the Grasshopper (page 149), a little bit of Fernet-Branca puts the pedal to the metal on the mint character while adding an underlying pang of bitterness. She thinks this makes the menthe qualities seem sharper and more focused, creating more of an obvious contrast with the warmth of the brandy. Her spec: 2 ounces of Cognac plus 1½ ounces of crème de menthe, and ¼ ounce of Fernet. Mint garnish, natch. A riff? Depends on who you ask, I guess.

TOM COLLINS

Rocking chair with
toes in the air

Is there another cocktail that better evokes the notion of whiling away a lazy afternoon on a three-season porch, favorite book in hand, warm breeze against your cheeks, more than the Tom Collins? A breezy adult lemonade spiked with gin, best quaffed quickly in the doldrums of summer while wearing your best seersucker or sundress, the Tom Collins is a simple but sophisticated highball. Unassuming and eager to please. A cocktail with all the characteristics of a fine Gin & Tonic, served without the impolite imposition of quinine. Like a loyal Golden Retriever, or reruns of your favorite vintage sitcom, it will always be there for you. Remember, it may taste like lemonade, but it's more like lemonade with a shiv, because that spike of gin WILL come for you if you're not careful.

Serve:
Shaken,
on the rocks

Tools:
Jigger, shaker,
Hawthorne
strainer, offset
serrated knife,
cocktail pick

Glass:
Collins, chilled

Garnish:
Orange or
lemon wheel,
cherry

RIYL:
Aviation
(page 73),
Breakfast Martini
(page 105),
Martini (page 205)

SPEC

Old Tom gin	2.0 oz
Fresh lemon juice	.75 oz
Simple syrup (page 29)	.50 oz
Sparkling water, to bottom	4 to 5 oz

OUR APPROACH

I struggle telling people why I like this drink so much. I think it's because it's uncomplicated. Just perfectly itself. It doesn't put on any airs or try to brag or boast. It's yummy. Comfort can be found in many places in cocktails, and I'm not talking about the effect of ethanol on the brain chemistry, but rather the Proustian (*Ratatouille*) memories that hark back to an idyllic childhood memory or feeling of being on vacation without any flight delays. The Tom Collins, in its purest state, and when made with attention to small details, evokes those feelings of comfort, so I'm not going to ruin that by messing with any of its elements. That includes using Old Tom instead of a London dry gin—Old Tom is the O.G. way to make the drink, a historic style of gin from Old Timey England that has a touch more sweetness and less of a juniper note than London dry.

CHOOSE YOUR INGREDIENTS

Old Tom gin is a marvel—try Hayman's or Ransom for a good introduction to the style. Also, this is a prime moment to revisit the discussion about the different types of bubbly water that exist and how to choose one that's gonna work well in your cocktail, because the key to a great Tom Collins lies in its fizzy effervescence. It must be cool, crisp, and full of tight bubbles. As discussed in the Aperol Spritz session (page 69), every brand of bubbly water has different mineral content and different size and intensity of bubbles. Using Topo Chico instead of San Pellegrino, for example, can be a personal touch that (slightly) changes the flavor and personality of the drink. The former has bubbles that'll scramble for the spotlight, whereas Pellegrino has a softer, less sprightly texture. Topo also blooms with minerals in a way Pellegrino does not. These comparisons could go on for days with other brands. Choose something that pleases YOU, or play around with making a few Collinses at once, each with a different brand, to find out which one you like the most.

HOW TO MIX

● **PREP THE GARNISH.** Cut the citrus wheel and stick the skewer through one side so it points toward you. Then skewer the cherry and push the skewer down through the other side of the wheel, away from you. This should resemble a big sun with a red center. Set aside.

- **MEASURE.** Take your shaker and toss in the simple syrup (if you don't have Old Tom gin, which has sugar in it, and are using a London dry, which doesn't have sugar added, bump the simple syrup up to ¾ ounce). Now, add the fresh lemon juice, followed by the gin, to the shaker.

- **STRAW TASTE.** To make sure everything is in the tin. You know that little Girl Scout down the street who opens a lemonade stand every summer and their product is so sweet it makes you cringe? That's what you want your Tom Collins to taste like before you add the sparkling water. If little Betsy adds too much gin, just tip her accordingly.

- **BOTTOM THE SPARKLING WATER.** Grab your Collins glass and fill it with ice and about two fingers worth of sparkling water and set aside. We use this method (called "bottoming") because the "body" of the drink (in this case, the gin, citrus, and sugar shaken together) will ease into the bubbles when you pour the cocktail from the shaker into the sparkling water. If you top with sparkling water instead, you have to stir the drink, which breaks up some of that perfect carbonation. Not ideal.

- **SHAKE.** Grab 5 pristine ice cubes, add them to the shaker, and Collins Shake (page 46), which is a little less vigorous and a lot shorter than a Coupe Shake (page 45). More like you are going through the motions of a shake but in a way that's kinda lazy. This should take about as long as it takes an orange tossed in the air to fall to the ground.

- **TASTE, ADJUST, AND STRAIN.** Straw taste. The mixture should be a big burst of sweet and boozy lemon and gin. It should be more robust than what you think you'd normally sip, because once it hits the ice and the sparkling water it'll smooth out into a properly balanced cocktail. Strain, pouring the liquid directly into the sparkling water instead of on the ice at the top of the glass, so you have a gentle incorporation. If you need to add a wee bit of sparkling water to correct your wash line—that is, how much space sits open between the top of the cocktail and the top of the glass—do that now. You want about one finger's worth of wash line here, because the garnish is going to take up a surprising amount of room.

- **GARNISH.** The garnish might seem like an afterthought, but it's not. Because I often describe this drink as "adult lemonade," leaning into that vibe with the garnish can really drive the point home. A freshly cut lemon wheel smells like lemon juice, not lemon oil, so it truly echoes the lemon juice (and the concept of lemonade) in this drink. While the cherry doesn't add any aroma, in this instance that's okay! It is a little reward for finishing your drink.

Sometimes when I want to change a classic, or put my own eeentsy beeentsy spin on it, I think about how I can further amplify the emotional experience of the drink—in this case, those warm, comforting, nostalgic emotions of drinking lemonade as a kid. For the Tom Collins, I've been known to bring in some warm cherry and vanilla notes via a barspoon of the syrup that Luxardo cherries come in, plus Peychaud's bitters. Think Cherry Lemonade versus a regular old lemon-lemonade. The small amount of syrup won't affect the balance of this drink—it just makes it a touch sweeter and changes the color to a pretty pink I love pink drinks. They taste better than yellow drinks. It's science. You'd make the drink the same way as before but dash the bitters and add the barspoon of cherry juice into the shaker tin before you add the simple syrup.

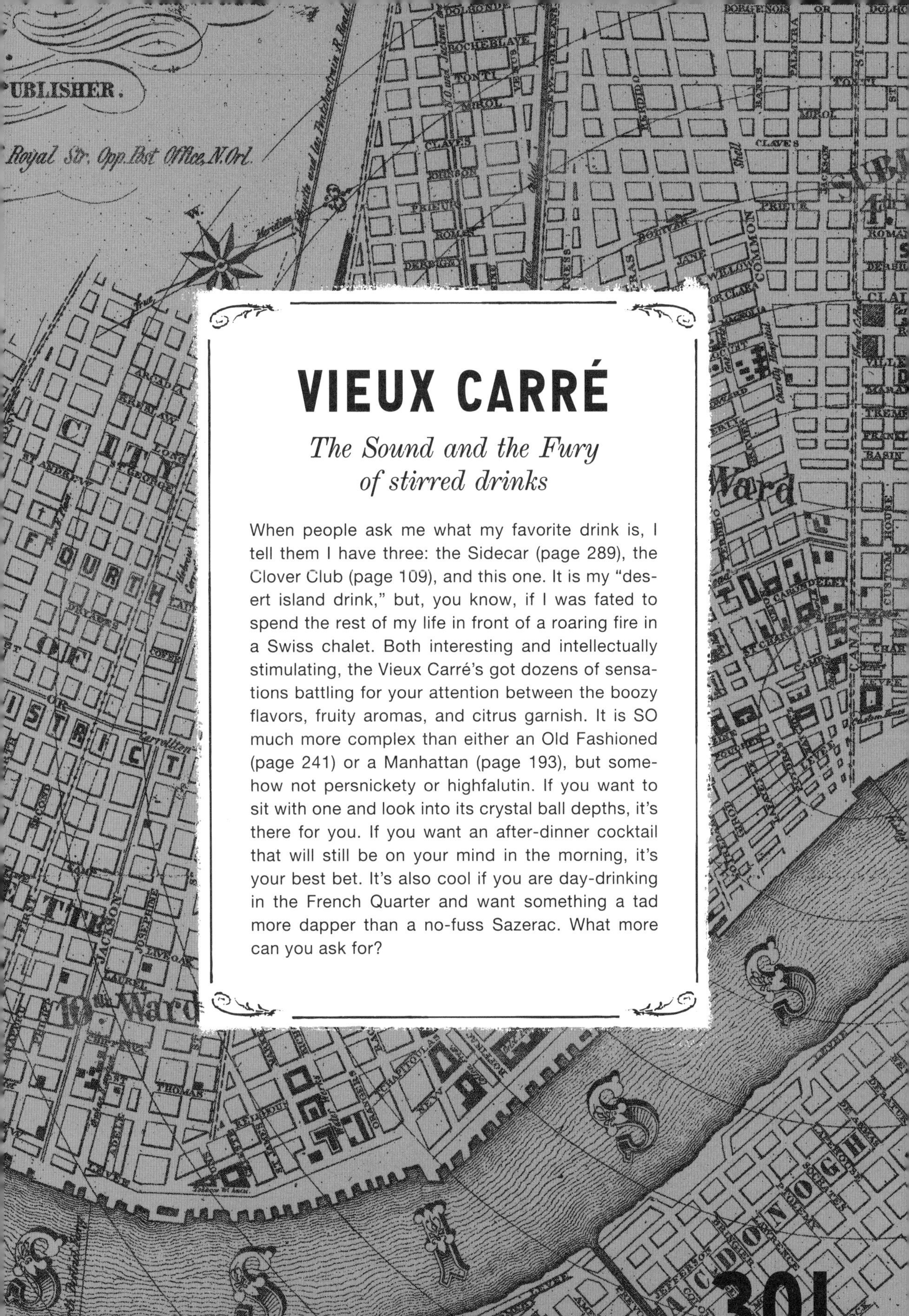

VIEUX CARRÉ

The Sound and the Fury of stirred drinks

When people ask me what my favorite drink is, I tell them I have three: the Sidecar (page 289), the Clover Club (page 109), and this one. It is my "desert island drink," but, you know, if I was fated to spend the rest of my life in front of a roaring fire in a Swiss chalet. Both interesting and intellectually stimulating, the Vieux Carré's got dozens of sensations battling for your attention between the boozy flavors, fruity aromas, and citrus garnish. It is SO much more complex than either an Old Fashioned (page 241) or a Manhattan (page 193), but somehow not persnickety or highfalutin. If you want to sit with one and look into its crystal ball depths, it's there for you. If you want an after-dinner cocktail that will still be on your mind in the morning, it's your best bet. It's also cool if you are day-drinking in the French Quarter and want something a tad more dapper than a no-fuss Sazerac. What more can you ask for?

Serve:
Stirred, large cube
or sphere

Tools:
Jigger, mixing
glass, barspoon,
Julep strainer,
Y-peeler,
paring knife

Glass:
Double Old
Fashioned, chilled

Garnish:
Orange or lemon
peel (or both)

RIYL:
Creole Cocktail
(page 198),
Cuba Libre
(page 121),
Old Fashioned
(page 241)

SPEC

Ferrand 1840 Cognac	1.0 oz
Rye whiskey	1.0 oz
Sweet vermouth	1.0 oz
Bénédictine	.25 oz
Angostura bitters	2 dashes
Peychaud's bitters	2 dashes

OUR APPROACH

Without a doubt, this cocktail has one of the most interesting narrative arcs of all time (page 44). It starts out with heavy citrus peel aromas on the nose, a little hot and sweet on the tongue, and then a few minutes in, the booze mellows, the brightness of the garnish fades, and the flavors open up in a symphony of botanicals—all honey and heather, like a picnic in a meadow of the French Alps—as the bitters whirl dervish and the sweet vermouth cuddles up to the aged spirits. In those last gasps, its full personality has fully opened, it's super cold, and the ABV has sunk into chuggable low-proof territory. I try not to knock it back like a shot, but before the empty glass hits the bar, I'm ready to get on that ride again. For all of these reasons, I'm sticking close to the way this cocktail has always been made.

CHOOSE YOUR INGREDIENTS

I like rich, sweet Cognacs in cocktails like the Stinger (page 293), but a Vieux Carré sparkles with a bold but dry brandy. I like Ferrand the most, because it's 90-proof instead of 80-proof like most others—this extra proof punches through in a pleasing way. Rémy would also work, because it has a nice lean quality. Something like Hennessy would be too round for me. You could also use Armagnac, which is often drier than Cognac, if you want to push the limits of balance. Regarding the whiskey: In this drink, the spirit should feel like the rustle of leaves in your ears, like woodfire and bark and dried summer flowers crawling into your head, like a rose-gold sunset shooting out of your eye sockets. Each style and land it comes from will inform its characteristics. Taste widely and find the bards in each category. Rye is aces in this cocktail, but if you are looking for bourbon, try the high-proof, high-rye ones like Wild Turkey 101 or Old Grand Dad Bottled-in-Bond—the extra bite from the proof helps tame the sweetness of the vermouth and Bénédictine.

- **PREP THE GARNISH.** We recommend orange peel oils first and foremost, but you could also use a lemon peel (or both lemon and orange) if you want a different aromatic experience. When prepping the garnish, know this is a sophisticated drink that deserves white glove treatment. Pull your citrus peel and trim it using a paring knife, so the edges look tidy as fuck. If that peel has any defects, deformities, or dents, it'll be a horrible eyesore, distracting from all the studied technique you're applying to your mixing practice! Don't ruin a delicious drink with a disgraceful garnish.

- **MEASURE.** Fill a mixing glass three-quarters of the way to the top with ice, then drizzle the bitters down the side of the glass so they don't just season the topmost cubes. You need to taste them inside the drink on the first straw taste, and that's not possible if they're clinging on for dear life to the topmost glacier. Next, donate the Bénédictine, add the sweet vermouth, and then stack the rye whiskey and Cognac. Do not let the full 2 ounces of spirit sneak above the rim, and do not let an extra glug escape from the bottle into the tin. Say it with me: Slow, steady movement, slow, steady measurement, equals better balance. Stir for a second to get all the liquids integrated with one another.

- **STRAW TASTE.** To make sure everything is in the mixing glass. Pay extra attention to the volume of the bitters and the character of the Bénédictine at this moment. Both will soften and hold hands waffle style with the spirits shortly, easing into a quiet admiration for one another, but at this moment you should be able to taste both relatively prominently.

- **STIR.** Employ a Chunk Stir (page 47) for this marvelous cocktail. Consider the proof of the rye and Cognac before you begin, and keep that in the back of your mind as you stir. If they are both high, like 100-proof, put on the song "Swimmers" by Zero 7 and just swim swim swim through that stir. Remember, this is a Southern cocktail, so there's no rushing it into existence.

- **TASTE, ADJUST, AND STRAIN.** Taste the drink as you stir; does it need a wee bit more bitters for depth? Just one more dash of Peychaud's, if you like that vanilla note, or Angostura if you want more clove and nutmeg. How about ⅛ ounce—just a whisper—of Demerara syrup to balance out the bitterness? The Bénédictine can be like a pesky liquor rep, assertive almost to the point of harassment, so on the second straw taste I often add a sploosh of Cognac to shut it up and give it a last stir. Once everything tastes right—a little sweet and a bit boozy because it's going over ice—strain into the glass onto the largest piece of ice you have.

- **GARNISH.** Express the oils of your chosen peel over the top of the drink, then insert it with the pretty side facing the drinker, at eleven o'clock if you are a righty, or one o'clock if you are a child of the devil.

For another version of the drink, I find inspiration in the maximalist hybrid style of John Bradstreet, a designer of objects and interiors in the early 1900s in Minneapolis who folded in Asian aesthetics with Arts and Crafts style. It's a mishmash of influences, but a mishmash that works. In short, I like a split-base of Cognac and apple brandy, then a split-base of sweet vermouth with Ramazzotti amaro, plus 2 dashes of Angostura bitters and 7 dashes of Peychaud's. There's still ¼ ounce of Bénédictine in there to keep the VC model intact. It's so wild. I love it. Emma's favorite version, on the other hand, is a bit simpler. Born from a brilliant improvisation made on-the-fly by Liz Kelley of Cure in New Orleans, the drink simply features a top-shelf Armagnac instead of Cognac. The chocolatey notes of the spirit bring great depths of soul to the classic build.

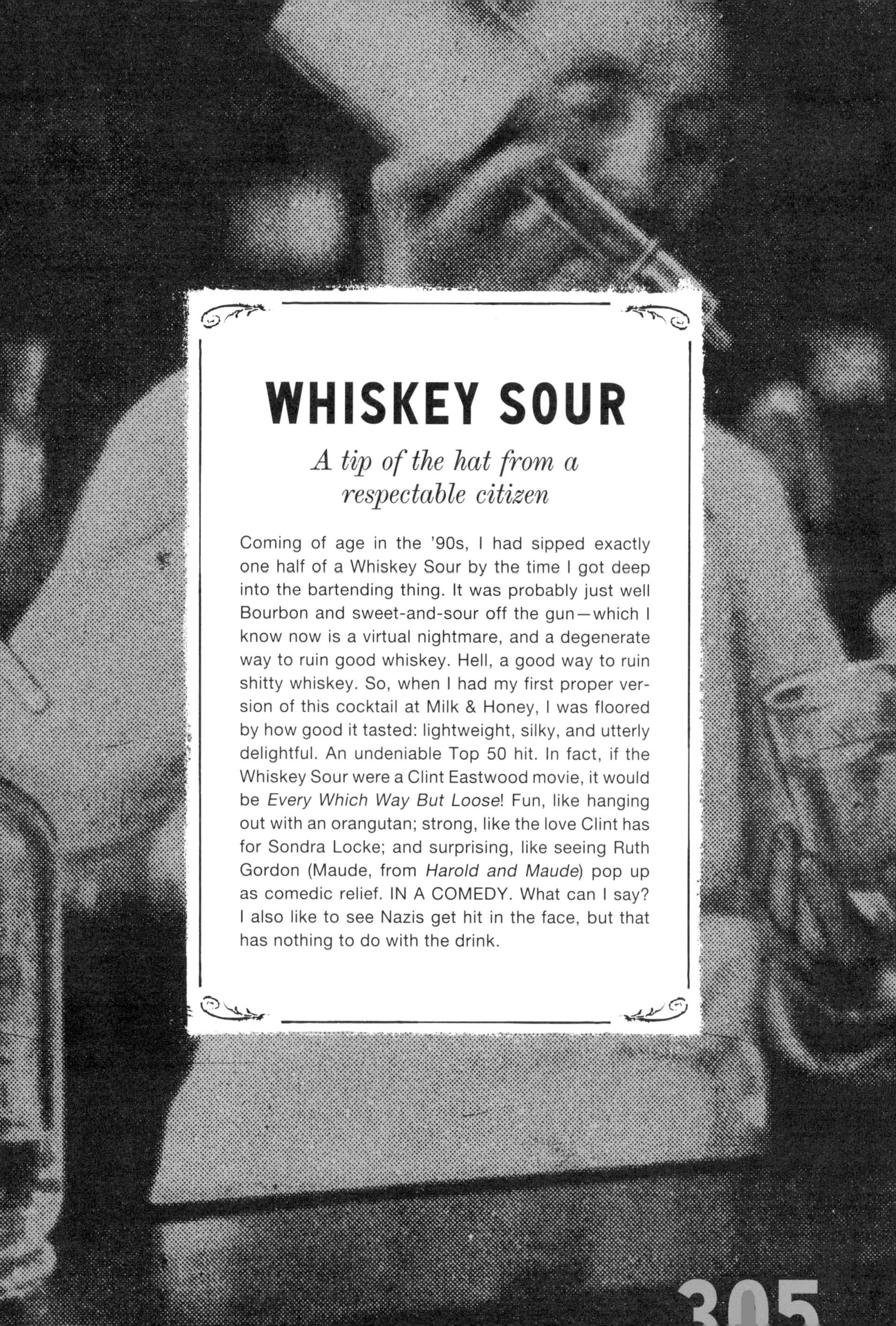

WHISKEY SOUR

A tip of the hat from a respectable citizen

Coming of age in the '90s, I had sipped exactly one half of a Whiskey Sour by the time I got deep into the bartending thing. It was probably just well Bourbon and sweet-and-sour off the gun—which I know now is a virtual nightmare, and a degenerate way to ruin good whiskey. Hell, a good way to ruin shitty whiskey. So, when I had my first proper version of this cocktail at Milk & Honey, I was floored by how good it tasted: lightweight, silky, and utterly delightful. An undeniable Top 50 hit. In fact, if the Whiskey Sour were a Clint Eastwood movie, it would be *Every Which Way But Loose*! Fun, like hanging out with an orangutan; strong, like the love Clint has for Sondra Locke; and surprising, like seeing Ruth Gordon (Maude, from *Harold and Maude*) pop up as comedic relief. IN A COMEDY. What can I say? I also like to see Nazis get hit in the face, but that has nothing to do with the drink.

Serve:
Shaken, up

Tools:
Jigger, shaker,
Hawthorne
strainer,
fine strainer,
channel knife

Glass:
Coupe + sidecar,
chilled

Garnish:
Angostura bitters,
lemon pigtail

RIYL:
Bee's Knees
(page 81),
Espresso Martini
(page 137),
Old Cuban
(page 237)

SPEC

Bourbon	. . . .	2.0 oz
Fresh lemon juice	. . . .	.75 oz
Simple syrup (page 29)	. . . .	1.0 oz
Egg white	. . . .	1

OUR APPROACH

Over time many barkeeps have decided to ditch the egg white in this recipe, but a Whiskey Sour sans egg white is just a Kentucky Daiquiri, and while there ain't no shame in that game, it's just not the same thing. The only reason to not use an egg is if you are sadly allergic to them. Oh, or if you have the good fortune to be a vegan, in which case you could use 2 tablespoons of aquafaba instead to get a similar texture. Who decided you could use chickpea juice in a quaffable cocktail? Beats me. Oh, the marvels of modern bartending! Anyway, I'm keeping the egg white in play because it lays down a structure and cushion for the whiskey to shine, and it stretches out the spirit's flavor in a different way than water or sugar do. In other words, it makes the whole cocktail taste more whiskey-forward to me.

CHOOSE YOUR INGREDIENTS

I've heard many barflies express the opinion that using expensive whiskeys in cocktails is a "waste," but I disagree. Nobody on their deathbed has ever said, "I'm so glad I used the rotgut when I made cocktails for my friends." By my book, your cocktail is only as good as its shittiest component, so go ahead and use that Willet when making Whiskey Sours, if the spirit moves you. Bourbon is standard for a Whiskey Sour, because the corn base makes it round and mellow and easygoing. I like Buffalo Trace or Elijah Craig in this build, because these are two of the bourboniest bourbons made on the Bourbon Trail. You don't *have* to use bourbon in this cocktail, though. Other types of whiskey will bring different flavors to the glass depending on what raw material they're made from, so think about how rye whiskey will have rye bread qualities (dry and savory) while corn whiskey will taste sweet and round, and wheat whiskey will have a soft and easygoing personality. Choose one according to your preferences, or pick a few different types and split-base to your heart's desire!

HOW TO MIX

● **MEASURE.** You want to get the lemon and the egg white canoodling as soon as possible, because the acid in the citrus mellows out the whites, so get that egg white into the tin and measure out the simple syrup and the lemon juice. Let that sit for a minute or so, then follow with the whiskey.

● **SHAKE.** Cap the tin. Mime Shake (page 45) first: That is, shake the contents of the tin without ice, just to get them all two-stepping together. Do this until you can feel the ingredients moving as a single unit inside the tin. Set the shaker down. Mosey over to the freezer and carefully grab your coupe and sidecar that have been chilling for at least 5 minutes. (You will need a sidecar if your coupe is less than 9 ounces, because this drink with all its foamy goodness gets really big.)

● **STRAW TASTE.** Uncap the tin and straw taste. It'll taste frothy, boozy, tart, and disjointed. You need to extrapolate what this is going to taste like when cold and with bright lemon in your nose. (Hint: It might taste a bit sweet now, but it'll dry out after you shake with ice and seem even more dry when you preface the first sip with lemon oil aromas.) Concentrate on the proof of the spirits as that will give you some idea of how long to shake with ice—if you've got 100-proof whiskey in there, it'll taste very pointy in this moment, and you'll need to shake for much longer than if it's lower-proof to smooth out those rough edges.

● **SHAKE AGAIN.** Add 3 cubes, recap, and Coupe Shake (page 45). Listen for when the ice starts to really turn into slush—that's when you can open the tins for the next straw taste.

● **TASTE, ADJUST, AND STRAIN.** Crack the tins, tap the tin with the cocktail in it on the counter to settle the foam. Straw taste: See how the egg white and the sugar came together during the shake? Magic. In the event it's crazy dry, you can add a bit of syrup now. Or, if for some reason all the white didn't come out into the tin, the drink may be too sweet, in which case you can add a bit of lemon and shake a bit more to integrate, then double-strain this into your glass. Move the fine strainer to above the sidecar and fill it with what's left in the tin.

● **GARNISH.** I like the way a pigtail works in an egg white sour. It's a very "Renaissance sea monster," if you will. Grab your lemon with the poles (the two bumps) by your thumb and forefinger. If you are right-handed, have the knife "upside down" so it curves away from you. Now pull the knife toward you while spinning the citrus away from you. Oil should shoot out in a mist over the top of the cocktail. Let this fragrant cloud settle on the top of your drink. Once you have about 5 inches of peel, or a little shorter than a $100 bill, start curling the peel into a tight curl, or cylinder shape, like a pig's tail. I like to whip the long end toward me each revolution, for speed, efficiency, and sheer swank. Now put about three-quarters of the spiral in the drink with a bit hanging onto the rim of the glass. See? LOCH NESS MONSTER! Add a few drops of bitters, take a toothpick or knife, and swirl them into a pattern that is pleasing to the eyes.

WHITE RUSSIAN

*You will abide. Oh yes,
you will abide.*

One of those maligned drinks that hit its stride in the 1970s—and found brief favor again among stoners who loved *The Big Lebowski* twenty years later—the White Russian is kind of like an adult chocolate milk, injected with a jolt of caffeine. I mean, there's no chocolate in the standard recipe today (though there was in its precursor, which was gin, crème de cacao, and cream), but its billowingly creamy, cozy vibes stir up the same nostalgic glow as grabbing a small carton from the lunch line. Pure comfort.

Serve:
Shaken,
on the rocks

Tools:
Jigger, shaker,
barspoon,
Julep strainer,
mixing bowl,
whisk, paring knife

Glass:
Double Old
Fashioned, chilled

Garnish:
Orange disk

RIYL:
Brandy Crusta
(page 101),
Mai Tai (page 189),
Ramos Gin Fizz
(page 273)

SPEC

Vodka	1.5 oz
Kahlúa coffee liqueur	.75 oz
Second coffee liqueur	.25 oz
Tempus Fugit crème de cacao (optional)	.125 oz
Heavy cream	.75 oz

OUR APPROACH

When free-poured into a Double Old Fashioned glass over wimpy ice cubes, the White Russian can be a real mess, but when approached with surgical precision, it becomes a proper nightcap (or brunch drink, if that's your vibe) that's worth writing home about. The cocktail's integrity lies in the relationship between strong and bitter and sweet and creamy: a four-way intersection of balance. For this version, we add more vodka than some other recipes do, because the punch of booze sets a sturdy base for the sugar and dairy. Then, taking notes from the team at Gus' Sip & Dip in Chicago, where the entire menu features classics dialed-in for modern palates, we hand-whip the heavy cream to give the drink a light-weight, fluffy texture. At the bar, they bottom the cream in the glass, but we're going to float it on top so the first sip is cozy and welcoming before it nosedives into bittersweet coffee and booze. A different narrative arc! Finally, we're giving you the option to add crème de cacao, because it'll sync up with (and sweeten) a bone-dry new-school coffee liqueur in ways both subtle and sophisticated.

CHOOSE YOUR INGREDIENTS

Start with the vodka—I know I waxed poetic about its neutrality in the Moscow Mule session (page 221), but depending on the raw material, the spirit can have slightly different textures. For example, Tito's from Texas is corn-based, so it's got a relatively round, balanced profile, whereas something like Nikka Coffey vodka, made with corn and barley, has an extra silky texture. Vodka made from wheat is going to have a different personality than one made from potatoes. And so on. Think about whether you want the vodka to cut through the dairy like a razor or cozy up next to it like a weighted blanket. Also: Split-basing Kahlúa with another coffee liqueur tends to work really well, because the Kahlúa brings that old-school vibe to the mix, while something new like St. George NOLA Coffee Liqueur, Tempus Fugit's Crème de Moka, or Borghetti di Vero Caffè Espresso will round out that classic flavor with interesting and unexpected nuance (like bitter chicory root, warm vanilla, and dark roast molasses notes, respectively). You can play around with the ratios of those two ingredients as long as they always come out to 1 ounce. Finally, the most important thing about a White Russian is that it needs to have a substantial heft vs.

resembling a watery puddle. Milk is a no-no, most alternative milks don't have the right texture, and while half-and-half kinda works in a pinch, the superstar in this drink is heavy cream, because it has the fat content to stand up to the other sharp and boozy ingredients.

- **PREP THE GARNISH.** Cut an orange disk from the citrus. You're discarding this after using its oils as garnish, so it doesn't have to be a showstopper, aesthetically speaking.

- **MEASURE.** If you're using crème de cacao for a little sweetness, add that now. Then stack the coffee liqueurs and add those to the tin. (You could also just use 1 full ounce of Kahlúa if you prefer.) Both of these ingredients have sugar, so stacking helps ensure you don't add too much of either one to the mix. Precise measurements are the first step on the yellow brick road to balance. Now, measure and pour the vodka.

- **STRAW TASTE.** To make sure everything is in the tin.

- **WHIP THE CREAM.** You have two options for whipping the cream. If you're old-school and want to use a whisk, you can: Pour the cream into a (chilled) bowl and go to town. If you want to save some time, add the heavy cream to an empty shaker tin and shake (without ice). When the texture is smooth and tight, like packed snow—not so thick you can't pour it—stop whisking or shaking. Set aside while you shake the cocktail.

- **SHAKE.** Add 5 ice cubes to the shaker tin and give the cocktail a nice and rough-and-tumble Rocks Shake (page 46) to bash together the booze and sugar. Stop shaking when the tin gets really cold and the ice still sounds like it's tumbling around in the tin like a rock tumbler.

- **TASTE, ADJUST, AND STRAIN.** Plunge your straw into the depths of the drink to snatch up a taste. Remember, the heavy cream is going to come into play soon and dampen the intensity of the ingredients you're tasting right now—the ice in the glass will also thin the drink out more over time—so the texture of the mix should be bombastic at this stage, overly sweet and almost chewy. If the texture is thin, or too bitter, you can add a barspoon or two of simple syrup or Demerara to plump it up in anticipation of its future. Strain this into a Double Old Fashioned glass over a few glistening ice cubes.

- **GARNISH.** First, the cream. Float ¾ to 1 ounce of whipped cream gently over the top of the cocktail. Then garnish with the oils from an orange disk to bring some aromatic interest to the experience. Cream smells relatively neutral, but when you bring in the soulful glow of a little orange oil, it brightens up the mood and sets the stage for the dark and bitter deliciousness to follow. Discard the disk.

This drink is primed for a "bitters make it better" moment. In the Sidecar (page 289) I talk at length about "echoing," which is pinpointing one ingredient in the drink and finding ways to integrate that ingredient into the drink in a few more ways. You could look at this drink in terms of the orange peel aroma and add orange bitters to the build—orange and coffee work SO well together, this is a real winner for the coffee drinkers out there. Coffee bitters also exist, so you could throw some of those into the tin and on top of the heavy cream, to create a kaleidoscope of coffee flavor in the drink. And if you like New Orleans–style coffee, try chicory coffee bitters! Angostura brings a cool cinnamon spice note to the drink, and cherry bitters could add a nice fruity note, if your new-school coffee liqueur is made with beans that lean into the fruity side of coffee.

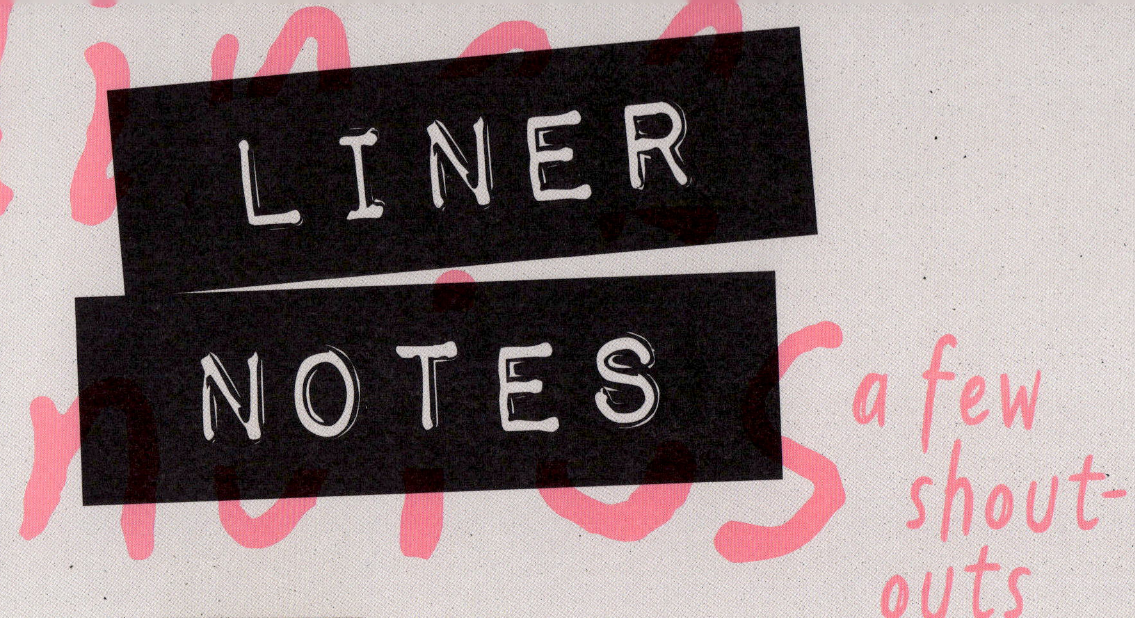

Writing a first book is easy, because you don't know what you are in for. To do a second one is absolute madness. These are the people who made this one feel less like work, and much more fun.

Emma, your dedication, patience, and ability to take my scribblings and make them coherent and erudite is Herculean. Thank you from the bottom of my heart and the top of my squirrel brain.

Kim Witherspoon, Jessica Mileo, and **Naomi Eisenbeiss** at Inkwell, thank you for the magic of getting this project greenlit and being steadfast navigators on every literary journey.

Jenn Sit, Ian Dingman, and all the other talented folks at Clarkson Potter for taking these ideas and a bunch of words and making it into a beautiful book. The difference between the manuscript and the finished product is the difference between warm gin and a perfect Martini.

I would like to raise a glass to all the intrepid readers and drink mixers who bought *The Bartender's Manifesto.* Those of you who reached out with a kind word or two, the next round is on me. You were instrumental in allowing us to write *The Classic Cocktail Sessions.*

To all the industry folks, chefs, servers, mentors, barbacks, and bartenders I have learned from over these many years, this is your book, too, thank you and I hope you see yourselves in it.

To **Neal** and **Kirk,** who allowed me behind their bars to test out a lot of these cocktails. You are gentlemen, scholars, and good judges of fine whiskey, thank you.

There are many people I wrote this book for: They were the audience in my mind, the inquisitive folks that I was trying to inform and impress. **Karen, Lisa,** and **Maranda** (The Tipsy Librarian), to name but a few of the many.

Otis and **Bella,** thank you for being a great sounding board, a safe harbor, and the best place in the world to write.

If you are new to making drinks, or just looking for a new perspective, thank you for picking this book up, and thank you for making the world more delicious.

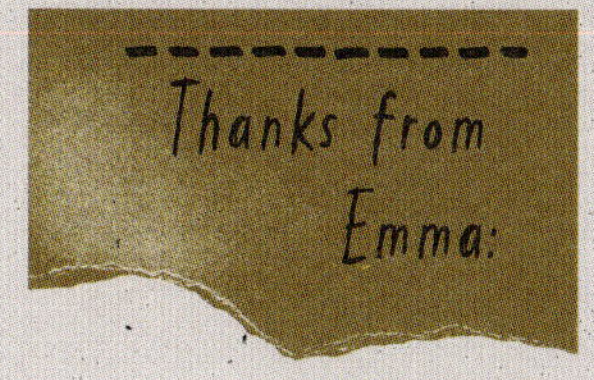

Toby, thanks for your willingness to jump into the fray again with me. Your endless supply of wit and wisdom makes the act of sitting at a computer for hundreds of hours feel like no time has passed at all. I'm a better editor, storyteller, and mixer of cocktails, thanks to you.

Kim Witherspoon (and **Jessica Mileo** and **Naomi Eisenbeiss**), thanks for your guidance and expert agenting skills. I am forever in your debt for the way you've helped me make this whole coauthoring habit more financially viable.

To the Clarkson Potter team: **Jenn Sit,** thanks for your creative guidance and eternal patience. You are a force of nature and a saint for putting up with our wordy rewrites and last-minute edits. I am so grateful that this is our fifth (!!) collaboration together. I wouldn't have it any other way. **Elaine Hennig,** you, too, have the patience of a saint and we appreciate all of your hard work on our behalf! **Ian Dingman,** as usual your sharp eye and impressive natural talent injected this project with so much life. Your enthusiasm and willingness to run with such a weird "vintage cocktails meet punk rock meets Andy Warhol" directive was truly impressive. Thanks a million to you and the rest of your production team, especially production manager **Jane Chinn.** Also: production editor **Liana Faughnan,** plus **Kate Slate, Eldes Tran, Hope Clarke, Sigi Nacson,** and **Mark McCauslin**—we are so grateful for your eagle eyes catching all of our typos and helping smooth out inconsistencies during your copyedits and proofreads!

The friends and brand folks who provided samples for recipe testing—this book is far more delicious for it! That's you, **Jake Parrott** of Haus Alpenz, **Simon Ford, Sacha Bell,** and the rest of the team at Rachel Harrison Communications, and **Ashley Ott** and the crew at Savona Communications. Also thanks to **Matthew Powell** of The Doctor's Office in Seattle for the last-minute advice on alcohol content vs. ABV; you are a gentleman and a scholar for helping us sort that graphic out, sir!

To all the bars and bartenders who let us shoot photos in your hallowed halls! In Chicago: **Victoria Koenig** at Mother's Ruin, **Dan Smith** at Queen Mary, **Danny Shapiro** at Scofflaw. In New Orleans: **Alex Anderson** at Peychaud's, **Lisa Nguyen** and **Neal Bodenheimer** of Cure and Cane & Table, **John Stubbs** and **Chris Hannah** of Jewel of the South, **Konrad Kantor** and **Rachel Johnson** at Manolito, **George LeBlanc, Matt Moore,** and **Josh Atterberry** at The Chloe. In San Diego: **Shannon Partrick** of C.H. Projects, plus **Gigi Barrett** and **Grant Northcutt** at Polite Provisions, **Keivon Dashtizadeh** and **Claire Freas** at The Lafayette Hotel & Club, **Tania Cornejo** and **Rachel Clark** of Ironside, **Daniel Brown** and **Fernando Loredo Sanchez** at J & Tony's Discount Cured Meats & Negroni Warehouse. And to my West Coast amigo **Jim Sullivan** for the sharp editing advice!

Zach, there aren't enough words to express how much your support means to me as I continue to say yes to too many projects at once. Thanks for your willingness to always put a critical eye on a manuscript (sometimes several times), to try eighteen versions of a Bijou on a weeknight, and to drop other (arguably more important) things to help with on-deadline crises like ABV calculations and running to the liquor store for more sweet vermouth. I also couldn't have done a book like this without my parents: **Mom and Dad,** thanks to you both for enduring my absence, listening to me fret about this and that, and for giving input on the recipes as I tested each one three or four or five times over.

INDEX

Egg whites
    Amaretto Sour, 65–67
    Clover Club, 109–11
    New York Sour, 233–35
    Pisco Sour, 261–63
    Ramos Gin Fizz, 273–75
    Whiskey Sour, 305–7
Errico, Enzo, 199
Espresso Martini, 137–39
Estopinal, Kirk, 165, 166, 282

 f

Falernum
    Jet Pilot, 177–79
    Saturn, 277–79
Fassionola, 31
    Hurricane, 165–67
    Saturn, 279
Fernet-Branca. *See also* Amaro
    Eeyore's Requiem, 230
    Grasshopper, 149–51
    Hanky Panky, 211
    Stinger, 295
    Toronto, 199
Fine strainer, 49
Fitty-Fitty, 210
Fortified wine. *See also* Sherry
    refrigerating, 41
French 75, 141–43

G

Garnishes, 49–51
    Gibson, 210
Gimlet, 145–47
Gin
    Alaska, 210
    Aviation, 73–75
    Bee's Knees, 81–83
    Bijou, 85–87
    Bloody Mary, 89–91
    Blossom, 210–11
    Bramble, 93–95
    Breakfast Martini, 105–7
    Chocolate Negroni, 230
    Clover Club, 109–11
    Corpse Reviver #2, 113–15
    Eeyore's Requiem, 230
    Fitty-Fitty, 210
    Fizz, Ramos, 273–75
    French 75, 141–43
    Gibson, 210
    Gimlet, 145–47

    Hanky Panky, 211
    Last Word, 185–87
    Martinez, 211
    Martini, 205–7
    Negroni, 225–27
    Pegu Club, 249–51
    Pimm's Cup, 253–55
    Saturn, 277–79
    Tom Collins, 297–99
    Tuxedo #2, 211
    20th Century, 57–59
    Vesper, 211
    White Negroni (Polka Dot), 231
Ginger beer
    Dark and Stormy, 133–36
    Moscow Mule, 221–23
Glassware
    chilling, 41
    types of, 33–35
Grapefruit bitters
    Martini, 205–7
    Paloma, 245–47
Grapefruit juice
    Hemingway Daiquiri, 153–55
    Jet Pilot, 177–79
    Paloma, 245–47
Grapefruit soda
    Paloma, 245–47
Grasshopper, 149–51
Green Chartreuse
    Bijou, 85–87
    Last Word, 185–87
Grenadine, 30
    Jack Rose, 173–75

H

Hanky Panky, 211
Hannah, Chris, 103
Hawthorne strainer, 49
Heavy cream. See Cream
Hemingway Daiquiri, 153–55
Herbsaint
    Sazerac, 281–83
Honey Syrup, 30
    Airmail, 61–63
    Bee's Knees, 81–83
Hotel Nacional, 157–59
Hot Toddy, 161–63
Howell, Maranda, 186
Hurricane, 165–67

I

Ice, tempering, 41
Irish Coffee, 169–71
Irish whiskey. *See also* Whiskey
    Hot Toddy, 162
Irish Coffee, 169–71
    New York Sour, 234

J

Jack Rose, 173–75
Jamaican rum. *See also* Rum
    Airmail, 62
    Daiquiri, 126
    Hemingway Daiquiri, 154
    Jet Pilot, 178
    Jungle Bird, 182
    Mai Tai, 190
    Old Fashioned, 242
    Piña Colada, 259
Jet Pilot, 177–79
Jiggers
    how to use, 42
Julep, Mint, 213–15
Julep strainer, 49
Jungle Bird, 181–83

K

Kingston Negroni, 230–31
Knives, 41
    safety, 50

L

Last Word, 185–87
Lemon juice
    Airmail, 63
    Amaretto Sour, 65–67
    Aperol Spritz, 69–71
    Aviation, 73–75
    Bee's Knees, 81–83
    Bramble, 93–95
    Brandy Crusta, 101–3
    Breakfast Martini, 105–7
    Clover Club, 109–11
    Corpse Reviver #2, 113–15
    French 75, 141–43
    Jack Rose, 173–75
    New York Sour, 233–35
    Pimm's Cup, 253–55
    Pisco Sour, 261–63
    Ramos Gin Fizz, 273–75

CLARKSON POTTER/PUBLISHERS
An imprint of the Crown Publishing Group
A division of Penguin Random House LLC
1745 Broadway
New York, NY 10019
clarksonpotter.com
penguinrandomhouse.com

Library of Congress Cataloging-in-Publication
Data
Names: Maloney, Toby [author] | Janzen,
Emma, 1986– [author photographer]
Title: The classic cocktail sessions: a
bartender's new-fashioned approach to
the world's most beloved recipes / Toby
Maloney and Emma Janzen; photographs
by Emma Janzen.
Description: New York: Clarkson Potter/
Publishers, [2026] | Includes index.
Identifiers: LCCN 2025026866 (print)
| LCCN 2025026867 (ebook) | ISBN
9780593798584 hardcover | ISBN
9780593798591 ebook
Subjects: LCSH: Cocktails | LCGFT:
Cookbooks
Classification: LCC TX951 .M253 2026
(print) | LCC TX951 (ebook) | DDC
641.87/4—dc23/eng/20250702
LC record available at https://lccn.loc.
gov/2025026866
LC ebook record available at https://lccn.loc.
gov/2025026867

ISBN 978-0-593-79858-4
Ebook ISBN 978-0-593-79859-1

Editor: Jennifer Sit
Editorial assistant: Elaine Hennig
Designer: Ian Dingman
Production designer: Christina Self
Production editor: Liana Faughnan
Production: Jane Chinn
Prepress color manager: Jane Chinn
Compositors: Merri Ann Morrell and
Zoe Tokushige
Copy editor: Kate Slate
Proofreaders: Eldes Tran, Hope Clarke,
Sigi Nacson, and Mark McCauslin
Indexer: Elizabeth Parson
Publicist: David Hawk
Marketer: Emily Hotaling

Manufactured in China

10 9 8 7 6 5 4 3 2 1

First Edition

The authorized representative in the EU for
product safety and compliance is Penguin
Random House Ireland, Morrison Chambers,
32 Nassau Street, Dublin D02 YH68, Ireland,
https://eu-contact.penguin.ie.